Sex, Culpability and the Defence of Provocation

The partial defence of provocation is one of the most controversial doctrines within the criminal law. It has now been abolished in a number of international jurisdictions. Addressing the trajectory of debates about reform of the provocation defence across different jurisdictions, *Sex, Culpability and the Defence of Provocation* considers the construction and representation of subjectivity and sexual difference in legal narrations of intimate partner homicide. Undeniably, the most vexing exculpatory cultural narrative of our times is that of a woman 'asking for it'. This book explores how the process of judgment in a criminal trial involves not only the drawing of inferences from the facts of a particular case, but also operates to deliver a narrative. Law, it is argued, constructs a narrative of how the female body incites male violence. And, pursuing an approach that is informed by socio-legal studies, literary theory and feminist theories of the body, *Sex, Culpability and the Defence of Provocation* considers how this narrative is constructed through a range of discursive practices that position women as a threat to masculine norms of propriety and autonomy. Once we have a clear understanding of the significance of narrative in legal decision-making, we can then formulate textual strategies of resistance to the violence of law's victim-blaming narratives by rewriting them.

Danielle Tyson is a Lecturer in Criminology at Monash University, Victoria, Australia. Her research interests include legal and social responses to intimate partner homicide.

Discourses of Law

Series editors: Peter Goodrich, Michel Rosenfeld and Arthur Jacobson
Benjamin N. Cardozo School of Law

This successful and exciting series seeks to publish the most innovative scholarship at the intersection of law, philosophy and social theory. The books published in the series are distinctive by virtue of exploring the boundaries of legal thought. The work that this series seeks to promote is marked most strongly by the drive to open up new perspectives on the relation between law and other disciplines. The series has also been unique in its commitment to international and comparative perspectives upon an increasingly global legal order. Of particular interest in a contemporary context, the series has concentrated upon the introduction and translation of continental traditions of theory and law.

The original impetus for the series came from the paradoxical merger and confrontation of East and West. Globalization and the internationalization of the rule of law has had many dramatic and often unforeseen and ironic consequences. An understanding of differing legal cultures, particularly different patterns of legal thought, can contribute, often strongly and starkly, to an appreciation if not always a resolution of international legal disputes. The rule of law is tied to social and philosophical underpinnings that the series has sought to excoriate and illuminate.

Titles in the series:

Nietzsche and Legal Theory: Half-Written Laws
Edited by Peter Goodrich and Mariana Valverde

Law, Orientalism, and Postcolonialism: The Jurisdiction of the Lotus Eaters.
Piyel Haldar

Endowed: Regulating the Male Sexed Body
Michael Thomson

The Identity of the Constitutional Subject: Selfhood, Citizenship, Culture, and Community
Michel Rosenfeld

The Land is the Source of the Law: A Dialogic Encounter with Indigenous Jurisprudence
C.F. Black

Shakespearean Genealogies of Power: A Whispering of Nothing in Hamlet, Richard II, Julius Caesar, Macbeth, The Merchant of Venice, and The Winter's Tale
Anselm Haverkamp

Novel Judgments: Legal Theory as Fiction
William Macneil

Visualizing Law in the Age of the Digital Baroque: Arabesques and Entanglements
Richard K. Sherwin

Forthcoming:

The Scene of the Mass Crime, Peter Goodrich and Christian Delage

Shakespeare's Curse, Bjoern Quiring

Crime Scenes: Forensics and Aesthetics
Rebecca Scott Bray

The Rule of Reason in European Constitutionalism and Citizenship
Yuri Borgmann-Prebil

The publisher gratefully acknowledges the support of the Jacob Burns Institute for Advanced Legal Studies of the Benjamin N. Cardozo School of Law to the series *Discourses of Law*.

Sex, Culpability and the Defence of Provocation

Danielle Tyson

Routledge
Taylor & Francis Group

LONDON AND NEW YORK

First published 2013
by Routledge
2 Park Square, Milton Park, Abingdon, Oxon OX14 4RN

Simultaneously published in the USA and Canada
by Routledge
711 Third Avenue, New York, NY 10017

Routledge is an imprint of the Taylor & Francis Group, an informa business

British Library Cataloguing in Publication Data
A catalogue record for this book is available from the British Library

Library of Congress Cataloging in Publication Data
Tyson, Danielle.
  Sex, culpability, and the defence of provocation / Danielle Tyson.
    p. cm.
  Includes bibliographical references and index.
  1. Provocation (Criminal law)   2. Criminal liability (International law)
  3. Justification (Law)   4. Defence (Criminal procedure)   5. Women, Violence
  against.   I. Title.
  K5086.T97 2012
  345'.05044—dc23

                                                                    2011052173

ISBN 978-0-415-56017-7 (hbk)
ISBN 978-0-415-56020-7 (pbk)
ISBN 978-0-203-11640-1 (ebk)

Typeset in Minion
by RefineCatch Limited, Bungay, Suffolk

Printed and bound in Great Britain by
TJ International Ltd, Padstow, Cornwall

For Imogen
with love

Contents

Legal cases cited

Legislation cited

Acknowledgements

This book grew out of my honours and doctoral theses and so I want first to thank my supervisors, Andrea Rhodes-Little and Alison Young, respectively. Thanks are also due to Peter Rush who offered invaluable and incisive comments throughout the writing of my doctoral thesis. Without their encouragement, support and intellectual contribution, these research projects would never have come to fruition. I am also deeply indebted to a number of people who have assisted me along the way on what now seems like a very long journey. In the early stages of conceiving this book, particular thanks are owed to Dean Wilson who encouraged me to see that there was a book in the thesis after all. For their help, humour, good counsel and feedback throughout the early stages of writing this book, I thank Rebecca Scott Bray and Suzanne Fraser and, in the final stages, Anita Spitzer, Bree Carlton, Paddy Rawlinson, Derek Dalton, Anna Eriksson and Mark Davis. I owe a particular debt to all my colleagues in Criminology at Monash University who, in those final heady days, came through with enthusiasm and support when I needed it most. I am also particularly grateful to Bronwyn Hammond who was the Manager of Policy and Research at the Office of Public Prosecutions, Melbourne, Victoria during the period when I collected the data for my doctoral research. I have also gained an enormous amount from the insights and stories of anti-violence-against-women activists, particularly Phil Cleary and Jane Ashton. I also owe special thanks to Debbie Kirkwood, Sarah Capper and Mandy

McKenzie, whose enthusiasm and willingness to collaborate on related projects has enriched my experience of undertaking this research.

I have presented papers at conferences on this work and I would like to thank all those who have given feedback and supported my work, particularly Myrna Dawson to whom I am particularly grateful for hosting me as a Visiting Scholar at the University of Guelph in Canada in 2010. Thanks are also due to the series editors, Peter Goodrich, Michel Rosenfeld and Arthur Jacobson. Parts of Chapters 2 and 3 include material that was previously published in Tyson D (1999) *Australian Feminist Law Journal* 13: 66–86. Part of Chapter 3 also includes material that was previously published in Tyson D (2007) 'Rewriting the event of murder: provocation, automatism and law's use of a narrative of insult', *Law Text Culture*, 11: 286–317 and part of Chapter 4 includes material that was previously published in Tyson D (2011) 'Victoria's New Homicide Laws: Provocative reforms or more stories of women "asking for it"? *Current Issues in Criminal Justice* 23(2): 203–33. Finally, and most importantly, I want to thank the people at the centre of this project – Alex whose love, encouragement, support and critical insights throughout have been unwavering and our daughter Imogen, whose love, loyalty and optimism knows no bounds.

Introduction: Murder and culpable subjects: the standard tale of a woman 'asking for it'

> Affectively speaking, I think that words can be much more harmful than actions. There's a sting in words, which no action can replicate.[1]

When undertaking court observation for my doctoral research, I witnessed the above exchange. The statement was delivered by Cummins J during legal argument in the absence of the jury in *Leonboyer*. Counsel for the defence had asked the judge to make a ruling that the partial defence of provocation be left for the jury on the ground that words allegedly spoken by the deceased *caused* the defendant, her fiancé, to feel insulted and *lose all self-control*. While under the influence of that loss of self-control, he inflicted at least 24 stab wounds to her head, back, groin and shoulder, thereby causing her death. The words allegedly spoken by the deceased were that she had been 'fucking' another man, which she followed with a taunt, in Spanish, about the defendant's lack of sexual prowess ('he did it better than you did').[2]

Cummins J was of the view that there were no authoritative cases that established mere words as a sufficient ground to raise the partial defence of provocation and therefore he did not intend to leave it as a matter for the jury (*Leonboyer* 1999: 1142). To register his disagreement, counsel for the defendant cited an Australian case from 1975 in which the presiding judge left the determination of whether provocation had occurred to the jury on the ground of mere words. In that case the defendant claimed to have been wounded by the words spoken by his former spouse 'at a time when he was under a lot of stress', and those words caused him to lose all self-control and kill her. The alleged words were described as a 'final rejection' by the defendant's 'angry spouse' that took the form of 'a statement that he wasn't going to see the children' (*Leonboyer* 1999: 1146). As such, counsel for the defence sought to convince Cummins J that a confession by a woman of adultery accompanied by a taunt about a man's sexual prowess was sufficient to raise the partial defence of provocation.

A short while later, the prosecuting counsel also sought to clarify the question of whether there were any authoritative cases that established words alone as a sufficient ground to raise the defence of provocation (*Leonboyer* 1999: 1163). He then cited the leading case on the doctrine of provocation in Australia, that of *Moffa*,[3] which he understood to have affirmed the House of Lords decision in *Holmes v Director of Public Prosecutions* ([1946] AC 588) that 'a confession of adultery without more is never sufficient to reduce an offence which would otherwise be murder to manslaughter'.[4] He then submitted that 'the proposition that mere words cannot amount to provocation as a "be all and end all" proposition is no longer correct' (*Leonboyer* 1999: 1166). He added: 'it's a question of looking at the words in the context in which they are uttered' (*Leonboyer* 1999: 1166). It was at this point that the judge replied: 'Affectively speaking, I think that words can be much more harmful than actions. There's a sting in words, which no action can replicate' (*Leonboyer* 1999: 1168). On hearing this a number of those seated in the courtroom – the prosecuting counsel, counsel for the defendant, their respective solicitors, the judge's associate and even the tipstaff – leaned back in their chairs and nodded their heads as if in agreement.

This exchange highlights some of the themes that are explored in this book: the problem of law's masculinist bias related to the constitution of subjectivity, sexual difference and assessments of culpability in provocation cases. Specifically, this scene illustrates my understanding of legal reasoning and language as a social practice and discursive formation. Law, observes Goodrich, is a linguistic register or literary genre that can be described in terms of its privileging of legally recognised meanings (modes of inclusion) and simultaneous rejection of competing meanings (modes of exclusion) (1987: 1–3). From this, it follows that if murder 'is to exist for us', it must first 'be articulated' and like any and all events will already 'have been articulated in numerous contexts and in a variety of ways' (Young 1997: 129).[5] Attaching this (and not that) explanation for the event of the deceased's death and invoking the idiom 'there's a sting in words which no action can replicate', demonstrates the ways in which a judge uses the linguistic device of metaphor. Literary tropes, such as metaphor, are employed in the process of judging because of their all-inclusive universal properties to explain social values and behaviours to various audience groups, ranging from the parties to a particular case, legal counsel, the jury, the appellate courts and the wider community.[6] I maintain that this process is not simply reducible to questions of style or adornment. Such treatments of language presume that: 'like law, [we can put our] faith in language as the instrument through which polyvalent signs can be reduced to a single truth and deliver both justice and narrative closure' (Aristodemou 2000: 106). On this view, the meaning of an event such as the killing of a woman by her intimate partner or ex-partner is assumed to be self-evident or to speak for itself, thus requiring no further justification; it is 'as if the statement of the case is a correct reflection and reproduction of the state of affairs in the world' (Philadelphoff-Puren and Rush 2003: 201).

Cummins J's resort to metaphor in the case observed – the idiom[7] that words have a sting – assists in the conveying of an idea, observation or opinion to the audience (legal counsel in the absence of the jury). When framed in this way, the idiom invoked by the judge appears as a relatively straightforward, commonsense observation about people's behaviour; that is, there is a limit to everyone's endurance and that everyone has a breaking point. When posed as commonsense knowledge, the phrase 'there is a sting in words which no action can replicate', simply appears to refer to a natural state of affairs in the world. Moreover, the person using the phrase does not need to claim responsibility for creating meaning because he or she is simply calling on pre-existing knowledge, which is assumed to be self-evidently true. Metaphor, writes Mills, 'conventionally works at the level of the phrase rather than at the level of words in isolation'. The use of metaphor enables a person to draw on a body of thought or background knowledge that might in fact skew the analysis or thinking of that particular object (Mills 1995: 136). Young has argued that '[r]easoning by analogy is unsurprising – it is, after all, the favoured mode of legal reasoning – but what has to be noted is the productive force that inheres in metaphor' (1996: 55).[8] In stating a similarity between two disparate things or domains (one context and another), 'analogies displace the invisible with the visible' (Young 1996: 55). Metaphor inscribes the event of murder with new meanings. Every deployment of the 'stinging speech' analogy repositions the victim as an illegitimate (active) subject rather than a legitimate victim and recasts the accused as the unwitting object of the speech act's insulting trajectory, compelled to restore his subjectivity by killing the verbal antagonist. As Dijkstra succinctly states: 'metaphors do the dirty work of ideology. They telescope complex ideas into simple imagery and encourage us to see others not as person but as patterns' (1996: 311).[9]

On this analysis, the metaphor that words have a sting carries with it a whole host of associated meanings, a sedimented narrative history,[10] that 'begin in myth, legend and religion and continue in representations in film, art, pornography, poetry and popular and domestic fiction and through to traditional common-law legal categories' such as the defence of self-defence and partial defence of provocation (Threadgold 1997a: 229). Interrogation of these scripts provides some insights as to the fears and fantasies that dominate the cultural and legal imagination. Foremost of these is the long held assumption about the capacity of the female body to incite male violence, which is illustrated by the qualifier: *she asked for it*.

The idea that words can wound is well established (eg compare Matsuda et al 1993 with Butler 1997). In the context of the criminal law of provocation, the allegedly provocative behaviour, whether through words or conduct, is understood 'by the defendant and the judiciary as saying something about *who* the defendant is (a cuckold in adultery cases, for example)' (Rush 1997: 342). As Rush observes, both self-control and its loss, however, 'are mental states that, like *mens rea*, cannot be observed and thus only appear in law as legal fictions' (1997: 341). As Chief Justice Gleeson remarked in the Australian case of *Chhay*, the judiciary's resort to metaphor to describe the loss of self-control is not only 'necessary', but 'disconcerting' and seems 'calculated to confound, rather than assist analytical reasoning'.[11] What is often meant when an accused claims to have 'lost it' or that his mind suddenly 'snapped', 'went blank' or he 'blew a fuse', 'saw red' etc is in effect that he lost his mind. Other examples found in provocation cases include the metaphor 'the straw that broke the camel's back',[12] feeling 'wound up like a clock spring'[13] or that my 'eyes' went 'black'[14] or that my mind 'exploded'.[15]

This brings me to a key reason for this book: to challenge and subvert the all too familiar cultural commonplace:[16] the convention that when a woman responds to the performance of men, she is not so much speaking back but asking for it and hence deserving of what she gets. For too long this narrative, what I term throughout this book a narrative of insult and its gendered trope of 'she asked for it', has come to inform the repertoire of 'commonsense' understandings that judges use to interpret 'facts', justify their decisions, arrive at their conclusions and reproduce their 'hegemonic tales' (Ewick and Silbey 1995: 211–217). A detailed discussion regarding the debates leading up to the decision, in some jurisdictions, to abolish the controversial partial defence of provocation will follow in the next chapter. For present purposes, I provide some preliminary remarks to give an indication as to the book's aims and concerns and where the discussion is headed.

The demise of provocation: a 'classic masculinist apology' for violent men[17]

The rule of law that provocation reduces the crime of murder to manslaughter has now been repealed in a number of jurisdictions: in the Australian states of Tasmania, Victoria and Western Australia (*Criminal Code Amendment (Abolition of Defence of Provocation) Act* 2003 (Tas), *Crimes (Homicide) Act* 2005 (Vic), *Criminal Law Amendment (Homicide) Act* 2008 (WA)), and also in New Zealand (*Crimes (Provocation Repeal) Amendment Bill* 2009 (NZ) (passed 26 November 2009). In these jurisdictions, provocation is to be considered along with other multiple aggravating or mitigating factors that a court must take into account when deciding an appropriate and proportionate sentence (Stewart and Freiberg 2008: 284). Its demise has also been contemplated in the Australian state of Queensland (Department of Justice and Attorney-General (DJAG) *Discussion Paper: Audit on Defences to Homicide: Accident and Provocation* 2007) and in England and Wales (Wells 2000: 85). The debates about whether to abolish the provocation defence in Queensland and England and Wales were constrained by their respective governments' intention to make no change to the existing penalty of mandatory life imprisonment for murder. Consequently, the *Criminal Code and Other Legislation Amendment Act* 2011 (Qld) was passed by the Queensland Government in 2011 and significantly revised the partial defence of provocation. In 2009 the *Coroners and Justice Act* 2009 (UK) replaced the provocation defence and implemented a new partial defence of loss of control. The partial defence of provocation still operates in one of the common law and four of the code jurisdictions in Australia. In South Australia, the qualified defence of provocation is governed by the common law.[18] In the Australian Capital Territory and New South Wales, there are statutory provisions governing the defence (*Crimes Act* 1900 (ACT) s 13; *Crimes Act* 1900 (NSW) s 23), and in the Northern Territory and Queensland (*Criminal Code Act* (NT), *Criminal Code* 1899 (Qld)), both of which carry a mandatory sentence of life imprisonment for murder.

In those jurisdictions in which it can still be raised it applies to situations where the accused 'understandably' loses self-control owing to the behaviour of the deceased. Broadly speaking, for the provocation defence to succeed, there are several elements that must be satisfied. The deceased must have said something and/or acted in a way that was provocative. The accused must have lost self-control as a result of the provocation and killed the deceased while experiencing that loss of self-control. Overriding both of these legal requirements is the further demand that the accused must have acted as a hypothetical 'ordinary' person would have acted.[19] What runs through each of the requirements of the formal legal definition is a construction and representation of what the deceased said and/or did and the effect of those words and/or behaviour on the accused. For some decades now, feminist scholars in almost all jurisdictions have expressed a sense of injustice with the way the partial defence of provocation has been too restrictive for women defendants who kill their violent abusers, but in cases involving men who kill their current or former female partners, they have been able to use it with relative ease. Some of the most scathing criticisms of the provocation defence have been in regard to how such cases operate to construct the female victim as partially to blame for, and hence deserving of, her own death. This was outlined by the National Association of Women and the Law (Côté et al) in a report submitted to the Federal Department of Justice Canada, entitled *Stop Excusing Violence Against Women*:

> By placing the focus on the victim's behaviour, the law capitalizes on historic judeo-christian (sic) ideologies that blame women for the evils of mankind, and that immunize men from responsibility for their behaviour. The plausibility of the provocation hypothesis in spousal femicide cases rests on sexist assumptions about female maliciousness and male vulnerability. It excludes the real context and dynamic of male domination and patriarchal violence.
>
> (2000: 21–22)

A key aim of these criticisms of provocation has been to find ways of challenging and subverting what this book argues is the most vexing exculpatory 'narrative of excuse' for men's murderous anger and rage against women. Numerous problematic cultural assumptions about masculinity and femininity underscore this narrative: one is an understanding that male violence is an expected and therefore 'normal' characteristic of masculinity and the other is the degree of blameworthiness that attaches to the woman victim depends on her performance of appropriate femininity (Edwards 1987: 158–61; Bandalli 1995: 401–402; Morgan 1997: 238; Howe 1999: 131, 2002: 41). In an effort to expose and unsettle the truth-claiming function of this exculpatory narrative, many feminist scholars have turned to legal storytelling, which is now a well established strategy of critique (Graycar and Morgan 2002: 66, 56–81).

Legal storytelling and narrative

Legal storytelling or narrative approaches to law emerged from the Critical Legal Studies movement in the early 1980s whereby feminist and critical race scholars sought to use narrative as a way to illuminate an understanding of race or gender oppression, or both, and to enable social and legal change (see for example Scheppele 1989; Symposium, 'Legal Storytelling', 1989; Matsuda 1987; Williams 1991). In characterising law as narrative, the legal storytelling approach debunks law's claims to autonomy and of absolute meanings and objective truth (McBarnet 1981). Law's reliance on storytelling is a source of its power; indeed, the narrative foundations of legal practices provide a justifiable basis for law's legitimacy. In this respect, the legal storytelling approach takes up Foucault's (1980) insight that discourses form the objects of which they speak, that discourses are an exercise in power in that they not only operate by defining a field of interest, but also by establishing what is a viable perspective on this field as well as who can legitimately speak about a particular issue or concern (eg experts – psychiatrists, doctors, judges, criminologists etc). Moreover, departing from conventional or positivist legal approaches, legal storytelling scholars reject pretensions of legal formalism, and understand courts as normative, adversarial and interpretive institutions that are deeply ingrained in popular culture. As Amsterdam and Bruner have argued, from this it follows that judges do not simply *find* law, they make it, but they do this within particular interpretive boundaries that shape but do not ultimately determine their decisions (2000: 7).

Delgado (1989) divides narratives into two types of stories: 'stock stories' and 'counter-stories'. Delgado developed the term 'stock story' to describe those stories that are not part of the dominant discourse but are legal narratives that silence the point of view of 'outsiders' (1989: 2411), those whose perspectives are excluded in the law's construction of an official story for the particular case. The key here is what Scheppele describes as the 'we-they' structure in legal discourse: the implicit contrast between the stories told by 'insiders' – '[t]hose whose stories are believed have the power to create fact' (typically those who are white, privileged and male) and those told by 'outsiders' – 'those whose stories are not believed and whose versions are discredited' (typically those who are not white, not privileged and not male) (1989: 2079). The idea of 'counter-storytelling' is seen as potentially subverting the mindsets and stories of dominant 'insiders' by disclosing alternative stories, experiences and new meanings. This recognition has been an important one for feminist legal scholars. As Graycar observes, it has not only 'led to a feminist concern about the stories told about women in law', it 'has been the developing interest in legal storytelling, or feminist narrative scholarship' more generally (1996: 298). Graycar and Morgan have also noted that many legal scholars have found the focus on 'how alternative stories can be told' to be a vital way of challenging law's stories (2005: 74). As such, there is 'now a powerful literature on the difficulties faced by 'outsiders'; by the disadvantaged, in telling their stories in law' and this has been a 'logical progression from the recognition that one of the major projects of feminist scholarship has been the recovery of suppressed stories of women from the official or accepted accounts of events or conditions of the world' (Graycar 1996: 298. See also Estrich 1988; Graycar and Morgan 1990; Mahoney 1991; Naffine 1994; Sarmas 1994; Kaspiew 1995; Puren 1995; Morgan 1997; Taylor 2004; Erlich 2001; Burns 2005; Gavey 2005; Larcombe 2005). Graycar notes, however, that while it is essential to find ever new ways for law to hear alternative stories, 'the framework within which those stories are told' must also be dismantled and rearranged (1996: 298).

The 2005 reforms to the laws of homicide in Victoria drew heavily on the critique of Morgan as outlined in an Occasional Paper, *Whom Kills Whom and Why? Looking Beyond Legal Categories*. Morgan's critique followed the approach of the then Vice President and President designate of the Law Commission of Canada, Nathalie Des Rosiers, which endorsed a focus on 'reality' or 'people's lives' and not 'legal categories' as a starting point (Morgan 2002: 1). According to Des Rosiers, a reconsideration of the defences to homicide, informed by the social context in which such homicides arise, was 'extremely productive since it helps to ensure that we do not take for granted abstract legal categories that may obfuscate rather than clarify the resolution of a legal problem' (cited in Morgan 2002: 1). Although the focus on storytelling and narrative as an approach to reform of the criminal law is not made explicit in Morgan's occasional paper or by the VLRC in its final report, arguably the claim that women's lives have traditionally been excluded from, or distorted by, legal categories is one that sees their voices, particularly the stories they tell about their own experiences of violence, as paramount. Indeed, it is a moot point that 'the place of the victim in the evolving court narrative is most problematic in a murder case'. As Gewirtz observes, 'the victim is dead – dead and silent, unable to tell his or her own story' (1996b: 866). This absence can only be filled by other people's utterances and writings. Morgan puts it as follows: 'dead women tell no tales, tales are told about them' (1997: 237).

An early example of the focus on storytelling as a feminist strategy to highlight the deficiencies of legal responses in cases of domestic homicide can be found in one of the most groundbreaking feminist works of the past two decades. Written almost 15 years ago, the book, *Blood on Whose Hands? The Killing of Women and Children in Domestic Homicides* (published by the Women's Coalition Against Family Violence, Melbourne, Victoria, 1994), tells the stories of nine women and children and documents their lives before they were killed, and then their lives as constructed by law.[20] Specifically, the stories tell of experiences that 'leave no doubt that domestic murder is an aspect of domestic violence: these deaths were not so-called "crimes of passion"; each was the culmination of an ongoing campaign around control and terror'. One of the most depressing findings relates to 'the sheer injustice and total inadequacy of the legal system's response to the death of these women and children' (1994: 105), a failure the authors trace to the lack of adequate response to victims of domestic homicide by the police, magistrates, judges and lawyers. This, they argue, is inextricably linked to community attitudes towards domestic violence that ignore or minimise its seriousness. Indeed, for the authors, this systemic failure is dependent on *how the victim's story gets told*. As the critical assessment of the case studies makes clear, the sympathy shown towards the men who killed their partners and children often went hand-in-hand with a verdict of guilty of manslaughter rather than murder.

Sex, Culpability and the Defence of Provocation builds on this important work, but from a slightly different perspective. Rather than telling the stories of the victim from the perspective of family and friends, the specific focus of this book is the underlying values and assumptions about sex, gender and the female victim's culpability that have underwritten provocation's victim-blaming narratives. This book uses case studies that are primarily drawn from the Australian legal context, but includes a range of international examples to explore the trajectory of debates about reform of the criminal defence of provocation. Pursuing an approach to reading law and legal texts that is informed by socio-legal studies, feminist theories of the body and literary theory, this book shows how the process of judgment in a criminal trial involves not only drawing inferences from the 'facts' of a particular case, but delivers a narrative. Law, it is argued, like literature and film, constructs a narrative of how the female body incites male violence.

In the language of the now classic work of Carol Smart, law is described as a particularly powerful social discourse because of its 'claims to truth', which in turn enables it to disqualify or silence alternative voices which challenge law.[21] Smart's seminal essay, 'The woman of legal discourse' (1992), argued that the power of law resides in the ways in which it operates as a 'technology of gender' (de Lauretis 1987), as a process that produces gendered subjectivities and identities rather than simply reflecting a previously gendered subject. As Smart observes, 'Woman is a gendered subject position which legal discourse brings into being' (1992: 34). Informed by Foucauldian discourse theory, Smart's understanding was that although law may be constituted as masculine (in the sense that there is a congruence between the idea of 'doing law and identifying as masculine' or 'doing masculinity' (Thornton 1986: 7 cited in Smart 1989: 86)), it is important to recognise that:

> ... law does not serve the interests of *men* as a homogenous category any more than it serves the interests of *women* as a category.... the idea of it as gendered allows us to think of it in terms of processes which will work in a variety of ways and in which there is no relentless assumption that whatever it does exploits women and serves men. Thus we can argue that '[t]he same practices signify differently for men and women because they are read through different discourses'.
>
> (Hollway 1984: 237 cited in Smart 1992: 33–34)

Building on Smart's discourse theory approach, this book explores the ways in which certain, preferred understandings about femininity, masculinity, heterosexuality and indeed, culpability, are embedded in the rhetorical practices of legal discourse (Young 1998: 445; see also Goodrich 1987). This approach positions law as essentially a literary genre or enterprise. In doing so, it opens up the possibility of examining how the meanings of the texts produced in one context (eg in the courtroom) are always connected to the meanings produced in other discursive contexts (such as popular culture). In short, my focus on the intertextuality of provocation cases seeks to interrogate how law's stories are *written* so we can begin to rewrite them. From this, it follows that the contexts that come before the courts are not as determinate as law's appeals to the 'facts' would appear to suggest. Rather, contexts 'travel' with pre-determined subject positions, forms of character, genre and discourse already attached. As Philadelphoff-Puren and Rush observe: 'as soon as judgment is understood as writing, then it is opened out to the very contexts which in fact structure it [eg literature] but that it must permanently disavow or repress' (2003: 202).[22]

Judges and juries alike have long listened to defence narratives of men's murderous anger and rage at their nagging, unfaithful and departing wives to receive a reduction in culpability for the crime of murder. So have feminist activists, lobbyists and scholars who have long sought to expose and eliminate law's masculinist bias. Now that the provocation defence is finally provoking its own demise across an ever increasing number of jurisdictions, there is an urgent need to ensure that insidious court narratives that portray the female victims of domestic homicide as to blame for their own deaths are no long able simply to be redeployed in the guise of other defences to homicide or at other stages of the legal process such as sentencing.

The public criticism generated by the 2004 decision of a Victorian Supreme Court jury to find James Ramage guilty of manslaughter on the ground of provocation for killing his wife, Julie, from whom he had recently separated, coincided with the Victorian legislature's decision to implement a key recommendation made by the Victorian Law Reform Commission (VLRC) in its *Defences to Homicide: Final Report* (VLRC 2004) to abolish the provocation defence and make other substantial changes to the laws of homicide through the *Crimes (Homicide) Act* 2005 (Vic). Indeed, the *Ramage* case is now well known to many of provocation's critics and provides a stark illustration of how law's narratives in cases of domestic homicide are anchored in cultural commonsense assumptions about 'unruly' and/or 'unchaste' women who are to blame for their own deaths. The accused's version of events at trial was that he lost self-control and attacked the deceased after she allegedly told him that the relationship was over, admitted to having a new lover, said that sex with him repulsed her and then screwed up her face.[23] There are restrictions that apply to evidence concerning sexual history and the history of the relationship that is led at a criminal trial. However, in this case, the defence adduced evidence of the deceased's sexual history including her sexual relationships to establish that Julie's words and behaviour triggered the accused's loss of self-control.[24] Mental health professionals testified that the accused had been 'extremely anxious, obsessed and emotionally fraught' over his wife leaving the relationship.[25] While there was evidence of previous incidences of violence within the marriage,[26] the history of Jamie's controlling behaviour, his affairs and abuse of Julie throughout their relationship was largely excluded as it was 'inadmissible' because it 'was hearsay, happened too long ago or was unduly prejudicial to the accused' (Kissane 2004b: 4). In an article, 'Honour killing in the suburbs', Karen Kissane (a leading journalist with *The Age* newspaper), highlights how the defence narrative suggested 'that she was likely to have lost her temper and verbally provoked her husband: "She was in love, and her hormones were such – you will find tampons in her handbag, and Dr Lynch (who performed the autopsy) will say that at the time she was menstruating ... Men tend to think women get a bit scratchy around that time"' (Kissane 2004b: 4). Describing the killing as one that 'shocked the comfortable inhabitants of Melbourne's leafy suburbs',[27] Kissane passionately observes how the trial had 'blown up into an ever darker storm over the way Julie Ramage's voice seemed to be strangled out of her a second time'. Indeed, for Kissane, as for 'her family and many independent observers', the case highlighted how 'ideas of "good" and "bad" women are still enshrined in the legal system and how the notion of "crimes of passion" favours the passions of men' (2004b: 4). The message sent to the legal and wider community and the Victorian legislature, as a result of public criticism generated by the *Ramage* case, was overwhelmingly in support of the abolition of the defence of provocation. This book tells the tale of how we, in the state of Victoria (Australia), got there.

Overview and organisation of chapters

Chapter 1 includes a theoretical discussion of feminists' criticisms of the partial defence of provocation and addresses the trajectory of debates about reform of the provocation defence across different jurisdictions.

The purpose of Chapter 2 is to show how historic and culturally specific beliefs in the inherent subversiveness of women and the capacity for 'the speaking woman' to incite male violence have become ingrained in the legal imagination. The chapter begins by invoking a scene from the film *Jackie Brown* involving a verbal exchange between a male and a female character, wherein the man shoots and kills the woman. The scene illustrates that law is just one of many fields which (re)produces commonplace cultural narratives about women who 'ask for it'. The familiar plot-lines, conventionally gendered subjectivities and subject positions that give shape to, and support pleas of provocation in, murder cases can also be found in popular culture. The chapter then discusses the work of feminist historians and critical attention to the literal and literary regulation of disruptive female speech, which reached its peak in England in the 16th and 17th centuries. The aim here is to show how these historical, cultural and legal materials performed a regulatory social function in that they both represent heterosexuality as normative at the same time as they reproduce in their audiences, heterosexual subjects. It is argued in this chapter that these texts provide a rich avenue through which to understand how discourses of power – law being one such discourse – respond to and deal with the body of the speaking woman.

Chapter 3 provides evidence for the book's argument that, like literature and film, law also constructs a narrative of how the female body incites male violence. The primary focus of this chapter is the Victorian case law relating to provocation, but the chapter's claims have general implications for provocation law in other jurisdictions. The cases analysed provide particular examples of the different discourses (such as the romance narrative) drawn upon by the authors of these narratives (eg legal counsel, the presiding judge, witnesses, legal experts and so on). The chapter draws on the concepts of desire, plot and character in narrative to illustrate the ways in which feminine excess is understood to drive wounded males to restore their masculinity – their voice – by killing their verbal antagonist.

Chapter 4 considers recent developments in Victorian case law in light of substantial changes to the laws of homicide, which included the abolition of the partial defence of provocation. In this chapter, I explore lingering concerns about whether, and to what extent, the decision to shift claims of provocation to the sentencing stage of the legal process will put an end to what is perhaps the most vexing exculpatory narrative of excuse for men's violence towards women: the narrative of women 'asking for it'. This chapter asserts that the decision to abolish the controversial partial defence of provocation in a number of Australian jurisdictions and elsewhere was only in part designed to redress the problem of provocation's victim-blaming narratives. It argues that a decision to abolish the partial defence of provocation in most jurisdictions is most often made alongside the introduction of other quite substantial legislative changes to the laws of homicide. Most of the legislative changes to the laws of homicide in Australian jurisdictions have been designed to make it easier for women who kill in the context of family violence successfully to claim self-defence. In some jurisdictions, such as the Australian state of Victoria, the decision to abolish provocation was accompanied by the introduction of a completely new legislative scheme for self-defence, whereas the changes introduced in Western Australia were more moderate, unlike those adopted in Queensland, which provided for a specific defence to murder for battered persons. Given the scope of the changes to the laws of homicide in these different jurisdictions, their impact remains to be seen. However, recent developments in Victorian case law would appear to suggest that provocation-type arguments are still being made in the guise of other defences to homicide – particularly the new offence of defensive homicide.

Chapter 5 engages with recent theorising on the relationship between men, masculinities and crime, which has become a hot topic in criminological and legal scholarship over the past 15 years. The chapter examines particular strands of thinking in the area of criminology that has sought to ask 'the man question', and places this discussion more generally in the context of the 'narrative turn' in critical studies of men and masculinity. Taking issue with the claim that masculinity is currently experiencing a 'crisis' and that violence is an effect of this masculine crisis, the chapter first offers a critique of the theoretical focus on the concept of 'hegemonic masculinity', which has been strongly endorsed within criminology. It then considers significant shifts in theorising the relationship between men, masculinities and men's violence, focusing on the growing trend towards psychosocial approaches that have sought to understand contemporary meanings of masculinity in somewhat more complex, and sometimes contradictory, ways. The chapter concludes by arguing that the thematic of these authors' own narratives share similarities with those found in the narratives mobilised by defence counsel in provocation cases; that is, the idea that a fragile masculinity is somehow threatened, impoverished by real or perceived feminisation.

In the concluding chapter, I return to the theme of the importance of (re) reading and (re)writing as a strategy of law reform in order to consider some of the implications for what I have argued in this work and some future directions feminist critique could take.

Notes

1 Trial transcript, Supreme Court of Victoria, Australia (19 October 1999) at 1168 (Cummins J) (*Leonboyer*).

2 *DPP v Michael Erick Gonzalez Leonboyer* [1999] VSC 450 at 3 (Cummins J).

3 *Moffa v The Queen* (1977) 138 CLR 601.

4 The prosecuting counsel also cited the Victorian Court of Appeal's decision in *R v Tuncay* [1998] 2 VR 19, a case where the victim was the wife of the accused. Both were of Turkish background and there had been a history of unsettled relationship between the two of them. Before he killed his wife, according to the accused, the wife had said that she intended to leave him and take the children with her, because of his drinking, and that she would look for a man who adhered to the religious beliefs of Islam. The accused said that if she left him he would commit suicide. The wife replied that if he did then she would be free of him, whereupon the accused killed the wife in what was described as 'an appallingly brutal attack upon a defenceless woman'. The decision of His Honour, Acting Justice of Appeal Hedigan, in dismissing the application and ruling that the issue of provocation should not be left to the jury, was not that mere words could not amount to provocation but that '[n]o reasonable jury, even taking the case at its highest in terms of the evidence that might be thought to be in support of the provocation, could have concluded that any incident of the behaviour by words or conduct of the deceased could have caused an ordinary person to form an intention to inflict serious bodily injury of death'.

5 Philadelphoff-Puren and Rush argue that such a scene represents the disaster that lies at the heart of all murder trials: this is that the dead body cannot speak until it has the voice or utterance of the other (2003: 210 fn 26).

6 There is a presumption that judgments 'will generally follow a predetermined pattern' and 'should be relevant and as succinct as possible'. Judges frequently make use of literary sources and linguistic devices such as narrative, in order that their ideas are more easily understood by their audiences. As Elms puts it: 'the deft use of literature can help the judicial writer to express important ideas in ways better than they could muster unaided' (2008: 57).

7 An idiom is an expression, word or phrase that has a figurative meaning that is comprehended in regard to a common use of that expression, separate from the literal meaning or definition of the word or words of which it is made.

8　Goodrich (1986: 198) explains in *Reading the Law* that:

> We can refer to a number of rhetorical functions that are either performed by the
> analogy or by associated figures … As a variant form of metaphor, the legal
> analogy can persuade in several different ways. First, as a statement of factual
> similarity between past and present cases, it can act as a figure of presence and
> bring the issue faced to life. The figure of *hypotyposis*, for example, is defined as
> argument 'which sets things out in such a way that the matter seems to unfold, and
> the thing to happen, under our eyes' … Second, the very notion of precedent as
> doing the same thing in similar circumstances (analogy itself is the rhetorical
> figure of *similitude*) incorporates several of the figures of repetition as persuasion
> and as a means of 'presencing the argument'.

9　My thanks to Patricia Rawlinson for pointing me in the direction of this quote.
10　I am using the term in a similar way to Threadgold and her analysis of how the legal
　　category of provocation is thoroughly embedded in a 'sedimented narrative history'
　　(1997a: 220).
11　Chief Justice Gleeson remarked in *R v Chhay* ((1994) 72 A Crim R 1 at 9) that:

> … [t]he necessity to resort to metaphor in expounding the law on this subject is
> disconcerting. References to supposed raising or lowering of blood temperature,
> reason becoming unseated, and passion mastering understanding, seem calculated
> to confound, rather than assist analytical processes. However, our understanding
> of consciousness and mental processes, as compared to our understanding of
> more readily observable physical phenomena, is so limited that metaphor seems
> generally to be regarded as essential in the expression of ideas which guide us in
> this area of discourse.

12　*Trisnadi*, Trial transcript, Supreme Court of Victoria (December 1996) at 560 (Eames J)
　　(charge to jury); Transcript of interview with police and Ian Leslie Brown (answer to 'Q'
　　385).
13　*Trisnadi*, Trial transcript, Supreme Court of Victoria (December 1996) at 33 (Eames J)
　　(charge to jury).
14　*Tuncay*, Trial transcript, Supreme Court of Victoria (November 1996) at 284 (accused's
　　sworn statement).
15　*R v Turan* [2000] VSC 207 at 287 (Teague J) (charge to jury).
16　I am using the term 'commonplace' in the way Young describes to point to how
　　'the habitual connotation of one thing with or for another becomes, by convention
　　and repetition, part of everyday knowledge and expectation, just part of the plot'
　　(1990: 4, 103).
17　The argument that the partial defence of provocation is '[t]he classic masculinist apology'
　　for men's violence against women has been well rehearsed (see for example McDonald
　　1993: 127 and Howe 2002: 54).
18　The elements of the partial defence of provocation are set out in *The Queen v R* (1981)
　　28 SASR 321.
19　The subjective and objective elements of the partial defence of provocation are set out in
　　Stingel v R (1990) 171 CLR 312.
20　In the book's opening pages we are told that the authors of these stories 'felt strongly that
　　they wanted the whole story told, including the names of the murdered women and

children and those who killed them', despite the risk of further abuse by the killers; some had 'already received threats to their lives and safety by these men' (Women's Coalition Against Family Violence 1994: ix).

21　As Smart observed more than 20 years ago (1989: 10–11):

> If we accept that law, like science, makes a claim to truth and this is indivisible from the exercise of power, we can see that law exercises power not simply in its material effects (judgments) but also in its ability to disqualify other knowledges and experiences. . . . Of course parties are not always silenced but . . . how they are allowed to speak, and how their experience is turned into something that law can digest and process, is a demonstration of the power of law to disqualify alternative accounts. . . . Law sets itself outside the social order, as if through the applications of legal method and rigour, it becomes a thing apart which can in turn reflect upon the world from which it is divorced.

22　The judgment that features in Philadelphoff-Puren and Rush's analysis is the sentencing decision of the Victorian Supreme Court in the case of *R v Whiteside and Dieber* [2000] VSC 260. They argue that: '[f]irst, literature appears in the judgment as the citation of *Julius Ceasar* and *The Merchant of Venice*. Second, literature appears as plot. Here we are referring to Cummins' self-conscious literary ordering of the facts around what he calls four steps of an "unfolding tragedy" . . . Third, literature appears as rhetoric. This can be identified not only as persuasion, but also as the specific tropes and figures of speech that are marshalled in the judgment, and their efficacy and truth effects. Fourth, literature appears in the judgment as genre. Here, we are referring to the genres of tragedy and courtly love . . . Finally, literature appears as concept. The literary concept of fate forms the very stuff of the legal narration of fatality' (Philadelphoff-Puren and Rush 2003: 203).

23　For a comprehensive discussion of the facts in the *Ramage* case see Coss 2005; McSherry 2005; Maher et al 2005; and Ramsey 2010. McSherry observed, for instance, how the majority judgments in the Australian High Court case of *Moffa* 'seemed to imply that insulting words may amount to provocation if they are violently provocative or of an "exceptional" character'. Yet, in *Ramage*, the deceased's words – alleged comments about the relationship including an expression of disgust in response to the thought of having sex with the accused – 'could hardly be seen as '"violently" provocative or of an "exceptional" character' (2005: 8).

24　*R v Ramage* [2004] VSC 391.

25　*R v Ramage* [2004] VSC 508, 29.

26　See McSherry's discussion of how some of this evidence relating to James's violence was excluded from the trial (2005: 6–7, 17).

27　Kissane notes how '[f]rom the outside, the Balwyn-based Ramages seemed to have it all. There was a son at Scotch and a daughter at Lauriston. James was director of a company that re-porcelained baths and Julie was a financial controller for a fashion house. Their dinner-party companions included lawyers and CEOs' (2004: 4).

CHAPTER 1

Feminist dilemmas with the partial defence of provocation: international debates

Introduction

The doctrine of the partial defence of provocation is one of the most controversial doctrines in the criminal law. Over the past 20 years, feminist scholars in almost all Western criminal jurisdictions have virtually been in agreement that the partial defence has historically operated, and in some jurisdictions continues to operate, as a profoundly sexed excuse for male anger and violence towards women that allows them to avoid a conviction for murder (Edwards 1987; Allen 1987; Horder 1989, 1992a; Coker 1992; Howe 1994; Bandalli 1995; Morgan 1997).[1] Feminists writing in Australia (Greene 1989; Tarrant 1990; Tolmie 1991; Stubbs 1992; Easteal 1993a; Stubbs and Tolmie 1994, 1995; Hubble 1997; Tolmie 1997; Easteal 2001; Bradfield 2002; Tolmie 2002; Stubbs and Tolmie 2005), England (Radford 1984; Edwards 1987; Radford and Russell 1992; McColgan 1993, 2000; Wells 1994; Carline 2005) and North America (Schneider 1980; Taylor 1986; Castel 1990; Maguigan 1991; O'Donovan 1991; Sheehy et al 1992; Sheehy 1994, 2001; Baker 1998; Maguigan 1998; Schneider 2000) have largely remained preoccupied with the ways in which the law of murder operates in relation to the practical availability of the defences to homicide (self-defence and provocation) for battered women who kill their violent abusers. They have continued to struggle to ensure legislative provisions are in place that better reflect and respond to the different circumstances in which such killings take place. When women kill an intimate partner, they typically do so in circumstances where they are not responding to a specific triggering incident that is legally required before a successful defence of provocation can be made out (Tarrant 1996). Rather, when women kill they are usually responding to a past history of violence and abuse by the deceased. Jeremy Horder (1992: 188–89, cited in Edwards 1984: 365) has described the legal predicament faced by battered women when seeking to raise the provocation defence as follows:

> Many battered women do not lose their self control prior to the killing of the batterer. Following long term abuse, some battered women appear to have taken a calculated decision to kill that was not triggered by any very recent provocation; still others appear to have acted in the face of recent provocation, but with more or less deliberation at or close to the moment of the fact.[2]

Although deserving of mitigation, women who kill their violent abusers often fail to satisfy the rules and requirements that structure the partial defence. It has been argued that the provocation defence has tended to reflect male attitudes and responses to violence and, for this reason, it has been seen as too restrictive for female defendants. Thus, the circumstances in which women kill their violent abusers have either had to be distorted to fit the existing requirements or been excluded altogether.

In contrast, men who kill their intimate partners or ex-partners usually kill in response to the slightest provocation – she either 'nagged', 'taunted', 'insulted' or 'goaded' him, 'flirted' with another man, 'flaunted' her infidelity, left the relationship or threatened to leave him (Bandalli 1995). Historically, the law has extended 'sympathy to the rage of the cuckold' (Kahan and Nussbaum 1996) and, as a result, men have been able to resort to the partial defence with relative ease.[3]

The argument that provocation is a profoundly sexed excuse for men to murder women can be situated within feminist legal scholarship and its demonstration that while law claims to be impartial, neutral and objective, beneath the façade the authoritative definitions, rules and categories that have come to inform legal doctrines were developed by men by reference to their own values and experiences. What is undisputed in this feminist criticism is that both the defence of self-defence and the defence of provocation are based upon standards of behaviour and experience that are more commensurate with male patterns of behaviour and male standards of acceptable conduct (Schneider 1980; O'Donovan 1991; Horder 1992a; Edwards 1996). As Edwards has observed, law 'is saturated and entrenched with a gendered vision of what constitutes manslaughter, provocation in particular, and what constitutes self-defence' (1996: 364). Writing about provocation cases in the English context in the late 1980s, Allen's examination of the use of the concept 'reasonable man' in criminal law persuasively demonstrated the sheer impossibility of this operating as an 'objective' standard of *mens rea* (guilty intent). Accordingly, Allen argued that the supposedly gender-neutral reasonable person standard in provocation cases is couched in sex-specific terms. In her now infamous analysis of *Camplin* ([1978] AC 705), Allen showed that at the very moment when the House of Lords sought to establish 'that the term "the reasonable man" is to include in principle "a reasonable woman" . . . we discover the limits of the law's capacity to confront and override the shared assumptions of the ordinary reality. At this deepest level', Allen resolved, '"[a] reasonable woman with her sex eliminated is altogether too abstract a notion" for anyone to grasp' (1987: 31). The most scathing feminist critique to emerge in response to this insidious fiction that the legal institution constructs and maintains (and that is illustrated by the law's claim of there being '[o]ne law for all reasonable persons' (Allen 1988),[4] is in relation to the provocation defence's exculpatory 'narrative of excuse' for men's anger and violence that operates to inscribe the body of the woman victim as partially to blame for and hence, deserving of, her own fate.

Masculinity has historically, philosophically and politically been constructed positively and treated as normative in terms of culture, reason and rationality; the feminine, in contrast, 'has been socially constructed as "other" to the masculine norm and is invariably associated with nature, the body, disorder, and irrationality' (Thornton 1996: 1; see also Thornton 1989). Since the late 1980s, women's engagements with law have demonstrated that failure to approximate appropriate standards of feminine behaviour (the good woman) can detract from the woman's status as victim, while condoning the violence perpetrated against her by her male intimate partner.[5] Edwards, for instance, recognised the need to focus on the legal construction and representation of the female victim and women's culpability. In her discussion of provocation cases in the English legal context, she showed that where it can be alleged that the deceased woman failed to approximate behaviour deemed appropriate to her expected feminine role, by either challenging male authority or appearing sexually non-conforming, 'she is held responsible' and 'such men are regarded as justifiably provoked' (Edwards 1987: 158, 165). Bandalli traced the problem of provocation to the ways in which its historical origins and development are based on male patterns of behaviour and male standards of acceptable conduct. The paradigmatic case of provocation was the sudden discovery of a wife in the act of adultery, 'a concept based historically on the protection of property rights, which included access to one's wife' (Bandalli 1995: 299). Bandalli's review of provocation cases in the English legal context demonstrated that the idea 'of being provoked by women's words' has a long legal and cultural history. In Bandalli's account because 'women can rarely compete in bare-fisted physical fighting, their weapons are frequently *words*' (1995: 400). In cases in which a husband killed his wife, the provocative incident invariably related to the wife's allegation of adultery, or her 'nagging' or 'taunting' behaviour (Bandalli 1995: 402). Moreover, in the cases analysed by Bandalli, the ease with which the husbands' accounts were accepted was evident in the empathy they were afforded in judges' comments. For Bandalli, a judge's perception as to whether a husband's claim to provocation is acceptable was paramount as it assisted 'in reducing the responsibility of the offender by "trying the victim", sympathizing with the plight of the husband, and voicing moral assessments' (Bandalli 1995: 402). Thus, this work convincingly demonstrated that:

> ... [w]hatever the *formal* structure of the law, ultimately the success or failure of a provocation defence depends on ingrained cultural judgment about the hidden agenda of this partial defence, as it operates in practice in spousal homicide, is one of *female responsibility*, whether as victim or offender.
>
> (Bandalli 1995: 398)

Since these early feminist critiques, these debates about the ways in which the partial defence of provocation operates to inscribe the body of the woman victim as provoking her own demise have been reignited following public outcry over a number of controversial verdicts. In response to these criticisms, law reform bodies in Australia and overseas have published various discussion papers and reports on the partial defences to murder and, in some cases, made specific recommendations about the abolition or reform of provocation.

While it would appear that the propensity for defence narratives that mobilise outdated gender norms about unruly woman victims who provoke their own demise are less likely to succeed in post-abolitionist jurisdictions (Howe 2002: 42), Kahan and Nussbaum attribute this 'to the law's emerging (if contested) receptiveness to the fear of the domestic violence victim – and its receding sympathy to the rage of the cuckold' (1996: 274). In some post-abolitionist jurisdictions such as Victoria, Australia, for instance, recent developments in case law would appear to suggest a continuation of 'cultures of excuse' for men's violence against women and that partially blame the woman victim for her own fate. These discussions and developments are taken up and explored in more detail in subsequent chapters. For present purposes, the aim of this first chapter is to provide an overview of the feminist literature that has examined the law in relation both to women who kill their violent abusers and men who kill their current or former partners. It does this, first, through a review of the empirical literature on the social context of homicide. This is in preparation for a discussion of recent controversies and cases that have driven debates about reform of the criminal law defences and, particularly, the continued use of the provocation defence, which, in some jurisdictions in Australia and overseas, have resulted in its abolition. This discussion demonstrates that the demise of provocation in an ever increasing number of jurisdictions is a sign that inappropriate gender norms are being challenged. In this chapter I set the scene for the discussion in subsequent chapters by outlining my critical approach to reading the law, legal texts and specifically provocation's victim-blaming narratives.

The social context of intimate partner homicide

Men are the overwhelming majority of victims of homicide, a consistent finding in both recent research conducted by the National Homicide Monitoring Program (NHMP) at the Australian Institute of Criminology (AIC) and research internationally (Wallace 1986; Mouzos 2000). The AIC data shows that in 2007–2008 there were 161 male (59 per cent) and 112 female (41 per cent) homicide victims. However, this gender pattern varies depending on the type of homicide. Men were the overwhelming majority of victims of those killed by an acquaintance or stranger (n=92, 84 per cent) whereas, within the category of domestic homicide in 2007–2008, 78 per cent (n=62) of victims of homicide were women killed by an offender with whom they were in an intimate relationship (Virueda and Payne 2010: 19).

The incidence of intimate partner homicide – variously 'domestic homicide' or 'femicide' or 'intimate femicide' – is a serious and ongoing social problem that has been well documented in feminist research since the 1960s and 1970s. According to the NHMP data, in 2007–2008, there were 260 homicide incidents involving the deaths of 273 victims (Virueda and Payne 2010: 2). By far the largest category of homicide is domestic homicide involving the death of a family member or other person from a domestic relationship (n=134 or 52 per cent) (Virueda and Payne 2010: 7). Of the 134 domestic homicides in 2007–2008, incidences of intimate partner homicide comprised the largest proportion of all domestic homicides (n=80 or 60 per cent) (Virueda and Payne 2010: 9).

Indigenous women were seven times more likely than non-indigenous women to be a victim of homicide and, of all domestic homicides (n=16), intimate partner homicide was the largest category involving indigenous victims (42 per cent) (2010: 22–23). This finding that indigenous people are overrepresented as victims of homicide has also been a consistent finding in previous research on homicide in Australia (Mouzos 2000, 2001). A study by Neil Websdale conducted in the United States found that African Americans are disproportionately overrepresented in intimate partner homicides and family homicides compared with their presence in the population (1999: 216–32).

A significant feature in incidences of intimate partner homicide is that most women are killed by their partners in the context of a prior history of family violence and abuse (Hore et al 1996; Mills 2003). In very close to half of the spousal homicide cases, there was preceding violence (Websdale 1999: 78–84). Research on family violence more broadly has shown that women are most at risk of violence from an intimate partner when they attempt to leave or terminate the relationship (Mahoney 1991; Bagshaw and Chung 2000). There is a significant body of research in the United States, the United Kingdom and Canada that has shown that just over one-third to one-half of women killed by an intimate partner had already separated or intended to separate at the time they were murdered (Wallace 1986; Dawson and Gartner 1992; Easteal 1993a; Wilson and Daly 1993; Wilson et al 1995; Dawson and Gartner 1998; Browne et al 1999; Websdale 1999; Johnson and Hotton 2003; Dobash et al 2007; Mills 2008; Johnson and Dawson 2011). This work has emphasised the importance of jealousy, sexual refusal, possessiveness and a desire for 'ownership' and control and perceived or actual infidelity on the part of women as motives in cases where men kill their current or former intimate partners (Daly and Wilson 1988; Polk and Ranson 1991a, 1991b; Campbell 1992; Radford and Russell 1992; Polk 1994; Wilson and Daly 1998; Websdale 1999; Dobash et al 2004; Serran and Firestone 2004; Shackelford and Mouzos 2005; Adams 2007). In Polk's (1994) extensive qualitative study of homicides in Victoria that examined data from coroners' files for the period 1985–1989, he notes (1994: 56) that:

> The overriding theme that runs through these killings is masculine control, where women become viewed as possessions of men, and the violence reflects steps taken by males either to assert their domination over 'their' women, or to repel males who they feel are attempting to take control of their sexual partner.

In relation to his other sub-category of male offender/female victim killings, Polk notes (1994: 24) that killings committed in the context of 'depression/ suicide' are no less proprietary:

> since in many of the accounts where the homicide is part of the male suicide plan the woman is clearly seen as a possession, or commodity, which the man must dispose of prior to his own death. In these cases as well, the killing represents the ultimate control of the man over the woman (there were no cases where a depressed woman killed her male partner as part of her suicide plan).

Morgan's discussion of Polk's data concurs that homicide is fundamentally a gendered social problem, but sees 'domestic' homicide as gendered in particular ways. Morgan observes that: 'some instances of men killing men share much in common with some instances of men killing women and should be connected, notwithstanding the different gender of the victims' (2002: 23). Furthermore, in order to understand the way the partial defence of provocation is often used, it makes better sense of the data to combine 'the male offender/female victim sub-category of "jealousy/control"' with 'the male offender/male victim sub-category of "sexual rivals"' (Morgan 2002: 23–24). By merging these sub-categories, Morgan notes that it means that (in Polk's sample), there were a further 13 cases where males killed a male sexual rival (70 per cent of killings by men in the context of sexual intimacy were out of jealousy/control reasons) (2002: 24 fn 91). The consequent picture that emerges from research in Australia is that a vast proportion of all homicides involving men as offenders (where the victims are either women or men) take place in the context of sexual jealousy.

In contrast, when women kill they almost never kill their intimate partners for the same reasons (Wallace 1986: 103). Rather, when women kill an intimate partner they are much more likely to do so in response to men's controlling and other violent behaviour (Polk 1994: 146–48). As numerous critical studies have reported, a prior history of family violence or fear of further violence was both the prevalent background and cause of killings of males by their intimate female partners (Bacon and Lansdowne 1982: 67–93; Radford and Russell 1992; Websdale 1999: 119–30). As noted by Morgan, homicides committed in the context of an intimate relationship raise the most controversy in the context of the legal system, in particular due to this large body of international empirical evidence that men and women kill for very different reasons and in very different contexts. Indeed, a key concern driving debates about the need for reform of the defences to homicide in Australia was that 31.5 per cent of all homicides involved a situation where a person killed his or her partner, or a former partner or a sexual rival. The overwhelming majority of these killings were committed by men who tended to be 'motivated by jealousy, or a desire to control their partner' (over three-quarters or 78.6 per cent). About half the homicide incidents in the context of sexual intimacy involved allegations of family violence against the accused (95.5 per cent of these involved a woman victim) (VLRC 2004: 15; VLRC 2003; Morgan 2002). It is to a discussion of the key areas of feminist concern with the partial defence of provocation that I now turn.

Women who kill their violent abusers

Australian courts inherited the defence of provocation when the English common law was introduced into Australia in the second half of the 19th century. While early courts approached the question of what kinds of words and/or conduct could amount to provocation for the purposes of raising the defence on a largely ad hoc basis, by the close of the 19th century it was accepted that a killing will be reduced from murder to manslaughter in circumstances where the provocation offered by the deceased was sufficient to deprive a reasonable man of the powers of self-control (Fairall and Yeo 2005: 188).[6] Although there is some variation in those jurisdictions in which it can still be raised, broadly speaking, the elements that are to be proven if the defence is to be successful are as follows: (i) the deceased must have said something and/or acted in a way that was provocative; (ii) the accused must have lost self-control as a result of the provocation and killed the deceased while experiencing that loss of self-control (these first two elements constitute the subjective requirement or test of the defence). Overriding both of these requirements is (iii) an objective requirement that the accused must have acted as an ordinary hypothetical person would have acted (the common law test for provocation was stated in *Masciantonio v The Queen* (1995) 183 CLR 58 at 67). The objective element of the partial defence has characterised debates in such cases ever since (see for example Yeo 1987a, 1987b, 1996; Fairall and Yeo 2005: 188).

Historically, provocation was developed as a concession to human frailty – a recognition that under certain circumstances everyone has the potential suddenly to 'snap' and kill another person. The standard formulation was expressed by Devlin J in *Duffy* ([1949] 1 All ER 932), which recognises that an accused person may find themselves in circumstances in which:

> . . . some act, or series of acts done (or words spoken) by the dead man to the accused, . . . which would cause in the accused, a sudden

and temporary loss of self-control, rendering the accused so subject to passion as to make him or her for the moment not the master of his mind.

Chief Justice Gleeson of the NSW Court of Criminal Appeal aptly described the problem with provocation: 'the law's concession to human frailty was very much, in its practical application, a concession to male frailty' (*Chhay v R* (1994) 72 A Crim R 1). Many critics have put this argument much more strongly, having argued that in practice the defence of provocation operates as a legal licence for men to kill women (Women's Coalition Against Family Violence 1994) or, indeed, 'womanslaughter' (Radford 1984; Radford and Russell 1992).

Both the defence of self-defence and the defence of provocation have generated much debate therefore with regard to battered women, largely due to the recognition that their acts and behaviour rarely conform to the masculine model (and metaphors) of behaviour and experience. Moreover, in cases involving women who kill, there has usually been a high degree of violence perpetrated against them in an ongoing relationship. As such, it is not these killings that the law deems 'normal', 'reasonable' or 'ordinary'. As Naffine, among others, has argued, the legal model of the reasonable or ordinary person 'is a man, not a woman. . . . he is a man, he is a middle-class man, and he evinces a style of masculinity of the middle classes' (1990: 100).[7] From this it follows that the tropes which feature in judicial debates about self-defence and provocation are overwhelmingly 'masculine ones, which emphasise masculine metaphors of temperature, speed and pressure' (as illustrated by expressions such as 'in the heat of the moment' or where anger is said to 'build up') (Young 1993: 771). In consequence, 'lawyers have had to match and often distort women's accounts and experiences in an effort to make them conform to law's standard universal subject' (Edwards 1996: 365).

The difficulties that women who have killed their violent abusers have faced when seeking to have their stories aired and heard in court can be illustrated by a number of high profile cases in Canada and England that dominated debates about reform of criminal law defences in the 1990s. The Canadian case of *Lavallée* (*R v Lavallée* [1990] 1 SCR 852) was the first time in which courts recognised the social reality of domestic violence through the use of expert evidence of Battered Wife Syndrome (BWS).[8] In *Lavallée*, the appellant shot her common law partner, Kevin Rust, in the back of the head as he was walking away from her and leaving the room. The shooting occurred after an argument where Ms Lavallée had been physically abused and was fearful for her life after being taunted with the threat that either she kill him or he would kill her. Ms Lavallée was charged with second degree murder, which at the time carried a sentence of 10 years before parole could be allowed. At trial, she pleaded self-defence. The traditional concept of self-defence involved a response to an immediate threat to one's safety. In this case, there was a pre-emptive strike in self-defence (Holland 2007: 138). A psychiatrist, Frederick Shane, gave evidence that Lavallée was a victim of BWS in support of her plea of self-defence, evidence that was based on the work of Lenore Walker on the 'cycle of violence' experienced by battered women (Boyle 1990: 171), and she was acquitted. The Crown appealed and a new trial was ordered by the Manitoba Court of Appeal. The case was then heard by the Supreme Court of Canada, which reinstated the acquittal. Many feminist lawyers and academics who have written about the case have since applauded it as a 'victory' for women because the judgment explicitly recognised that an aspect of Canadian criminal law, the defence of self-defence, had developed and operated in a gender biased way (Martinson 1999; Young 1993; Boyle 1990; Martinson et al 1991). Wilson J's majority judgment broke new ground in its criticism of the elements of the law of self-defence that she said had evolved from a male model of experience with violence and hence male evaluations of appropriate responses to violence, a bar room brawl encounter between two strangers relatively equal in size and strength (Martinson 1999: 381). The court recognised that the requirements for invoking the doctrine, particularly the im-minence requirement, incorporated assumptions based on a male model of experience and response to violence that neither coincides with nor incorporates the actual experiences of battered women.

As a result of *Lavallée*, evidence pertaining to the broader context is admissible so that the 'facts' are assessed from the perspective of the accused, rather than the standard of the 'reasonable' man (Castel 1990: 257; Sheehy 1992, 1994, 2001). Although this means that in principle the male bias of the provisions of self-defence, even when there is no immediate attack, has to some extent been addressed by *Lavallée*, many still claim that the criminal law fails to accommodate the experiences of battered women.

The English decisions of *Ahluwalia* and *Thornton* were also landmark cases for battered women who kill their violent abusers and highlight the complex relationship between the legal construction of women and dominant or conventional understandings of femininity.[9] Comparing it with the case of Sara Thornton, who also killed her abusive husband, but who was subject to quite a different narrative from that of Kiranjit Ahluwalia (*Thornton* [1992] 1 All ER 306; *Thornton (No 2)* [1996] 2 All ER 1023, [1995] *NLJ*) (1994: 737–74), Nicolson's analysis demonstrates that the question of whether female defendants are treated as mad or harshly treated as bad depends on a cultural judgment. Both cases, argues Nicolson, 'illustrate the long-standing tendency for the prosecution of women to be transformed into trial of their character, with their perceived conformity or non-conformity with the standards of appropriate femininity determining their treatment (1995: 188–89; see also Nicolson 2000: 172; Rollinson 2000).[10] Kiranjit Ahluwalia killed her husband by pouring a mixture of petrol and caustic soda over the bed on which he lay sleeping and then set it alight (*Ahluwalia* [1992] 4 All ER 889). At trial, Mrs Ahluwalia pleaded not guilty to murder and relied on the partial defence of provocation in the alternative. Despite evidence adduced at the trial showing that she was suffering from BWS (having suffered years of physical and mental abuse at the hands of her husband), the jury convicted her of murder and she was sentenced to life in prison. As a consequence of her case coming to the attention of the London based campaign group, Southall Black Sisters, she became a symbol of the oppression of Asian women in Western society and the group pressed for a retrial. Three grounds of appeal were argued: the first two alleged jury misdirections on the subjective and objective conditions of provocation, respectively, and the third that there was fresh evidence of diminished responsibility. On the latter ground alone, the Court of Appeal set aside Mrs Ahluwalia's conviction as unsafe and unsatisfactory and ordered a retrial. At the retrial, a plea of manslaughter was accepted and she was sentenced to 40 months' imprisonment, exactly that period already served (Nicolson and Sanghvi 1993).

In *Ahluwalia*, the judge's comments emphasised her conformity with an idealised form of femininity. According to Rollinson, Ahluwalia's allotted passivity and submissiveness functioned to paint a picture of her experience as a passive victim of conjugal violence, and appeared to encourage Lord Taylor CJ to speak of it as a 'tragic case' (2000: 114). In contrast, Sara Thornton's experience as a battered woman was downplayed to the point of almost becoming invisible (Rollinson 2000: 115). Whereas Sara Thornton's biography and actions were perceived as aggressive, fickle and devious and as outside of appropriate standards of femininity, the sympathetic rendering of the facts in Kiranjit Ahluwalia's case depicts her as a feminine woman and legitimate victim of conjugal violence (Rollinson 2000: 115). While neither image comes close to the experiences of battered women, according to Rollinson 'both are facilitated by a construction of the legal narrative that is held out as an "institutional regime for the production of truth"' (Kritzman, cited in Rollinson 2000: 114). The 'narrative either maps out an intent from the factual evidence that masculinises the defendant (constructing her as bad) or, alternatively, that effaces any conception of intentionality in favour of a traditional concept of female behaviour that is emotive, rather than rational (constructing her as mad)' (Rollinson 2000: 114).

In Australia, a number of criticisms followed the High Court Decision in *R v Osland* ((1998) 197 CLR 316), which at the time was only one of two appeal cases to have debated the issue of whether BWS evidence should be introduced.[11] In 1996, Heather Osland relied on expert testimony of BWS to found both the defence of self-defence and provocation but was convicted of the murder of her violent husband, Frank Osland, and sentenced to a term of 14 and a half years' imprisonment. At a separate trial, the first jury could not decide whether her adult son, David, who struck the blow that killed his stepfather was guilty, but the second jury acquitted him of murder on the grounds of self-defence. Heather Osland unsuccessfully appealed against her conviction to the High Court in 1998. Following her conviction and sentence, a campaign was initiated to advocate for her release from prison and reform of the partial defences to murder. The campaign group named *The Women Who Kill in Self-Defence Campaign* was comprised of individual women, Brimbank Community Centre, Domestic Violence and Incest Recourse Centre (DVIRC) (now known as Domestic Violence Recourse Centre Victoria or DVRCV) and community legal centres. An offshoot of this campaign group was the *Release Heather Osland Group*, which was formed in collaboration with the Victorian Women's Trust (VWT) and whose primary aim was to work towards Heather Osland's release. In 2005, Heather Osland was released after serving nine and half years of her sentence (Farouque 2005). According to one member of the *Heather Osland Support Group*, although Heather Osland's case became the catalyst for the 2005 reforms to the laws of homicide in Victoria, she personally endured a long and hard fight for justice. Over the last 10 years, the Victorian Government has implemented quite significant reforms in response to family violence issues as they relate to homicide laws, and '[y]et there does not seem to be an explanation as to why the government could not show mercy to a woman who was clearly a victim of long-term family violence, who acted to protect herself, and for whom there was widespread community support' (Kirkwood 2010: 169; see also Milovanovic 2010a, 2010b).

As noted by Fairall and Yeo, the controversy surrounding the *Osland* decision persuaded the Victorian Law Reform Commission (VLRC) who, in its earlier report on homicide in 1991 concluded that the experiences of battered women who kill were sufficiently accommodated by the partial defence of provocation, to change its mind. In its 1991 report, the VLRC drew on the findings of an empirical study conducted in Victoria that suggested that while the defence is used more frequently by men who kill women than women who kill men, it is not operating in a gender-biased way because the women who raise provocation appear to be more successful with the defence than men. This position was essentially reversed by the VLRC in 2003 when its *Defences to Homicide: Options Paper* found the opposite (Fairall and Yeo 2005: 214). The specific concerns driving debates surrounding whether or not the defence is biased against women defendants and unduly favoured male defendants are explored in more detail below. For present purposes, it can be noted that most feminist legal scholars would now be in agreement that the allowance of BWS testimony has allowed some recognition and contextualisation of women's experiences and has assisted in dispelling commonly held myths about battered women (Rix 2001; Schuller et al 2004; Douglas 2008). Wells has observed that feminist narrative efforts to ensure the experiences of battered women who kill their abusive partners are seen and aired in court have fast become part of the vocabulary with which domestic violence and the women who kill as a result of it are talked about. However, she also recognises that it has increasingly become more common to note a number of unintended 'essentializing and syndromizing' effects (2000: 91).[12] Although self-defence law may allow for the incorporation of battered women's experiences, 'the spirit of that law is still at the mercy of its judicial interpretation and application . . . [i]n practice . . . [it] . . . largely remains the preserve of men, with battered women still relying on the far less appropriate defence of provocation' (Manning 1996: 16–17, cited in Morrissey 2003: 98–99). Others concur, noting the shift away from narrow constructions of BWS towards recognition of the need for broader 'social context framework evidence' (see for example Maguigan 1991) to assist juries and the judiciary to better assess the reasonableness of a defendant's claim to self-defence. Stubbs and Tolmie, writing together and separately, have repeatedly demonstrated that notwithstanding the decision in *Osland v The Queen* ((1998) 197 CLR 316), Australian case law remains preoccupied with 'the psychological individualism of the criminal law' more generally, which they find 'is not confined to the trial stage but also shapes prosecutorial discretion and sentencing' (2008: 155; see also Stubbs and Tolmie 1995, 1999, 2005). Despite the fact that many Australian feminists have looked to best practice in Canada, a number of scholars have noted Canadian legal decisions that have not applied the principles in *R v Lavallée* sympathetically, preferring instead to resort to 'the '"syndromisation" of what is essentially a social problem' (Holland 2007: 139; see also Grant 1991; Sheehy 1994; Shaffer 1997; Stubbs and Tolmie 1999; Parfett 2001; Tang 2003; Gillis et al 2006). Osthoff and Maguigan have observed similar trends in decisions in the United States (2005).

Previous law reform efforts to ensure that the criminal law is as responsive to women's experiences and values as it is to men's experiences and values have been limited in their effectiveness, such limitations having been traced by other critics to the failure of equality concepts to bring about social and legal change (Fineman 1991; Sheehy 1991; Baker 1998; Carline 2005; Hunter 2006a; Forell 2006; Douglas 2008). Others, such as Morrissey, however, are of the view that battered women who kill need a 'new legal narrative' that can 'uphold their claims of self-defence' and 'would base representation upon a concept of determined agency'. In this way their act of killing their abuser could more appropriately be understood as 'a rational choice' and the result of being 'coerced into that decision through lack of societal support and recognition of their situation' (2003: 102).

This approach, as Hunter illustrates, highlights the persistence of:

> ... legal characterisations [that] 'transform the lives of victims into cases, taking away from the stories the meaning behind their circumstances and unique identities'. This is both a 'process of objectification and subjection' and also a normalising process, erasing complexities and contradictions in favour of a clear, black-or-white story.
>
> (Bumiller 1988, cited in Hunter 2006b: 40)

Thus, for Davies, it is important to continue 'working to achieve change along at least two fronts, one "internal" to law and accepting (however conditionally) its power to define and refine; the second from a position of scepticism and critique of law' (2003: 169).

Provocation: the jealous lover's defence?

The preceding discussion focused on feminist arguments that the doctrines of self-defence and provocation were too narrow and did not allow the broad context of women's behaviour to be accommodated. The discussion below examines another sex-specific area of the law of murder that has come in for considerable feminist criticism – where the partial defence of provocation is relied on in cases involving men who kill out of anger, jealousy, possessiveness or loss of self-control. The argument that the partial defence of provocation operates as a deeply sexed excuse for men to murder women has been traced to its historical (masculine) origins. The foundations of the doctrine of the partial defence of provocation were laid in the 16th- and 17th-century English common law at a time when the death penalty was mandatory for those convicted of murder.[13] In recognition of the need for law to make a concession to 'human frailty' (or 'human infirmity'),[14] it distinguished between those murders where a person acted out of malice or premeditation, where the use of force was presumed illegitimate, and those where a person killed in cases of 'chance medley' – where the person's use of force is presumed partially justifiable (Brown 1963). The provocation defence initially developed as a common law doctrine about men defending their honour.[15] Until the 19th century, the legal rules and requirements that structured the partial defence treated men and women differently. Provocation's 'primal scenes' are listed by Chief Justice Holt in 1707 in *R v Mawgridge*, in which provocation in an adultery context appears for the first time in English homicide law.[16] In the context of murder between intimate partners or ex-partners the paradigm of provocation cited in legal texts is a situation where a man suddenly discovers his wife in the act of 'infidelity' with another man (see *R v Maddy* (1671) 1 Vent 159, reprinted in 83 ER 112). If the man kills the adulterer, it is manslaughter, 'for jealousy is the rage of a man, and adultery is the highest invasion of property' (*R v Mawgridge* (1707) 84 ER 1107: 1114–15 (Lord Holt CJ (KB) UK). A man in this situation is seen to have struck out in the 'heat of passion' or a 'hot-blooded rage'.[17] 'Sexual provocation', writes Leader-Elliott, 'the claim that infidelity, desertion or sexual humiliation drove to the offender to kill a rival or a sexual partner – is a distinct variety of the defence, with its own particular history' (1997: 151). Whereas originally cases of 'sexual' provocation appeared to be limited to a husband killing his male rival, Leader-Elliott has shown that it was not until well into the 19th century that a reported case conceded the possibility that provocation might provide a partial excuse to a husband who killed his wife (1997: 153). The modern law of provocation is, as Leader-Elliott notes, 'far removed from the stark simplicities of *R v Mawgridge* and early 19th century cases. Modern courts are far more hospitable to pleas based on jealousy and possessiveness' (Leader-Elliott 1997: 153).[18]

Bradfield has observed that the standard 'narrative of provocation' is that of the 'jealous husband', one that recounts a familiar story of 'jealousy, betrayal and infidelity' (2000:5; see also Gorman 1999: 478–500). This standard provocation narrative involves a number of assumptions about male anger and jealousy as culturally understandable and male violence as justifiable. This restrictive view of what counts as provocation for the purposes of raising the defence has, as highlighted above, meant that the experiences of battered women and their stories 'of fear, violence and oppression' have been inaudible. The deficiencies of this restrictive view of provocation have been addressed by expanding the circumstances in which it may be raised in order to recognise that, in the case of the battered woman, the provocation could be cumulative, rather than sudden and based on fear, rather than anger. However, many feminists have remained critical of the ways in which the courts have continued to empathise with the murderous rage of husbands who kill their 'provocative' wives.

While the modern law of provocation can be found to draw on various and specific fictions of masculinity, what is equally clear is that the stories that are told about the murderous rage of jealous (cuckolded) husbands and lovers transform the woman's death into *his* tragedy for the purposes of his redemptive narrative and, in so doing, reduce her murder 'to the moral ambiguity of manslaughter' (Leader-Elliott 1997: 162–63)[19] As Howe observes: 'the standard provocation tale is a man's tale of his aggravation by a . . . "nagging, unfaithful or departing wife, more recently a man making an unwanted sexual advance to another man"'. Moreover, 'only the killer's story is narrated' whereas the victim, 'whether female or feminised', having already been silenced once by being murdered, is silenced once again in the context of the trial (2002: 60).

While the courts have not always been in agreement that 'words alone' should amount to provocation (Morgan 1997), perhaps the most scathing critique to emerge within feminist legal scholarship with regard to provocation is in relation to those cases where the grounds for blame reduction includes the 'nagging' or 'taunting' behaviour of the deceased (Edwards 1987; Lees 1992, 1997; Coker 1992; Bandalli 1995; Howe 2002, 2004b). If women's use of violence has hardly figured in the definition of the 'reasonable man' standard in cases of self-defence, in provocation cases the purported capacity of the female body to incite men's violence has loomed large in legal narrations of women victims as provokers of their own demise. As Sue Bandalli's analysis of provocation cases in the English legal context has persuasively revealed, matrimonial transgressions such as 'shouting', 'swearing', uttering a 'constant stream of abuse', using 'cutting and hurtful phrases', 'needling him, by removing his food before he had finished it and switching off the television when he wanted to view it' and 'treating him with disdain' all substantiated a plea of provocation (1995: 400). Moreover, Bandalli illustrates that 'only one side of the story is heard' and that is typically that of the 'good' or 'hardworking' husband whose culpability is reduced, and who was 'let down' by his wife or who caused him to suffer 'through no fault of . . . [his] . . . own' (1995: 402).

Bandalli's analysis is important in another respect. She insightfully demonstrates the link between the apparent acceptability of the idea of being provoked by a woman's words in provocation cases to the historical and cultural association between unruly speech and gendered forms of punishment meted out on the literal and literary figure of the scold (1995: 399 fn 19, 406–407). Up until the late 18th century, the legal and social consequences for women who were thought to have exercised an excess of feminine agency, either by talking too much and/or behaving in a way that was thought to be sexually non-conforming or challenging male authority, was to subject them to direct physical punishments that were sometimes quite brutal and painful. A method that was used at that time was to punish the offending woman by the application of the branks or the scold's or gossip's bridle. Citing Dobash et al (1986: 19, cited in Bandalli 1995: 406–407), Bandalli observes that 't]he branks was an iron cage placed over the head, and most examples incorporated a spike or pointed wheel that was inserted into the offender's mouth in order to "pin down the tongue and silence the noisiest brawler"'. Although references to the actual word 'scold' or 'scold's bridle' are often discursively absent in contemporary cases of so-called 'provoked' killings, subsequent chapters will demonstrate that we nonetheless find similar tensions around conceptions of women's agency and responsibility being played out in provocation cases with disingenuous or devastating effects. As this book aims to illustrate, while the exculpatory script of a woman 'asking for it' reflects, on the one hand, long held legal and cultural assumptions and sensitivities to 'loquacious', 'unruly', 'malicious' and 'angry' wives, these assumptions, on the other hand, are not only value-laden; indeed, they are value-judgments about what appropriate womanhood should be; they are *stories*. That is to say, these assumptions about the female victim and women's culpability are themselves literally brought into being by virtue of a whole host of linguistic techniques and devices of narrative that are mobilised by lawyers and judges to portray the woman victim as the 'antagonist', rather than the victim in the narrative ('a shrew'), and the violence as an attempt both to 'control' and 'discipline' her.[20] It is precisely the *sexed* aspect of provocation's victim-blaming narratives that has been a driving force behind calls for reform of the partial defences to homicide, which in some jurisdictions, has successfully resulted in the abolition of the provocation defence.[21]

More recently, feminist arguments have observed that while a woman-blaming provocation narrative is less likely to succeed in an Australian court today, the same cannot be said where provoked men kill other men, rather than women. For Howe, norms relating to sexuality and, in particular, male homosexuality, have not changed much at all (2002: 42). This insight brings me to a third area of concern in relation to the partial defences to murder: where the provocation relied on is in response to an alleged non-violent (homo)sexual advance.

Provocation and 'homosexual panic'

The concept of 'homosexual advance defence' (HAD) or 'homosexual panic defence' (HPD) was originally employed by lawyers in the United States in cases where the defendant pleads insanity or diminished responsibility in answer to a charge of murdering a homosexual victim. However, in Australia, since the late 1990s we have seen the emergence of what is ostensibly a 'new' criminal defence: the HAD (Statham 1999). It has been successfully relied on by heterosexually identified men as a de facto defence, available to a defendant in Australia and other common law jurisdictions (Howe 1998: 466–67) and operates either to absolve the defendant from criminal liability or to mitigate that liability (Howe 1999: 339; see also Comstock 1992; Mison 1992; Tomsen 1994, 1998; Dressler 1995; Johnson 1996; Howe 1997, 1998, 2000; Bradfield 2001; Lee 2008). The most recent case to provoke comment and outrage to which this claim of HAD can be tied is the New South Wales High Court decision in *Green*[22] (Bradfield 1998; Howe 1998; Statham 1999; Meure 2001; Young 2001; de Pasquale 2002; Golder 2004a, 2004b). In Golder's account, his criticism is with the ways in which 'legal inscriptions' in such cases 'legitimise, produce and reproduce violence against homosexual men' (2004a: 54). Golder demonstrates that discourses of predatory homosexuality and paedophilia are articulated together in HAD narratives. Other scholars who are also critical of this informal provocation defence have commented on how the narratives that are produced are predicated upon a logic of (hetero)normativity in which the threat of the 'homosexual' advance is not homosexuality per se, but rather, 'symbolic feminization' (Lunny 2003: 311). Golder identifies that the particular inscription of the bounded nature of the male heterosexual body in legal discourse, 'its impermeable and unbreachable status, leads to a parallel inscription on the homosexual as penetrator/predator' and is itself a form of legal violence (2004a: 67–68; see also Howe 1998; Statham 1999; Tomsen 2002; Rudland 2001). This idea developed from the now classic work of Robert Cover, who commented that the defining characteristic of the act of legal interpretation was necessarily connected to the imposition of state sanctioned violence. The point Cover was making here concerned the violence of legal interpretation (1986: 1601). Citing the work of Sarat and Kearns, Hunter observes that from this it follows that the law's 'violence may be understood in disciplinary, discursive and cultural as well as physical terms' (2006b: 33). Thus, for Golder, the most effective strategy is that of 'rewriting the body'. The 'metaphoric and utopian challenge to the logic of the bounded body . . . is [one] . . . in which we are all implicated, and whose pressing call none of us can ignore' (2004a: 68, 2004b). What the work of feminist and queer theorists shows is that while the law purports to prohibit violence, '[n]ot all extra-legal force is disallowed. As feminist and lesbian/gay/queer theorists have observed, law does allow – indeed, it allows considerable scope for – violence by men against women and children, and homophobic violence against gay men and lesbians' (Hunter 2006b: 30).

Law reform inquiries: cases and controversies

It is now possible to cite a number of recent cases from different national and international jurisdictions that have attracted significant public criticism. The debates surrounding these controversial verdicts have typically involved allegations that the standard provocation narrative of a man who kills his 'nagging, unfaithful or departing wife' is anachronistic, that it shifts the responsibility for his anger and violence onto the dead body of the woman victim, and that it should be abolished. In response to these criticisms, law reform bodies in Australia, England and New Zealand have made various and specific recommendations to reform the defences to homicide, which has resulted in either the abolition of the partial defence of provocation and, in some cases, its retention and reform.

The demise of provocation in Tasmania, Victoria and Western Australia

In the mid 1990s, a Standing Committee of the Attorneys-General discussed the development of a national model criminal code for Australian jurisdictions. The committee, now known as the Model Criminal Code Officers' Committee (MCCOC), published a report on fatal offences against the person entitled *Model Criminal Code, Fatal Offences Against the Person Discussion Paper* (MCCOC 1998). In contrast to the earlier reports on homicide (LRCV Report No 40 1991 and NSWLRC Report 83 1997), the committee came to the conclusion that there was overwhelming evidence that the defence of provocation was so deeply male-oriented that it should be abolished and further recommended that claims of provocation be left to the sentencing phase (MCCOC 1998: 91, 93, 101, 103).

In apparent support of the view of the committee, the Tasmanian legislature abolished the defence of provocation to murder in 2003 (Bradfield 2003). The *Criminal Code Amendment (Abolition of Defence of Provocation) Act* 2003 (Tas) repealed section 60 of the Tasmanian criminal code (Fairall and Yeo 2005: 215–16).[23] Although the Tasmanian legislature acknowledged the growing empirical literature showing that men and women kill their intimate partners or ex-partners in very different circumstances (Bradfield 2003), it is the only Australian state to have abolished provocation as a stand-alone decision (Ramsey 2010: 69).[24]

In Victoria, the decision to abolish the provocation defence was made by the Victorian Law Reform Commission (VLRC) in its final report entitled *Defences to Homicide* (2004: xlv, 58, Recommendation 1). The VLRC were concerned about the inequitable treatment of men and women who kill their current or former partners in light of the empirical evidence that men and women kill in very different circumstances (2004: 27–30; Morgan

2002: 21–29). The VLRC was particularly concerned that continued use of the provocation defence would only serve to legitimate killings committed in anger (2004: 31–32). A related issue was that it would operate to the disadvantage of people who were exercising their equality rights: for instance, leaving a relationship or starting a new relationship with another person (VLRC 2004: 56–58). Accordingly, the VLRC was of the view that '[p]eople should be expected to control their behaviour – even when provoked'. The VLRC stated that 'the historical justification for retaining a separate partial defence on the grounds of compassion –a "concession to human frailty" – is, we believe, difficult to sustain'. The Victorian Government was also persuaded by these concerns that retention of the provocation defence would only serve to send an inappropriate message that the deceased is somehow partially to blame for their own death (VLRC 2004: 58, 32) and the defence was abolished through the *Crimes (Homicide) Act* 2005 (Vic). Thus, it recommended that the provocation defence be abolished and that considerations of provocation mitigation could more appropriately be dealt with at the sentencing phase (VLRC 2004:32).

Although there had been a long history of feminist criticism of the partial defence of provocation prior to the controversial verdict in *Ramage*,[25] as noted by one commentator: '[f]ew cases display more effectively the injustice of the provocation defence.... [and] ... the double devastation experienced by the deceased's family and friends when a provocation plea is successful' (Coss 2005: 135). While public criticism of the *Ramage* case[26] coincided with the release of the VLRC's final report (2004), it did not have a direct bearing on the recommendations made in the report because it was published prior to the controversial verdict. However, many are of the view that it was the case that not only swayed public opinion but also, and perhaps more importantly, the Victorian legislature (Ramsey 2010: 67; see also Coss 2005; Maher et al 2005). In 2004 James Ramage (the last man in Victoria to rely successfully on the provocation defence) was convicted by a Victorian Supreme Court jury of the manslaughter of his wife, from whom he had been separated for six weeks prior to her death on 28 October 2004.[27] The jury was persuaded that James had been provoked to kill Julie after she allegedly told him 'that she had had sleepovers and how much nicer than you the new man was, that they shared interest and he cared for her. She then said that sex with you repulsed her and screwed up her face and either said or implied how much better her new friend was'.[28] James struck Julie at least twice to the face, causing her to fall to the ground, and then strangled her until she was dead. After clearing up all the evidence, he placed her body in the boot of his car and drove some distance out of Melbourne before burying her in a shallow grave. Later that evening, he had dinner with his son. At some point during dinner, he spoke to his daughter on the phone who was concerned about her mother's whereabouts, but he said he didn't know where she was. Some hours later, he confessed to police. He was sentenced to a maximum period of imprisonment of 11 years, with a minimum non-parole period of eight years on 10 December 2004.

From the very outset, critics launched a scathing attack of the ways in which 'the trial' in the *Ramage* case 'was seen to become an examination, and ultimately crucifixion, of the deceased wife, Julie' (Coss 2005: 136). Media reports emphasised how Julie Ramage was 'a duplicitous, pleasure seeking, hormone-driven flibbertigibbet', while 'the jury was told that James Ramage was controlling but heard little detail about what form this took' (Kissane 2004a: 4). It was argued in the *Ramage* case that evidence of the history of the relationship provided the background context to the exchanges that were made between James and Julie at the time she was killed.[29] While the defence sought to place 'particular reliance upon the sequence of events in the six days prior to the killing of the deceased, counsel for the Crown, in contrast, sought to rely on this evidence to demonstrate that 'the accused had great difficulty in dealing with rejection; that he not only desired to restore the marriage but to remain in control of the situation' and 'that the deceased had a continuing underlying fear of the accused'.[30] Jane Ashton, Julie's twin sister, said after the verdict: 'I'm just devastated. Females can have their characters blackened and their struggles as victims trivialised, whereas the abuser's testimony as to how he was provoked and his emotional state before that is sanctioned by law' (Kissane 2004a :4). As Maher et al observed, the trial quickly descended into a 'tragic' and 'shocking' tale about James's desperate but thwarted attempts to win back the affections of his estranged wife whereas Julie, in contrast, was positioned as an obstacle in the narrative (an 'agent in the marital difficulties') (Maher et al 2005: 156; see also Coss 2005).[31] In response to the verdict, Jane Ashton spoke of how '[s]he (Julie) was being portrayed as the person who provoked him who had somehow brought it on herself by defying him. This woman was leaving him purely because she found him cruel and no longer wished to have a relationship with him' (Gough 2004: 3; see also Packham and Ross 2004: 16). According to another commentator on the *Ramage* case, Phil Cleary (2004: 4), whose sister was murdered by her violent ex-boyfriend, Peter Keogh, and who has since been an advocate for its abolition, said:

> If Julie Ramage's behaviour was the kind that might have caused an ordinary man to lose control and strangle her, no woman is safe. As long as we offer juries the chance to blame a woman for her murder,

as this jury has effectively done in handing down a manslaughter
verdict, we're a party to the violence.

In another recent case of intimate partner homicide, the jury was not offered
the chance to blame the woman victim for her own fate. Mazin Yasso, like
James Ramage, killed his estranged wife, Eman Hermiz, from whom he had
been separated for a number of months. According to Maher et al's analysis
of the case, both were Iraqi nationals and had married in Baghdad in 1990.
Eman arrived in Australia in 1999 having been sponsored by her sister and
brother-in-law. Mazin arrived some months later, with the plan that Eman
would sponsor his permanent residency application. The couple had been
separated some months prior to Eman's death. On the day she was killed,
Mazin had followed her to a shopping centre where he confronted her about
some items he wanted returned. According to Mazin, at some point during
the confrontation, Eman spat at him (which was interpreted by him and his
defence counsel as a culturally offensive gesture) causing him to lose self-
control and stab her multiple times (Maher et al 2005: 153). Unlike James
Ramage, however, the trial judge ruled that the defence of provocation
should not be left to the jury. This decision was overturned on appeal,
resulting in a retrial. At his second trial, the presiding judge did allow the
defendant to rely on the defence of provocation, but the jury did not find
that he was sufficiently provoked and convicted him of murder.[32]

Media reports of the killing of Julie Ramage by her estranged husband,
James Ramage, identified it as an 'honour killing' (Kissane 2004a: 4–6). Yet,
as Maher et al observed, media responses to the *Yasso* case did not present it
as 'honourable'. Furthermore, Maher et al convincingly demonstrate that
'the rhetoric surrounding the "war on terror"' with its 'accepted conventions
of white masculinity' underpinned the discourses deployed by the
prosecution, the defence and the judge. Consequently, 'Yasso's responses
[were presented] as culturally specific' and his reactions were compared
'unfavourably with what would be expected of an "Australian" man'.
Moreover, his 'behaviour was seen as a reflection of his status as "other", as
foreign'.[33] Maher et al's analysis of the differential media coverage and legal
responses to these two cases reveals that 'when violent masculinity is practised
by white middle-class men [eg James Ramage], it is likely to be interpreted
differently than when it is practised by those identified as culturally "other"
[eg Mazin Yasso]' (2005: 148). It also 'suggests that the form of masculinity
supported by the law is raced, as well as gendered' (Maher et al 2005: 159). A
similar observation has been made by de Pasquale in his discussion of the
Australian High Court decision in *Green*.[34] For de Pasquale 'an unmarked,
heterosexist legal regime asserts its cultural dominance in provocation cases'.

He argues that while provocation cases involving ethnic minority defendants are generally perceived as raising cultural issues (and rightly so), cases in which men allege a homosexual advance are no less culturally inscribed. In his analysis, '[s]pecific cultural assumptions about unruly women being somehow blameworthy or partially deserving of their own deaths may well be linked to the latest aspersions that courts, including the High Court, have assembled about gay men' (2002: 117).

In the wake of other controversial verdicts and shortly after Victoria enacted its reforms to the laws of homicide in 2005, Western Australia initiated similar changes to the law of homicide to that taken in Victoria and abolished provocation through the *Criminal Law Amendment (Homicide) Act* 2008 (WA). Until 2008, the partial defence of provocation to murder was governed by s 281 of the *Criminal Code* (WA).[35] Unlike other Australian jurisdictions, Western Australia was the only state to maintain a distinction between wilful murder, murder and manslaughter. However, this division was abandoned as a result of a recommendation of the Law Reform Commission of Western Australia (LRCWA) in 2007 (LRCWA 2007).[36] Other changes include the introduction of a new offence of 'unlawful assault causing death' (a 'one-punch' homicide offence) and changes to the defences of duress, accidence, self-defence (acknowledging its debt to the VLRC) and the defence of property (Office of the Attorney General Western Australia 2008, Hayward 2008).[37]

The controversial verdict in the case of *Sebo* in Queensland also prompted calls for the abolition of the partial defence of provocation.[38] However, given the Queensland government's stated intention that no change be made to the existing penalty of mandatory life imprisonment for murder, the Queensland Law Reform Commission (QLRC) recommended that it be retained but that it be severely restricted in its application (QLRC 2008: 10-11, 497-500).

The legal reforms in Queensland

In Queensland the partial defence of provocation is provided for in section 304 of the *Criminal Code Act* 1899 (Qld) (QLRC 2008: 213; Burton et al 2011: 78).[39] To provide some context to the debates surrounding calls for the abolition of the provocation defence, the case of *R v Sebo* is one of the cases that prompted an audit undertaken by the Queensland Department of Justice and Attorney-General (DJAG) of homicide trials and the use of the excuse of accident and the partial defence to murder of provocation (DJAG 2007), and attactred significant public commentary. Damian Karl Sebo was convicted of manslaughter after he repeatedly bashed his former

16-year-old girlfriend, Taryn Hunt, to death with a steering wheel lock on 9 September 2005. At his trial, Sebo claimed that he lost self-control and killed the deceased, who was allegedly affected by alcohol and 'taunted' him with claims of having slept with a number of other men. It was at this point that he said he stopped the vehicle on the roadside and made her get out. When she said that she would continue to deceive him, he struck her a number of times with a steering wheel lock, continuing after she had fallen to the ground. The blows caused injuries which were described as 'severe' and she died two days later in hospital. He was sentenced to 10 years' imprisonment.[40] According to media reports, the unsuccessful campaign to abolish provocation was being driven by Taryn's mother, Jennifer Tierney and the Queensland Homicide Victim's Support Group, who were critical of how 'provocation is being used as an excuse for attackers who "snap and kill" to be convicted of the lesser charge of manslaughter or acquitted' (Edmistone 2007a, 2007b; Anonymous 2007; Stigwood 2007: 12).

The results of the audit were published in 2007 in the Department's Discussion Paper, *Discussion Paper Audit on Defences to Homicide: Accident and Provocation* (DJAG 2007), which was followed in 2008 by the Queensland Law Reform Commission's (QLRC) review of the excuse of accident and the partial defence of provocation (QLRC 2008).[41] The Commission's view was that the partial defence of provocation contained in section 304 of the *Criminal Code* (Qld) 'should be abolished' but only if 'mandatory life imprisonment for murder is replaced with presumptive life imprisonment for murder, so that circumstances that might otherwise give rise to the partial defence could be taken into account at sentencing' (QLRC 2008: 500). It recommended that legislation be drafted to give effect to a number of recommendations including that 'the partial defence of provocation cannot be based on words alone or conduct that consists substantially of words' (recommendation 21-2) and that '[s]ection 304 of the *Criminal Code* (Qld) should be amended to include a provision to the effect that, other than in circumstances of an extreme and exceptional character, the partial defence of provocation cannot be based upon the deceased's choice about a relationship' (recommendation 21-3). It was also recommended that 'consideration should be given, as a matter of priority, to the development of a separate defence for battered persons which reflects the best current knowledge about the effects of a seriously abusive relationship on a battered person, ensuring that the defence is available to an adult or a child and is not gender-specific' (recommendation 21-4) (QLRC 2008: 500-501).'

Two years later Queensland Attorney-General, Cameron Dick, announced proposals to reform the laws of homicide, which were to be 'targeted at murderous ex-lovers, graveyard vandals and unfair landlords' (Office of the Deputy Premier and Attorney-General Media Release (24 March 2011); see also Trenwith 2010). In line with the Queensland Law Review Commission's recommendations, the reforms to the laws of homicide in Queensland only partially removed the defence of provocation (Sweetman 2010). The *Criminal Code and Other Legislation Amendment Act* 2011 (Qld) was passed by the Queensland Government on 4 April 2011 and received royal assent and commenced on 4 April 2011. The Act gave effect to key recommendations made by the Queensland Law Reform Commission to reform the provocation defence (QLRC 2008). As such, the new laws provide that the onus be on the defendant, rather than the prosecution, to prove on the balance of probabilities that provocation occurred. The changes also restrict the range of circumstances in which the partial defence may be raised and will no longer apply where 'the sudden provocation is based on words alone, other than in circumstances of a most extreme and exceptional character'. Nor will it apply, according to clause 5 of the amended section 304: other than in circumstances of a most extreme and exceptional character, where—

(a) a domestic relationship exists between two persons; and
(b) one person unlawfully kills the other person (the deceased); and
(c) the sudden provocation is based on anything done by the deceased or anything the person believes the deceased has done—
  (i) to end the relationship; or
  (ii) to change the nature of the relationship; or
  (iii) to indicate in any way that the relationship may, should or will end, or that there may, should or will be a change to the nature of the relationship.

In furtherance of the QLRC's recommendation to have 'regard to the limitations of existing defences for a person in a seriously abusive and violent relationship who kills his or her abuser' and 'that consideration be given to the development of a separate defence of battered persons (recommendations 21–24 of the Review),[42] the *Criminal Code (Abusive Domestic Relationship Defence and Another Matter) Amendment Act* 2010 (Qld) was passed on 16 February 2009.

The QLRC's recommendation to have 'regard to the limitations of existing defences for a person in a seriously abusive and violent relationship who kills his or her abuser' acknowledged that consideration be given to the development of a separate defence of battered persons (recommendations 21–24 of the Review).[43] The Department of Justice and Attorney-General

(DJAG) retained academics from Bond University, Professors Geraldine Mackenzie and Eric Colvin in July 2009, to examine the development of such a defence. The outcome was their report entitled *Homicide in Abusive Relationships: A Report on Defences* (Mackenzie and Colvin 2009) in which they recommended the introduction of a separate partial defence to murder into the Criminal Code applicable to victims of seriously abusive domestic relationships who kill their abusers, believing their actions are necessary for self-defence where there are reasonable grounds for such belief. In response to the recommendations of the independent review (Mackenzie and Colvin 2009), the Queensland government inserted the new s304B into the *Criminal Code* (Qld) and introduced a new separate, partial defence of killing in an abusive domestic relationship in February 2010 (the *Criminal Code (Abusive Domestic Relationship Defence and Another Matter) Amendment Act* 2010 (Qld) was assented to 16 February 2009). While the impact of the various and specific amendments to the laws of homicide in these Australian jurisdictions remains to be seen, provocation is still available in the Northern Territory,[44] New South Wales, the Australian Capital Territory[45] and South Australia.[46]

Provocation in New South Wales

In New South Wales (NSW), there are statutory provisions governing the provocation defence (*Crimes Act* 1900 (NSW) section 23). In 1997, the New South Wales Law Reform Commission (NSWLRC) recommended that the provocation defence be retained (NSWLRC) 1997).[47] The defence of excessive self-defence is found in section 421 of the *Crimes Act* 1900 (NSW).[48] It was enacted in 2001 in response to a 1998 Working Party publication on killings in response to homosexual advances, which recommended an amendment to the provocation defence but not to self-defence (Roth 2007). As noted by Yeo, the New South Wales legislature appears to be content to recognise these defences and retain their current structure (2010: 3).[49] However, from time to time, debates about reform of the laws of homicide have surfaced in response to public outcry over a series of controversial verdicts involving the 'homosexual advance defence' (HAD) in the context of provocation. I have already alluded to the contours of these concerns in a preceding section in relation to the High Court decision in *Green*. In 2004, the Australian Capital Territory (ACT) amended section 13 of the *Crimes Act* 1900 (ACT) so that a non-violent sexual advance could no longer form the basis of a defendant's claim to the defence of provocation (*Sexuality Discrimination Legislation Amendment Act* 2004 (ACT)).

The demise of provocation in New Zealand

In 2009, the New Zealand Parliament passed legislation repealing the partial defence of provocation (*Crimes (Provocation Repeal) Amendment Bill* (NZ)) (passed 26 November 2009). Prior to this, provocation was governed by section 169 of the *Crimes Act* 1961 (NZ). The decision to repeal provocation in New Zealand followed two reports by the New Zealand Law Commission (NZLC) in response to criticisms of the failure of the partial defences to murder to deal with domestic violence perpetrated on women by men and domestic violence in same-sex relationships. One was published in 2001, which found the submissions in favour of abolishing the provocation defence 'compelling'. It recommended that issues of provocation would be more appropriately dealt with by taking it into account as a mitigating circumstance when sentencing (NZLC 2001: 42). The other report was published in 2007 and the New Zealand Law Commission again concluded that section 169 of the *Crimes Act* 1961 (NZ) should be repealed (NZLR 2007: 48-49).

The New Zealand Government's decision to abolish the partial defence of provocation follows the controversial verdict reached by a Christchurch jury in the case of *Weatherston*. The jury found Clayton Weatherston guilty of the murder of his ex-girlfriend, Sophie Elliott. Weatherston, an economics lecturer, stabbed Sophie, an economics student at the same university, 216 times in her home on 9 January 2008. They had been in a relationship for about six months and had separated in December 2007. On the day she was murdered, Sophie was preparing to leave Christchurch for a job with the Treasury in Wellington. On 9 January 2008 she was in the middle of packing at home in her bedroom. Clayton Weatherston arrived at her house with a bag of items including a kitchen knife. According to Weatherston, 'he was provoked by the actions of Sophie Elliott (he said, by her lunging at him with a pair of scissors in the bedroom, against the background of their tumultuous relationship) and that the killing was the result of ... losing the power of self-control'.[50] Following the conviction, Sophie's mother, Lesley Elliott, announced her intention to establish the Sophie Elliott Foundation as a tribute not only to her daughter's memory but to raise money to fund a nationwide primary prevention programme and to support local community initiatives which align with the foundation (Wade 2010; Booker 2011). Indeed, public debate surrounding the case intensified following claims by Sophie Elliott's father in relation to what he perceived to be undue censoring of his version of his victim impact statement (Gower 2009). While many have welcomed the decision to repeal provocation (New Zealand Government Media Releases (19 August 2009, 27 November 2009)), others are of the view that it should have been retained and simplified to make it easier to apply and automatically exclude in circumstances that are 'common human experiences and, although emotionally painful', are not situations in which 'ordinary people respond ... with murder' (see for example Tolmie 2009; see also New Zealand Labour Party Media Releases (23 July 2009, 27 November 2009).

Reform of provocation in England: a revamped defence of 'loss of control'

Following the high profile cases of *Thornton* and *Ahluwalia*, feminist legal scholars and law reformers across national and international jurisdicitons have continued to voice concerns about legal responses to women who kill their violent abusers or who are killed by their current or former partners.[51] In England, these concerns have taken place in the context of a jurisdiction in which there is mandatory life imprisonment for murder (Lacey, Wells and Quick 2010: 726–46). In December 2002, the British Court of Appeal heard three combined Attorney-General's appeals against unduly lenient sentences for domestic homicide. Two cases concerned men who killed their ex-female partners and the third case involved a man who killed his fiancée.[52] Leslie Humes was sentenced to seven years' imprisonment after he pleaded guilty to manslaughter by reason of provocation. Humes, a solicitor, stabbed his estranged wife in front of her four children. He claimed he lost self-control after she told him she did not love him. Mark Wilkinson was found guilty of manslaughter by provocation after a trial and sentenced to four years' imprisonment. He said he lost his self-control and suffocated his ex-partner after she allegedly taunted him about her plans to start a new relationship with a boyfriend. Darren Suratan denied killing his partner but evidence that he had struck her at least twice causing her to suffer a haemorrhage formed the basis of his conviction for unlawful manslaughter. He was sentenced to three and a half years' imprisonment. The Attorney-General launched an appeal against the sentences on the basis that he wished 'the courts to impose tougher sentences on men convicted of manslaughter for killing their partners' (Dyer 2002). The Court of Appeal rejected all three appeals but, according to Burton, its interpretation effectively effaced the violence committed against the victims by putting their behaviour on trial. Thus, in *Wilkinson*, 'the defendant faced a dual threat of loss of possession of both his former partner and his children'. Although '[a] similar double threat was rather more implicit in *Humes*', the Court of Appeal agreed with the trial judge's decision to afford 'mitigation for stress with symptoms of not sleeping or eating properly in a period of separation prior to the killing'. And in *Suratan*, although the defence of provocation was not raised, it can be assumed that the Court of Appeal regarded the strain of putting up with the victim's excessive drinking 'as an appropriate factor for the trial judge to consider in mitigation in setting a sentence that was lower than the suggested appropriate term for a killing resulting from more than a single blow' (Burton 2003: 280–82).

The precursor to these debates about provocation in England and Wales came with the House of Lords' judgment in *Smith*.[53] As Burton notes, Lord Hoffmann's statement that 'male possessiveness and sexual jealousy should not today be an acceptable reason for loss of self-control leading to homicide' did little to loosen the hold of what she termed 'the jealous male defence' in England and Wales. Rather, she argued, the Court of Appeal sentencing decision in *R v Suratan, R v Humes* and *R v Wilkinson*[54] reinforced the apparent acceptability of 'British judicial attitudes to such a defence through current sentencing practices' (2003: 280). Thus, for Burton, the empathy afforded these three jealous male killers could only be redressed through substantive reform of the partial defence of provocation and/or the sentencing for domestic homicide: otherwise 'the families of victims will be left with an impression that men are still "getting away with murder"' (2003: 287–88)

The British Court of Appeal decision in *Suratan, Humes* and *Wilkinson* reignited calls for reform of the partial defences to murder and lenient sentences for domestic homicide (Hinsliff 2003). The proposals for reform were backed by Harriet Harman QC, the then Solicitor-General, and outlined in a consultation paper *Safety and Justice: the Government's Proposals on Domestic Violence* in 2003, which noted 'the concern about the way in which the law on murder operates in domestic violence cases ... about the level of sentencing by reason of provocation where the provocation relied on is sexual jealousy or infidelity' (Edwards 2003). As one commentator noted, when announcing the *Safety and Justice* proposals, the then Solicitor-General Harriet Harman said they were an important step in ending the 'culture of excuses' for men's violence against women.[55] The Home Secretary, David Blunkett, requested that the Law Commission instigate an inquiry into the operation of the partial defences to murder.

In 2004, in response to the realisation that provocation did not easily accommodate the circumstances of domestic violence, the UK Law Commission published its report on the defences to homicide (Law Commission Report No 290 *Partial Defences to Murder* 2004). It described the current law on murder as a 'mess' and recommended a complete review.[56] It recommended retaining the partial provocation defence, but proposed redrafting the legislation to redefine and narrow the circumstances in which it can be raised. This recommendation was eventually implemented by the government in sections 54 and 55 of the *Coroners and Justice Act* 2009 (UK), discussed in more detail below. It is significant that at this time it was the Commissioner's view that a wife's taunts may 'constitute some provocation' and the husband may well be said, at law, to have lost his self-control if he kills her in such circumstances (Law Commission 2004: 191–93).

In October 2004 the Home Office announced that a review of the law of murder would take place and this was confirmed by the Home Office in its Terms of Reference on 21 July 2005. On 20 December 2005 the Law Commission opened its consultation and on 29 November 2006 published its report, *Murder, Manslaughter and Infanticide*, in which it revealed that the Home Office would be taking over the review of the law and would be consulting on broader public policy issues such as sentencing (Law Commission Press Release (29 November 2006)). It was conceded in the 2006 report that the current law appeared 'especially user friendly to men ... because they are more likely to lose their temper or respond violently to such matters', and that it could also lead to lenient sentencing in cases where the provoked murder 'may have been little more than a reflection of the continuing cultural acceptability of men's use of violence in anger' (Law Commission 2006: 91). The Law Commission also set out its recommendation that instead of the current two-tier structure of general homicide offences, namely murder and manslaughter, there should be a new three-tier structure. In descending order of seriousness, the offences should be 'first degree murder' (mandatory life sentence), 'second degree murder' (discretionary life sentence) and 'manslaughter' (discretionary life sentence) (2006: 19–20). The report also detailed recommended reforms to complicity in murder, diminished responsibility, provocation and infanticide and that the government should undertake public consultation as to whether, and if so to what extent, the law should recognise either an offence of 'mercy' killing or a partial defence of 'mercy' killing (Law Commission 2006). In July 2008 when the government launched the consultation paper announcing its proposal to abolish the existing partial defence of provocation and to replace it with a new partial defence for those who kill 'in response to words and conduct which caused the defendant to have a justifiable sense of being seriously wronged', it provoked strong reactions including the criticism that it was discriminatory because it gave protection to certain groups (UK Ministry of Justice Media Release (29 July 2008); Slack 2008; Wooding 2008; Rozenberg 2008).

Historically in England, provocation was governed by common law but prior to its reform was also in part defined by statute.[57] Although the option of abolition has been taken up in various Law Commission recommendations, and in response to a series of high profile cases since the 1980s,[58] courts have not only struggled to more appropriately attune their responses to the gendered reality in which women kill their violent abusers, but they have also struggled to acknowledge the gendered basis of legal constructions of provocation as a partial defence (Lacey, Quick and Wells 2010: 781–93). The most recent changes to the law of homicide in England are those implemented through the *Coroners and Justice Act* 2009 which have been described as among 'the most sweeping changes to murder laws in 50 years' (Slack and Doherty 2009). It significantly revised the law of diminished responsibility and replaced the partial defence of provocation (Mackay 2010). The latter was achieved by creating a defence akin to the plea of 'excessive self-defence', called the partial defence of 'loss of control' (section 54) which, if successfully pleaded, would continue to lead to a manslaughter conviction. It is hardly surprising that the changes have been met with some disappointment. As Clough (2010: 121) notes:

> . . . shying away from the full reform of homicide is not the only criticism of the new law. While some responses to the Consultation Paper accused the government of pandering to pressure groups, others have been more critical of the sexual infidelity exclusion built into the new defence.

Section 55, which sets out the meaning of qualifying trigger for loss of self-control provides:

(3) This subsection applies if D's loss of self-control was attributable to D's fear of serious violence from V against D or another identified person.

(4) This subsection applies if D's loss of self-control was attributable to a thing or things done or said (or both) which—

    (a) constituted circumstances of an extremely grave character, and

    (b) caused D to have a justifiable sense of being seriously wronged.

(5) This subsection applies if D's loss of self-control was attributable to a combination of the matters mentioned in subsections (3) and (4).

(6) In determining whether a loss of self-control had a qualifying trigger—

    (a) D's fear of serious violence is to be disregarded to the extent that it was caused by a thing which D incited to be done or said for the purpose of providing an excuse to use violence;

(b) a sense of being seriously wronged by a thing done or said is not justifiable if D incited the thing to be done or said for the purpose of providing an excuse to use violence;

(c) the fact that a thing done or said constituted sexual infidelity is to be disregarded.

Clough further notes that 'without any provision demanding evidence of seeking help from the authorities prior to the killing . . . it allows the defence to be raised without any real evidence that the person killing from fear of serious harm had no other option' (2010: 122).

Others, too, have noted that although this policy shift is away from condoning men's anger, there still needs to be a 'qualifying trigger', namely fear of serious violence or circumstances of an extremely grave character giving rise to a justifiable sense of being seriously wronged. As Ramsey has observed, anger in such a situation may be sudden, such as might occur in the case of a man, or the steadily mounting anger, such as the 'slow burning fuse' or the 'straw that broke the camel's back' such as might occur in the case of a woman subject to continuous beating or abuse by her husband. It is assumed the defence will not succeed where the accused person is simply very angry, or motivated by revenge, or responding to sexual infidelity. As such, Ramsey worries that 'the *Coroners and Justice Act* retains the possibility that mere words – things "done or said (or both)" – might rise to that level' (2010: 99). In attempting to resolve the criticisms of provocation,[59] the new 'loss of control' requirement amounts simply to an extension of old law (eg the common law of the defence of provocation) (Clough 2010: 123; see also Howe 2010; Norrie 2010; Withey 2011). In light of these criticisms, while the decision to introduce a new partial defence of 'loss of self-control' represents an important law change, it remains to be seen whether, and to what extent, 'ending the provocation defence in cases of "infidelity" . . . will put an end to the culture of excuses' for men's violence against women (Slack and Doherty 2009).

Conclusion; now that provocation has gone, is this the end of provocation's victim-blaming narratives?

This chapter has traced the trajectory of debates about the need for reform of the controversial partial defence of provocation and arguments that it should be abolished. These debates are grounded in a great deal of feminist legal scholarship that has demonstrated that the problems with provocation and indeed the defences to homicide more generally lie with the way in which such cases operate to normalise or condone men's anger and violence towards women, and to inscribe the body of the woman victim as to blame for her own fate. The chapter also considered that the provocation defence has now been abolished in a number of different jurisdictions. In these post-abolitionist jurisdictions, provocation will be considered alongside other aggravating or mitigating factors that a court must take into account when deciding an appropriate and proportionate sentence. It can also be noted that the decision to abolish provocation has been accompanied by other quite significant changes to the laws of evidence and self-defence. While the impact of these various and specific reforms to the laws of homicide in these different jurisdictions remains to be seen, the question is, now that provocation has gone, is this the end of provocation's victim-blaming narratives? As some critics have forecast, the gendered assumptions underpinning these narratives are likely to continue to underscore the arguments and judgments made about men who have killed their current or former female partners in sentencing. For instance, commenting on Victoria's new homicide laws, Phil Cleary has observed: '[t]here is nothing in the legislation to say a woman's infidelity, alleged or otherwise, won't be dissected in a murder trial. Certainly, it will not be excluded when a judge calculates a sentence' (2006: 21). This is an important point given the tendency for sentencing in cases of domestic homicide to undermine legal developments that potentially benefit women (Horder 1989; Easteal 1993b, 1994; Graycar and Morgan 1996; Burton 2003; Stubbs and Tolmie 2008).

My aim in the next chapter is to examine the 'intertextual history' (Threadgold 1997a: 210)[60] of the legal category of provocation. This will allow for an appreciation of the way in which 'the meaning of textual elements are always part of a much greater system than the word or text' and that '[t]here is a constant interaction between meanings, all of which have the potential to recontextualise and resignify others' (Threadgold 1997b: 67). Threadgold's insight is an important one because it opens up the possibility of 'rewriting' these meanings (1997b: 16–33). However, we also know that 'some stories never die: [t]hey are just told with different characters and different settings' (Rawlinson 2010: 1). Feminist cultural scholars have long observed how '[c]rime is an occasion for storytelling, for the generation of narratives which describe, respond to, or displace a rupture in the cultural order' (Young 1996: 79). While the 'facts' of a particular case 'are not just sitting out there with only one story to tell' (Morgan 1997: 247), these tales, as Morrissey observes, are founded on stock stories and stock characters in their promotion of stock theories of crime (2003: 12). Thus, the criminal trial is a struggle over narrative and juries require the format and structure of such stories to enable them to make sense of complex legal argument and evidence that is relied on by legal counsel. Aside from relying on stock stories, 'judges often tell jurors to use their "common sense" when making judgments' (Morrissey 2003: 13). But as Morgan reminds us: 'dead women tell no tales; tales are told about them' (1997: 238). It is for this reason that feminist scholars have argued for a closer analysis of the relationship between narrative and law reform and to work for changes in the structure of law, and the legal categories within which problems are defined and dealt with (Graycar 1996: 309; Graycar and Morgan 1996, 2005). However, my aim is not simply to suggest that 'the telling of feminist stories, or performing the self differently' is a 'sufficient agenda for change' (Threadgold 1997a: 212). Rather, my aim is to demonstrate the performative power of law's narratives.[61] A discussion of the sedimented history of provocation's victim-blaming narratives will take place in the next chapter.

Notes

1 As noted by Howe, '[d]evastating feminist critiques of the age-old concession to "passion" in the form of homicidal fury unleashed on women by furious men are now legion, and available in all western jursidictions' (2004b: 59).

2 Or as O'Donovan has argued: '[t]he very nature of prolonged violence, the apparent initial tolerance by the victim, and her failure to respond violently immediately is contrary to the "heat of the moment" quality which is required by the current definition of provocation' (1991: 223).

3 McColgan notes that 'for every example of a woman who kills in circumstances where she fears for her life at the hands of her abuser and receives a significant custodial sentence, examples may be found of men who kill "nagging", unfaithful or departing wives or girlfriends, and who escape comparatively lightly' (2000: 148).

4 For a recent critique of the reasonableness requirement in the American legal context see Lee (2003: 46–67).

5 For an extensive overview of feminist work on this theme see Naffine (1990: 136–48) and also Smart (1992).

6 This position comes from the English case of R v Welsh (1869) 11 Cox CC 336 (Keating J): '[T]here must exist such an amount of provocation as would be excited by the circumstances in the mind of a reasonable man, and so as to lead the jury to ascribe the act to the influence of that passion' (at 338).

7 This point, argues Naffine, comes from the work of third-phase feminists: that while law professes to be internally coherent and certain, to organise around clear and rational principles (such as the need for us to be treated as free, autonomous and rational beings), it is in fact shot through with contradictions (so that sometimes it perceives us as determined and dependent, as not fully in charge of our actions) (1990: 101).

8 On the phenomenon of 'battered woman syndrome' see Walker (1989, 1990).

9 For a compelling comparative critique of Thornton and Ahluwalia in light of Lavallée see Young (1993: 792–805, 1997: 127–55).

10 Nicholson draws on the work of Worrall to highlight how 'appropriate femininity' is 'clustered around three core ideas: domesticity, which requires good women to be good and caring mothers, loyal and supportive wives, competent housewives; sexuality, neither promiscuous nor frigid, and being a single woman (eg chaste and demure); and finally, pathology. All of these ideas 'are defined in contrast to their masculine corollaries. Moreover, these binary oppositions involve hierarchies, with the masculine side

constructed as superior and as the norm against which femininity is measured, thus rendering the "normal" woman always already abnormal' (1995: 188).

11 The other appeal case was *Runjanjic and Kontinnen* (1991) 56 SASR 114. For a discussion of *Runjanjic and Kontinnen* and the *Osland* decisions in relation to BWS evidence see Stubbs and Tolmie (1999: 720–27).

12 Morrissey concurs, noting that '[f]eminist discourses, both legal and psychological, have been enormously influential in position the new BWS narrative of battered women, which is fast on its way to becoming an alternative stock story for use in Western courts'. However, she argues that '[i]ts popularity for traditional legal and media discourses stems from the implicit denial of agency to battered women who kill . . . Battered women who kill are thus at one and the same time welcomed into a society which accepts the reality of domestic violence, yet also cast out as belonging to a brutalized minority group in which murder represents the only means of escape' (2003: 101).

13 See Coss (1991) for a detailed discussion of the historical origins of the doctrine of provocation in England.

14 See Tindall J in *R v Hayward* (1836) 6 C&P 157 at 159, where he referred to the need to extend compassion to human infirmity.

15 Brown notes that killing was excusable during 'embroilments to settle so-called "breaches of honour"' because of the absence of malice and the existence of provocation serious enough to deprive one of their self-control (1963: 310, 312–313). In Horder's discussion of the historical development of the provocation defence, he has argued that over time the focus changed from one of justifiable retribution or 'anger as outrage' as an appropriate response to a breach of masculine honour to the modern concept that we have now which is 'anger as loss of self-control' (1992a: 40; see also Horder 1992b). It is this modern understanding of the defence that centres on the idea that defendants are less culpable when they lose 'self-control' that has given rise to much controversy and concern. See Seldon (1610) for an account of the code of the *duello* (also known as 'trial by combat' or the judicially sanctioned duel) in England from the Norman Conquest.

16 Lord Holt defines the categories of conduct where provocation was available as follows: 'when a man is taken in adultery with another man's wife, if the husband shall stab the adulterer, or knock out his brains, this is bare manslaughter: for jealousy is the rage of a man, and adultery the highest invasion of property' (*R v Mawgridge* (1707) Kel 199, 84 ER 1107 at 1115).

17 Many provocation provisions expressly include the phrase 'heat of passion'; see Forell (2006: 31).

18 For a discussion of English cases where the law allowed provocation to be raised on the basis of an unfaithful wife, see Leader-Elliott (1997: 157). For a discussion of cases where the law allowed provocation in contexts other than domestic homicide, see Lee (2003: 19–20).

19 In Leader-Elliott's analysis of provocation, these fictions of masculinity include the 'man of reason' and his less than ideal counterpart, the 'man of passion'. Over time, these fictions have '[o]ffered opportunities to tell sympathetic stories as restraints on the defence of sexual provocation were modified or abandoned'. Indeed, as Leader-Elliott observes '[c]ompassion for the man who kills his wife or lover draws on the familiar Anglo-centric patterns of tragic narrative' and 'Shakespeare's *Othello* serves as a salient if stark reminder' (1997: 162–63). Reilly makes a similar point: '[i]n explanations of loss of self-control there are several tragic narratives. The story of a loss of self-control carries a powerful narrative in its own right. In addition, behind every story of a loss of self-control, there is a further tragic personal narrative of anger, failed relationships,

unfulfilled expectations, frustrated desires, revenge, love and social dislocation' (1997: 331; see also Finkel 1995).

20 Borochowitz has shown narrative devices such as these are often used in batterers' own constructions of their wives' narratives to achieve a sense of coherence when telling their stories and justifying their violent behaviour (2008: 1166). By portraying his wife as 'a shrew', the batterer is then able to blame her for failing to fulfil the expectations of what is ultimately a predetermined narrative of the idealised wife and/or relationship. Consequently, argues Borochowitz, batterers 'disciplined' their wives for deviating from 'the script' by using force. If the resort to the 'script' or story that 'she asked for it' explains the tendency for nagging to be seen as a reasonable provocation to murder, it has entered into the realm of 'common-sense' in cases where the provocation relied on is sexual infidelity and/or jealousy.

21 Drawing on Mahoney's insights into men's attempts at 'power and control', Morgan has observed that '[i]n many of the so-called "mere words" or "confessions of adultery" homicide cases, what is also happening is that the victim has announced her intention to leave or has, indeed, already left' (1997: 247–48). As Morgan makes clear, the legal narrative is one that emphasises 'the *sexual* aspects' of the alleged actions and taunting behaviour (1997: 249).

22 *Green v R* (1997) 191 CLR 334.

23 Prior to 2003, the law of provocation in Tasmania was governed by section 160 of the *Criminal Code* (Tas) 1924, which was closely modelled on the common law.

24 In a reference to the work of Bradfield, Ramsey has argued that there were two key rationales for the abolition of provocation in Tasmania in 2003: 'first, that repeal of Tasmania's mandatory death sentence for murder made heat-of-passion mitigation unnecessary and, second, that the partial defense tacitly endorsed male violence prompted by a man's inability to control his spouse' (2010: 68–69).

25 *R v Ramage* [2004] VSC 508.

26 Media reports featured headlines such as 'Women are angry' (Stewart 2004: 10), 'Call it what it was: domestic homicide' (Alexander 2004: 10), 'It's time women had a better deal from the law' (Crooks 2004: 17) and 'Honour killing in the suburbs' (Kissane 2004b: 4–6).

27 *R v Ramage* [2004] VSC 508. See also McSherry (2005: 15–22).

28 *R v Ramage* [2004] VSC 508 at 22.

29 *R v Ramage* [2004] VSC 391.

30 ibid paras 8, 9–10.

31 Maher et al also note how '[t]his empathetic identification with Ramage [was] intensified in the way Osborn J locates Ramage explicitly as father and as financial provider'. Accordingly, they argued that there was 'a sustained focus on the fatherhood of Ramage, both through repeated reference to the distress he exhibited and the involvement of his children as witnesses to the "facts" of the case' (2005: 157).

32 *R v Yasso* [2002] 130 VIC 468, [2005] VSC 75.

33 For a detailed comparison of the *Ramage* and *Yasso* cases see Maher et al (2005: 147–63).

34 For an alternative and equally thought provoking discussion of the High Court decision in *Green* see Young (2001: 305–27).

35 The Act provided:

> When a person who unlawfully kills another under circumstances which, but for the provisions of this section, would constitute wilful murder or murder, does the act which

causes death in the heat of passion caused by sudden provocation, and before there is time for his passion to cool, he is guilty of manslaughter only.

The term 'provocation' was not defined in this provision but was defined under s 245 of the Code (see LRCWA 2007: 204). For a full discussion of the arguments for and against abolition of the provocation defence see the Law Reform Commission of Western Australia's *Final Report: Review of the Law of Homicide* (Project No 97, 2007).

36 For an evaluation of the arguments which led to the abolition of the distinction between wilful murder and murder in Western Australia and whether it was desirable or appropriate to merge these offences see Crofts (2008, 2006).

37 Western Australia also repealed the mandatory life sentence for murder, and replaced it with a presumptive life sentence. In March 2010 Dimitrios Tsakiris was the first person jailed for life for fatally stabbing his wife in March 2008 under the new law. For an evaluation of the reforms to the laws of homicide in Western Australia see Hopkins and Easteal (2010: 132–137).

38 It can be noted that there were two other high profile cases – Jonathon James Little, who was acquitted of murder in relation to the death of David Stevens and Ryan William Moody, who was acquitted of the death of Nigel Lee – that prompted the initial audit on the defences to homicide – accident and provocation – undertaken by the Queensland Department of Justice and Attorney-General (DJAG 2007: 1).

39 The reference to 'provocation' in Queensland courts is a reference to the common law meaning of provocation and not to the definition of provocation as a complete defence to assault as it is elsewhere in the Code (e.g. section 268 and section 269). Section 269 provides that:

A person is not criminally responsible for an assault committed upon a person who gives the person provocation for the assault, if the person is in fact deprived by the provocation of the power of self-control, and acts upon it on the sudden and before there is time for the person's passion to cool, and if the force used is not disproportionate to the provocation and is not intended, and is not such as is likely, to cause death or grievous bodily harm.

40 My summary of the facts is drawn from the judgment of the Court of Appeal in *R v Sebo ex parte A-G (Qld)* [2007] QCA 426, who dismissed Sebo's appeal against sentence. A more detailed discssion of *R v Sebo* can be found in the Queensland Law Reform Commission's Review (QLRC 2008: 251–257).

41 The results of the DJAG Discussion Paper are discussed in the Queensland Law Reform Commission's Review (QLRC 2008: 228-230).

42 The relevant provision provides:

(1) A person who unlawfully kills another (the *deceased*) under circumstances that, but for the provisions of this section, would constitute murder, is guilty of manslaughter only, if—(a) the deceased has committed acts of serious domestic violence against the person in the course of an abusive domestic relationship; and (b) the person believes that it is necessary for the person's preservation from death or grievous bodily harm to do the act or make the omission that causes the death; and (c) the person has reasonable grounds for the belief having regard to the abusive domestic relationship and all the circumstances of the case.

(2)   References to the following are to be interpreted in the same way as they are interpreted under the Domestic and Family Violence Protection Act 1989 for that Act—(a) the existence of a domestic relationship between 2 persons; (b) an act of domestic violence in a domestic relationship.

(3)   An *abusive domestic relationship* is a domestic relationship existing between 2 persons in which there is a history of acts of serious domestic violence committed by either person against the other.

(4)   A history of acts of serious domestic violence may include acts that appear minor or trivial when considered in isolation.

(5)   Subsection (1) may apply even if the act or omission causing the death (the *response*) was done or made in response to a particular act of domestic violence committed by the deceased that would not, if the history of acts of serious domestic violence were disregarded, warrant the response.

(6)   Subsection (1)(a) may apply even if the person has sometimes committed acts of domestic violence in the relationship.

(7)   For subsection (1)(c), without limiting the circumstances to which regard may be had for the purposes of the subsection, those circumstances include acts of the deceased that were not acts of domestic violence.

43   The first inquiry into women offenders and the defences to homicide was the *Report of the Taskforce on Women and the Criminal Code* conducted in Queensland by the Office of Women (Office of Women, 2000). The *Taskforce* recognised the difficulties encountered by women who kill their violent abusers who use defences such as Battered Women Syndrome (BWS) to assist their defence. In particular, it recognised that the Queensland formulation of self-defence is fundamentally inconsistent with killings committed in response to family violence which usually stem from ongoing patterns of abuse and which often occur in non-confrontational circumstances.

44   Provocation is available as a qualified defence to murder under Part VI Division 3 subdivision 158 of the *Criminal Code Act* (NT) and is available for both fatal and non-fatal offences. More recently, there have been criticisms of the operation of the partial defence of provocation in the Northern Territory have tended to focus on the problems with the construction of the 'ordinary Aboriginal person'. Douglas, for example, has argued that the law finds it difficult to imagine the 'ordinary Aboriginal' benchmark without resorting to racist 'stereotypes, and problematic markers of cultural authenticity' (2006: 223). Douglas suggests that despite the motivations of some culturally sensitive lawyers and judges, their efforts to construct defendants as closely as possible to a model of cultural authenticity, often end up an oppressive tool which degenerate into a 'new version of assimilation'. In agreement with various law reform commissions, Douglas has called for abolition on the basis that the defence is unable to deal with the concept of culture (2006: 224). Other legislative changes enacted through the (*Criminal Reform Amendment Act (No 2)* 2006 (NT) include an amendment to provide that the provocation defence not be available in response to a non-violent sexual advance (s 158(5) inserted by *Criminal Reform Amendment Act (No 2)* 2006 (NT)s 17). Despite these reforms to the provocation defence, there does not appear to be any intention to reform the penalty of mandatory life imprisonment associated with murder in the Northern Territory (see for example Douglas 2006: 225 and Carrick 2010).

45   In the ACT, section 13 of the *Crimes Act* 1900 (ACT) provides for the partial defence of provocation in a trial for murder. In the ACT, the legislation was amended in 2004 to provide that a non-violent 'homosexual' advance is not, on its own, sufficient grounds

for raising the provocation defence (*Crimes Act 5* 1900 (ACT) s 13(3), inserted by the *Sexuality Discrimination Legislation Amendment Act* 2004 (ACT) s 3, sch 2 pt 2.1). However, a non-violent advance may be taken in account in deciding whether the defendant was provoked together with other conduct (*Crimes Act* 1900 (ACT) s 13).

46   In South Australia, the common law defence of provocation applies and a conviction for murder is punished by mandatory life imprisonment for murder.

47   The NSWLRC acknowledged concerns surrounding the application of the partial defence of provocation in relation to homicides committed in the context of family violence, and made a number of recommendations for reform, none of which has been adopted (ALRC Final Report 114, NSWLRC Final Report 128, 2010: 635). For instance, two key recommendations were rejected by the Commission. The first was 'the option of specifically excluding the operation of the defence in cases where men killed female partners after a relationship breakdown, or in cases of killing in response to homosexual advances'. The second was 'the option of removing the "loss of self-control" requirement in the defence to make the defence more available to battered women who kill' (Yeo 2010).

48   Section 421 states:

(a)   the person uses force that involves the intentional or reckless infliction of death, and

(b)   the conduct is not a reasonable response in the circumstances as he or she perceives them, but the person believes the conduct is necessary:

(c)   to defend himself or herself or another person, or

(d)   to prevent or terminate the unlawful deprivation of his or her liberty or the liberty of another person.

49   For an overview of developments in relation to the law of provocation in New South Wales see Eburn (2011), Roth (2007) and Yeo (2010).

50   *The Queen v Clayton Robert Weatherston* HC CHCH CRI 2008-012-137 (15 September 2009).

51   The website of the campaign group *Justice for Women* lists a number of significant cases in an effort to highlight the injustices women, whether as victims or offenders, face when seeking to have their stories heard in court, as does the group *Southall Black Sisters*.

52   I am very grateful to Burton (2003) for her critical insights concerning these cases on which my summary here primarily draws.

53   *R v Smith* [2000] 3 WLR 654. See commentary on the House of Lords decision in *Smith* by Elliott (2000: 594–600).

54   Attorney-General's Reference No 74, No 95 and No 118 of 2002 [2002] EWCA 2989.

55   For a detailed account and criticism of the merits of the *Safety and Justice* proposal and related policies that were initiated by the Home Office at this time see Howe (2008: 188–202).

56   In its Consultation Paper No 177 *A new Homicide Act for England and Wales?* (2005) the Law Commission detailed a draft report which included recommendations for a new three-tiered structure for homicide, in addition to additional proposals to reform the defences and partial defences, and also that it undertake a more substantial inquiry into the partial defences to murder.

57   Section 3 of the *Homicide Act* 1957 stated that:

Where on a charge of murder there is evidence on which the jury can find that the person charged was provoked (whether by things done o said or by both together) to lose his self-control, the question whether the provocation was enough to make a reasonable man do as he did shall be left to be determined by the jury; and in determining that question the jury shall take into account everything both done and said according to the effect which, in their opinion, it would have on a reasonable man.

58 As Clough (2010: 121) has argued: '[i]n 2005, the judgement in *R v Holley* ([2005] UKPC 23, [2005] 2 AC 580) succeeded in quashing developments in case law over the previous decade attributed to the reasonable man, reverting the law to a fixed capacity for self-control and not a variable standard as had previously been applied following the decision in *R v Smith (Morgan)* ([2000] UKHL 49, [2000] 4 All ER 289). Holley was convicted of murder for killing his girlfriend in the course of an argument. At trial he claimed that the deceased had said to him, 'You haven't got the guts' whereupon he struck and killed her with an axe. At trial, he relied on medical evidence of his chronic alcoholism arguing that it was a disease and, as such, a characteristic attributable both to the reasonable person and to the assessment of his capacity for self-control (Edwards, SSM 2006: 342). See also commentary by Csefalvay (2006) and Quick and Wells (2006), who also discuss the House of Lords decision in *Smith* (*R v Smith* [2000] 3 WLR 654) and Privy Council revision in *Holley*.

59 Lacey et al have observed that section 1(a) responds to the gender bias criticism of the defence by removing the need to establish a sudden loss of self-control, which they note was the product of the common law (eg *Duffy* (1949)). In relation to section 55, they note that the introduction of a new trigger of fear of serious violence sets a more exacting test in relation to 'things done or said'. In doing so, this is clearly designed with battered women in mind (2010: 794–96).

60 I have taken my understanding from Threadgold, who argues that the 'telling' of 'intertextual histories' is part of the broader project of feminist poetics. The term 'poetics' here is taken to mean 'to work on and with texts' (1997b: 2).

61 As Threadgold observes, Graycar's intervention does not address the idea that the court is a place of performance. Those who know the rules of the game or performative code are the 'insiders' (legal professionals and courtroom administrative staff). This means that the 'outsiders' (the female complainant of a rape trial or the defendant if it is a spousal murder trial) are at a considerable disadvantage because 'she has no code and therefore must hypothesise, abduct the meaning of what goes on around her, indeed of what is targeted at her. At the same time she is given no time for this reflective activity but is expected to improvise' (1997a: 212–213). Thus she has little if any performative power 'except within the frameworks of the stereotypes that rush to fill the semiotic void of . . . [her] . . . exclusion. . . . You are Desdemona to a murdering Othello. . .' (1997a: 214). I also note that Threadgold's use of the term performative comes from Judith Butler's theory of gender as a performativity (see in particular *Gender Trouble: Feminism and the Subversion of Identity* (London: Routledge 1990) and *Bodies That Matter: On the Discursive Limits of Sex* (London: Routledge 1993). As Carline explains, Butler's 'queer theory approach to law recognises that the law creates culturally intelligible scripts, gender performances, which bodies perform and are judged against' (2005: 38).

CHAPTER 2

Bridling scolds: insults, female sexuality and the unruly woman

Introduction: telling cultural tales

The major focus of this chapter is on the stories that are told about dead women who are said to have used words and/or behaviour to 'provoke' their own deaths. This necessitates an investigation of the values and assumptions, underpinning what is, I argue, the most vexing exculpatory cultural narrative of excuse for men's violence against women: the narrative of a woman 'asking for it'. My aim is to demonstrate that not only are the storytellers many and varied, but that the woman's story is excluded: 'the dead women can no longer tell the stories of their own lives; others are left to tell the tale' (Morgan 1997: 238) – but that these stories are shaped by unconscious fears and fantasies about the threat posed by the female body and its predisposition to transgress appropriate gender norms. These fears and fantasies about the threat of unbridled female sexuality have long dominated the cultural psyche.[1] This argument is not advanced in order to provide further insight into the lived narrative realities of the lives of women who kill or are killed by their current or former partners.[2] Rather, in this chapter I want to highlight the discursive construction of two figures that can be found to form or inhabit the structure of the narrative of a woman 'asking for it': a delegitimated figure (a figure of feminine excess) and a legitimated figure (a figure of masculine loss).[3] What will become clear in this and subsequent chapters is that legitimate and illegitimate subjects are mobilised through different kinds of narrative or genre. In this chapter, I discuss the textual production of these two figures in a number of historical, cultural and legal materials beginning with a discussion of the film *Jackie Brown* (1997, directed by Quentin Tarantino), feminist readings of the play *The Taming of the Shrew* (1594, written by William Shakespeare) and, in the 'leading case' on the doctrine of provocation in Australia, that of *Moffa v The Queen*.

This approach highlights the cultural production of *the crime* (Young 1996: 13–16; Knox 1998: 16–17; Williams 1999: 168).[4] The importance of Young's work lies in her connection of what she terms the 'crimino-legal complex' with 'the knowledges, discourses and practices' of criminology, criminal justice and criminal law and importantly popular culture (1996: 2).[5] As Puren and Young offer, '"Culture" here is to be understood, not as an empirical collection of images, but as a process, or *regime of imagination*, through which events come to have meanings as *texts*' (1999: 3, 4):

> [c]ommonplace cultural narratives, genres, scenarios and char-
> acters have a semantic life independent of the cases brought and
> heard before the law. Agile questioning practices in the trial deploy
> cultural devices in the production of meaning. The usual result is
> the narration of a culturally familiar tale to be recognised by the
> jury . . .; a legal narrative to be recognised by the judge . . .; and a
> story which will not be recognised by the . . . [victim] . . . as the
> story she [might have] told.

This alternative reading of law and legal texts means 'coming to terms with Robert Cover's provocative claim that the defining characteristic of the act of legal interpretation is its necessary connection to violence itself' (Cheah and Grosz 1996: 8). As Cover states, '[l]egal interpretation takes place in a field of pain and death' (1986: 1601). Cover here is saying more than simply that legal adjudication involves the necessary imposition of violence. Rather, in terms expressed by Cheah and Grosz, Cover is making a more profound link, which is that 'violence is constitutive of the meaning of law itself' (1996: 8). As Puren and Young note, to insist on 'the textuality of law', on '[v]iewing legal processes as textual recognises that any event is made legible (and legal) through strategies of signification'. Citing the example of how 'in the scene of the rape trial, the complainant's narration of the event is subjected to the toxic practices of the defence, which aim to demolish her story', Puren and Young also recognise that not all narratives come to have the same status as 'truth' (1999: 4).[6] Rather, law can be described as offering 'modes of reading/writing, which are formative of particular kinds of habitus and are inevitably partially constituted intertextually by and through mediations of popular culture' (Threadgold 2002: 26; see also Threadgold 1997a). This is in contrast to the traditional view of law that sees it as immune from influence from other cultural forms such as literature and film (Puren and Young 1999: 4–5). Whereas literature admits to the artificiality of its constructions, law persists in the concealment and denial of its literary sources and aesthetic arrangements (Aristodemou 2000: 2; Douzinas and Nead 1999; Goodrich 1996: 112). As Puren and Young have argued, among others, 'these scripts and genres are prone to erupt within the courtroom as much as in the cultural arena considered to be their proper place' (1999: 5; Threadgold 1997a: 214).[7]

The second section of this chapter focuses on the exculpatory and frequently misogynistic cultural script of a woman 'asking for it' within its historically contingent cultural terrain. The texts that concern me here are constructions of disorderly speech and particularly, female speech as a sign of domestic and political disorder in poetry, drama, ballads, theological treatises and local court records that betray a virtual obsession with 'scolding' women. There is now a growing body of work by feminist historians that has examined how women's speech could be both politically and socially empowering and, at the same time, could be sharply regulated, and in many cases, silenced. These writers argue that the regulation of women's speech can be traced to broader stories and concerns surrounding the connection between a certain kind of speech and a certain understanding of what it was to be a woman or man (Gowing 1996; Kamensky 1996; Snyder 2003; Bardsley 2006; Jones 2006). Drawing usefully on the insights of Judith Butler's theorising of gender as a performance, as an 'ongoing discursive practice', makes it possible to be attentive to the scenes and stagings that comprise masculinity and femininity in particular contexts (Kamensky 1996: 24; see also Gowing 1996: 5–7).[8] Comparing the doctrines of contempt and contempt in the face of the court with the doctrine of provocation highlights their connection with those cultural stories. It is worth reiterating at this point that the defence of provocation provides the accused with a partial excuse for the crime of murder. Unlike self-defence which results in an acquittal, a successful defence of provocation reduces the accused's culpability to that of voluntary manslaughter. The rules and requirements vary between Western jurisdictions but can generally be said to consist of several elements that must be satisfied before a successful defence can be made out. The accused and his lawyer must allege that the deceased uttered words and/or acted in a way that caused the accused to experience a sudden and temporary loss of self-control. The accused and his defence lawyer must also argue that the accused killed the deceased while experiencing that loss of self-control. Overriding both of these legal requirements is the further demand that the accused must be said to have acted as an ordinary hypothetical person would have acted. What is common to each of these elements of the formal legal definition is *a construction of what the deceased said or did*. In drawing attention to the ways in which the accused's position in provocation is assimilated with that of the court in contempt of court, we can see an endorsement by law of the notion that he who feels insulted and retaliates with violence is a legitimate subject of violence.

To set the scene, consider the film *Jackie Brown* (1997, directed by Quentin Tarantino). The scene involves a verbal exchange between two characters, a man, Louis (played by Robert De Niro), shoots and kills a woman, Melanie (played by Bridget Fonda). The two of them are to deliver the proceeds of a cash heist to a third character, Ordell (played by Samuel Jackson). Ordell is Louis's old-time criminal associate and Melanie's boyfriend. The scene begins in a department store outside a ladies' changing room where the cash is to have been left for them to collect by a fourth party. Melanie and Louis hover nervously outside the ladies' changing room. Feeling impatient, Melanie decides to take charge of the situation by marching into the changing room cubicle to get the cash herself. When she comes out, to the surprise of Louis, she greets him with a look of defiance and triumph and walks off in the direction of the parking lot outside. Feeling discombobulated, Louis scampers off after her as she marches toward the emergency exit. Once outside in the car park we witness Louis grab the bag from Melanie, his position of authority and control regained, only to be foiled a second time when we get the impression that he has misplaced something vital. It suddenly dawns on Melanie that Louis cannot remember where he parked the car. She laughs at his incompetence and begins to tease him about it. At first, Louis does not respond. Noticing that she has rattled him, she says to Louis:

> Jesus, but if you two aren't the biggest fuck-ups I've ever seen in my life [pauses and shakes her head]. How did you ever rob a bank? When you robbed banks, did you have to look for your car then, too? No wonder you went to jail ... What a loser (Tarantino 1998: 185).[9]

Louis does not respond and changes direction, cutting down another aisle looking for the car. She keeps on at him, 'Is it this aisle, Lou-is ... or is it the next one over?' Suddenly, Louis spins around to face Melanie and points his finger at her, 'Don't say anything else, okay? I'm telling you, keep your mouth shut'. Melanie pauses and opens her mouth as if to speak. Shaking his finger at her Louis warns, 'I mean it. Don't say one fuckin' word'. Silent for only a brief moment Melanie starts up again chanting in a sing-song voice, 'Okay, Louis . . . Lou-is? . . . Lou-is . . .?' Suddenly, he spins around a second time. The viewer looks over his shoulder along the length of his outstretched arm which is pointing directly at Melanie. He holds a gun. He shoots her – at close range. The camera remains focused on Louis. Melanie is no longer within the camera's frame. He steps forward and shoots downwards at an unseen body lying prostrate on the ground.

This is one of the most violent scenes in the film.[10] We never see Melanie again; there is no direct image of her corpse. All that remains is the posthumous conversation about her between Louis and Ordell. They are seated together in the getaway van. In an off-hand sort of way, during their conversation, Louis confesses to Ordell that he had to shoot Melanie. In a manner, reminiscent of a police interview, Ordell demands to know why Louis did not simply talk to her. He goes on to suggest to Louis that if talking to her did not work, surely he could have just hit her. As if a physical assault might have been a more reasonable mode of correction and containment than murder. Then he asks Louis if he is sure she is dead, '. . . we don't want that bitch surviving on us. Anybody but that woman'. Ordell shrugs it off.

The deployment of narrative is a retrospective way of giving meaning to an event by reference to an earlier event or series of events in time. It allows members of a culture to apprehend the significance of that event under a common storyline. First, the narrative erases the material body and puts in its place a subject. Melanie's performance becomes the cause of Louis's actions. In this way, the insult becomes the space of culpability. What is pertinent about the insult is that it is not the material body that matters but the reinscription of Melanie's subjectivity in the discourse of others (Louis and Ordell, audience, Tarantino). In short, *she* asked for it. Secondly, the narrative provides a structure of identification. The audience forms an allegiance with the character of Louis as the subject of violence. Despite any empathy the audience might feel for Melanie, she nonetheless remains the subject (*she* asked for it) and the object on which violence is justifiably enacted. Thirdly, not only does the film set up an instance of the provocation narrative but it illustrates a key trope of that narrative, namely that 'she asked for it'. It is by way of this trope that allegiances are formed and culpability is attached. It also shores up an all-too-familiar cultural commonplace: the convention that, when a woman responds to the performance of men, she is not so much speaking back but asking for it and hence deserving of what she gets. It is for this reason that, although the killing of Melanie was sudden, it was not altogether unexpected.

For any narrative to have coherence and plausibility, it requires validation of its plot and its conclusions by the audience (the viewer or reader). In the film, the murder of the character Melanie acquires meaning to the extent that it shores up a commonplace cultural narrative that positions the deceased as having 'asked for it' and to blame (albeit partially) for her own death. Although direct references to a key figure who inhabits or forms one part of the structure of this narrative (of sex and of culpability) – the literary (and literal) figure of the scold – are discursively absent in the film, it is through recourse to the gendered trope of 'she asked for it' that the murderer's character (Louis), his murderous act (shooting a woman) and his reasons for killing her (because she 'asked for it') makes sense. It is in this way that the viewer or audience is invited to accept the plot of the film and, in so doing, empathise with the acts and behaviour of some characters while condemning the acts and behaviour of other characters. It is also how filmic texts can operate to normalise some men's claims of provocation (that they were 'provoked' to kill by the words or behaviour of the deceased) in order to reduce murder to manslaughter.

My aim in recalling this scene in the film is to draw the reader's attention to a central theme of this book: that is, that like literature and film, law also requires an audience (a judge, members of the jury, the legal, feminist, academic community, the public and so on) to validate its stories and narrative conclusions. Although law's stories inevitably come from different institutional sites and different discursive formations, they have parallels with the ones we find in literature and film.[11] This leads me to *The Taming of the Shrew*, a play by William Shakespeare written in 1594. The play provides a classic caricature of the figure of the nagging, taunting woman in the cinematic text I am discussing here, which is the textual legacy of the dominant fiction of femininity running through so many of the provocation cases that I am attempting to chart in this book, and of which this play is but one explicit example. The literary and literal figure of 'the scold' or 'scolding woman' operates in cinematic discourse to evoke the female character, Melanie, into narrative possibility. There it invites the audience to accept the all too familiar convention that, when a woman responds to the performance of a man, she is not so much speaking back but asking for it and hence deserving of what she gets (which may include being hit, bashed, stabbed, strangled or shot to death by him). Conventionally produced gendered subjectivities and subject positions are realised in the texts of popular culture to elicit sympathy or blame for murderers, their murderous acts and their reasons for killing another person. In the same way, conventional femininities and masculinities play a key role in judicial assessments of culpability in provocation cases. As subsequent chapters will show, the narrative of a woman 'asking for it' is not only a feature of contemporary popular film but also preoccupies, informs and shapes assessments of culpability in provocation cases.

Telling literary tales: the scolding woman

The emergence of the figure of the 'nagging, shrewish, sharp-tongued women' has been dated from about the mid-14th century (Bardsley 2006: 106–120, 144). While some historians have suggested that scolding was mainly a phenomenon of the 16th and 17th centuries (eg Underdown 1985), others note that long before her appearance in legal discourse the evil- or idle-tongued woman was not only the mainstay of vernacular literature, she was also a regular theme in ancient and Christian literature.[12] Indeed, the invention of the scold needs to be seen in the context of what can only be described as obsessive cultural anxiety and fixation with oral and verbal transgressions.[13]

The mouth, along with its tongue, has long been inscribed as a potentially contaminating and unruly organ. A perceived lack of discipline of the tongue, mouth and speech was a key way of attributing culpability for all sorts of social transgressions. In Greek poetry, for instance, the tongue was metaphorised as a key, capable of unlocking or locking the teeth (or door) to sound, words or song (Drew Griffith 1995: 2), and in common proverbs in medieval times the tongue as a sword or destructive weapon was part of the popular imagery (Sheneman 1993: 398). In psalms and religious pamphlets, it was alleged that garrulity could quite literally subvert morality and truth.[14] A number of writers have described and examined several re-emerging key tropes and themes that organise this literature. For example, the metaphor of the tongue (as speech) pointed to a preoccupation with voicelessness, censorship or fear of castration (quite literally cutting the tongue out of the mouth) and of death (be it social and/or physical).

More broadly, Paster's examination of several city comedies, a sub-genre of early Renaissance theatre which dealt satirically with current events and life in and around London, links injunctions against breastfeeding, menstruating, urinating and defecating in public with imperatives of sexual difference (1987: 44–45).[15] Educational treatises and etiquette manuals were as much about social manners and class status as they were about 'natural' bodily functions. The question of outward bodily control, including anxieties about fertility and potency, culminated in numerous dramatic parodies that featured a leaky bladder, flatulence and gossiping. Drawing on psychoanalysis, Paster explains that comedy was a way to express a collective anxiety about what these 'slips' of the body might reveal about the nature of the self, including the subject of the unfortunate 'slip' and the object to whom it might have been intended or become attached (in these cases the audience) (1987: 44). The ritualised cultural preoccupation with a leaky bladder can also be linked to anxiety about another orifice: an undisciplined or unruly mouth and tongue. The discursive formation of a woman's orifices as signalling a lack of control constituted all women as potential subjects of insult in need of discipline and containment. A woman whose bladder leaked involuntarily invoked condemnation of her as irrational, unreliable and sexually incontinent: '[u]ncertainty in the lower parts bespeaks unreliability in the constructed woman; over production at one orifice bespeaks overproduction at the rest ... "A likerish tongue a likerish tail" says the proverb ...' (Paster 1987: 51).

This was a way for culture of all levels to stress gender difference and sometimes this took the form of extreme misogyny[16] while at other times, in popular literature ballads for example, the way gender was understood to determine social roles was through mocking their inversion (a reference to the work of Natalie Zemon Davis (1975) on upside-down rites and cucking and ducking stools) (Underdown 1985: 117; Bardsley 2006: 141–143, 149; Jones 2006: 2).

The scold's invention also needs to be seen in the context of wider developments in the regulation of disruptive speech. As Bardsley explains, the late medieval period in England saw an intensification of the regulation and control of the voices of common folk, who also became the focus of new repressive energies through which the Church regulated the daily lives of most people (2006: 16–18). Other researchers have observed that the regulation of disruptive speech peaked in the 16th and 17th centuries in Europe (Dobash et al 1986), North America (Bauman 1983; Norton 1987; Spindel 1995; Snyder 2003) and England (Sharpe 1980; St George 1984; Gowing 1996; Kamensky 1996, 1997). Scolding, however, was by no means an exclusively feminine offence. Indeed, as Bardsley and Jones have noted, it was a strongly femininised one; men were regularly punished for disruptive speech as women were, but for different kinds (eg swearing, blasphemy, sexual boasting and verbal abuse of officials) (Bardsley 2006: 88, 95–102, 151; Jones 2006: 104–109, 111–119). The designation of women's speech as disruptive, therefore, needs to be understood in the context of broader debates about the connection between a certain kind of speech and a certain understanding of what it was to behave like a proper woman or man (Norton 1987; Spindel 1995; Gowing 1996; Kamensky 1996, 1997; Snyder 2003; Bardsley 2006). However, as Bardsley notes, whereas men were punished for doing, women were punished for speaking and being: 'women with uncontrollable voices ... were connected with sexual immorality, violence and even keeping company with the devil' (2006: 146).

In Kamensky's study of the relationship between speech and society in early New England, for instance, she convincingly argues that early New Englanders believed that 'speech was conduct and conduct was speech' (1997: 5).[17] Moreover, insults were highly gendered. The 'freedom' to 'traffick in words', Kamensky observes, remained largely men's prerogative and was an essential part of what distinguished a certain kind of man from women and from boys (1996: 23). Accordingly, Kamensky's sources demonstrate that: '"Man alone is endowed" with speech . . . if the sounds that emanated from the human tongue were sometimes "exceedingly good" . . . they just as often proved "excessively evil"' (1996: 18). Indeed, the precise nature of the threat of the 'ungoverned' tongue was believed to be that of endangering social order (Bardsley 2006: 26–44). If it was acknowledged by any male author who cared to discuss the subject that the 'perils of misspeaking' could befall both men and women, it was 'Woman' who, 'for the most part, had the glibbest tongue' (Kamensky 1997: 71–99).[18] This is because it was her sex that was predisposed by nature to scold.[19] Although one of the key preoccupations with the scold's speech 'was that there was simply too much of it', 'the real danger' was that the scold spoke 'too *publicly*' (Kamensky 1996: 20–21; Bardsley 2006: 147). The scold not only threatened the peace, harmony and order of the family, but of the community at large. There lived, of course, '"good women, modest women, true women . . . ever chaste, ever glorious", ever silent', but according 'to 17th-century ears', there was no greater risk than that posed by the woman who appeared 'male in dress, hairstyle, and gesture, the notorious "Man-Woman" . . . [whose] . . . "vile and horrible profanations" . . . [rendered her] . . . "deformed", even "monstrous"' (Kamesky 1996: 21). For young women, silence was to be a permanent condition. This is illustrated in the writings of Richard Brathwait, author of *The English Gentleman* (1630), who said that: '"what is spoken of [young] Maids", is "properly applied . . . to all women: *They should be seene, and not heard*"' (Kamensky 1996: 29).[20]

The common law offence of scolding developed in England and Wales from about the middle of the 16th century and remained on the statute books until 1967.[21] It was also transported to North America (the United States) with the colonists. The common scold, *communis rixatrix* (law-Latin confined it to the female gender), referred to a species of public nuisance. According to the definition of the scold in William Sheppard's *A Grand Abridgment of the Common and Statute Law of England* (1675), it referred to 'a troublesome and angry woman who, by her brawling and wrangling amongst her Neighbours, doth break the publick Peace, and beget, cherish and increase publick Discord (cited in Spargo 1944: 121–22). Up until the late 18th century, various forms of direct physical punishment were meted out to control the behaviour of wayward members of the community.[22] The offence of scolding, for instance, was punishable by putting the head of the offender in a cucking or ducking-stool and submerging it in a river or pond, or tumbrel (a chair for the same purpose) (Bardsley 2006: 141–43).[23] Dobash et al note where men might be subjected to a '"cuckold's court" or forced to ride backwards on a donkey for allowing their wives to cuckold or dominate them', 'when women attempted to speak out against their husbands or other men within the community ... they risked being labelled public nuisances, shrews, nags and viragos' (1986: 19). As a consequence, women were more likely to be subject to more physical, direct and serious community chastisements.[24] Women labelled scolds were sometimes punished by putting the woman's head in the scold's or gossip's bridle or the branks. According to Dobash et al, 'the branks was an iron cage placed over the head, and most examples incorporated a spike or pointed wheel that was inserted into the offender's mouth in order to "pin the tongue and silence the noisiest brawler"' (1986: 18–19). In the United States, scolds or those convicted of similar offences could also be sentenced to stand with their tongue in a cleft stick, a more primitive but easier to construct version of the scold's bridle (Earle 1907: 96–106). However, as Bardsley points out, it was the presence of scolding stereotypes in English culture prior to and alongside their legal development that assisted in the creation of the scold as a category of femininity by which women could be branded, punished and controlled (2006: 27).

Shakespeare's play *The Taming of the Shrew* (1594) offers perhaps the most classic caricature of the figure of the scold (Underdown 1985: 117). As Boose notes, since its inception, the play's sexual politics have 'inspired controversy'.[25] If the play's 'vision of male supremacy' has continued to provoke anxiety in male viewers these past decades, such reactions would hardly compare with those it has produced in its women viewers (Boose 1991: 179). Boose is here referring to the most controversial and remarked-upon lines in the play, which take place in the final scene where Kate apparently accepts her own subjection.[26] Boose remains critical of the tendency for most critics of *The Taming of the Shrew* to adopt a kind of revisionist reading, which emphasises 'Kate's and Petruchio's mutual sexual attraction, affection, and satisfaction [and] deemphasizes her coerced submission to him'. What this reading misses, Boose forcefully argues, is the placing of this literary fiction within the historical realities that defined the lives of 16th century "shrews" – the real village Kates who underwrite Shakespeare's character' (1991: 181).[27] In Boose's account, the literary (and literal) practice of bridling scolds is an indelible part of the history of socialising women into silence. Women who remained otherwise paid a physical price for resisting patriarchal authority.[28]

Boose, too, takes issue with Underdown's claim about the 'significant increase in instances of crimes defined as exclusively female: "scolding", "witchcraft", and "whoring"' (1991: 184). The punishments that were meted out to women were less focused on controlling their sexual transgressions; rather, 'the veritable prototype of the female offender of this era seems to be, in fact, the woman marked out as a "scold" or "shrew"' (Boose 1991: 185).[29] The punishments meted out to scolds were part of the broader mechanism of shaming rituals through which patriarchal culture reinscribed its authority. Paradoxically, these shaming rituals were an equally powerful counter-site for the containment of men. As Boose notes, by the late 16th century, 'the political symbolism of the cross-dressed unruly woman' was 'appropriated for new uses' by those reacting against enclosure. In one peasant riot against enclosure in Wiltshire, the rioters adopted the name 'Lady Skimmington', which signified unruliness, and led 'skimmingtons' against 'Skimmington', an authority figure. Whereas the men convicted of the Wiltshire riot and another in Datchet were 'made to stand pilloried in women's clothing', the women rioters were 'sentenced to their usual punishment at the cucking stool, wearing their usual clothing' (Boose 1991: 192). As Boose argues, '[b]y signifying male rebellion against hierarchical privilege as a feminized act, the authorities located insurrection within the space where it could be most effectively controlled: in the inferiorized status of a "womanish" male'.[30] It would appear that the site of shame was the same for both sexes: 'the space of the feminine' (Boose 1991: 192).

What is being staged in *The Taming of the Shrew* is the benevolent version of the shaming of a scold in which Kate occupies both shamed object and chivalric ideal. As Boose notes, actual references to the 'iron bridle' are discursively absent in the play. What Shakespeare appears to be doing by effectively 'pushing' these more 'brutal patriarchal practices that were circulating' at the time aside 'is conscientiously modelling a series of humane but effective methods for behavioural modification' (Boose 1991: 198). Shakespeare's taming of the shrew narrative is not one of 'physical brutality'. Rather, he reshapes the trope of the 'old, usually poor women ... or nagging wife into the newly romanticized vision of a beautiful, rich, and spirited young woman' (Boose 1991: 192). While the scold's bridle is not materially present in the play's narrative, the various and specific tropes of unruliness – 'horse references or horse representations' – pervade the play and in doing so draw on the cultural discourse of 'the maiming/disfiguring of the mouth' as the means to control women (Boose 1991: 199).[31]

As such, Boose's reading is one in which she notes that the various and specific tropes of unruliness that are mobilised throughout the play initially serve to indicate the female protagonist's (Kate) desire for autonomy and agency. This is achieved by having modalised Kate from the speaking position of the 'I', which figures her as defiant, and as able to resist her husband's ill-treatment of her, including his desire to confine her within his dominion, which is the private domain of the home. However, by the end of the play, the conditions of possibility for Kate's subjectivity become 'trapped within the rhetorical co-options of a discourse that dissolve all difference between the 'I' and "you"'. In Kate's final speech, her 'disquisition on obedience', she is enunciated differently, having been shifted 'into an address targeted at some presumptive Everywoman'. The result is one in which the women in the audience are encouraged to identify with the ideological imperative of the play's own discourse and align themselves accordingly with the fate of the now heroine, which is one in which she 'apparently' accepts her own subjection (Boose 1991: 179–80). Within a political and gendered economy of sexual difference, we can see that the mouth and tongue have been marked as a sexed body part, a literal and figurative site of culpability through which to contain the speech and opinions of predominantly working-class women (and some men) (Stallybrass 1987: 210–20).

Similarly, as her study of the Tudor Stuart Church courts has demonstrated, Gowing has noted that 'men's blows were figured as, most justifiably, a response to women's words'. Indeed, '"[s]hrews" were an accepted problem and their "chastisement" by blows a familiar theme in popular literature, married life, and the courts' (1996: 181, cited in Wiener 2004: 176–77). By the 18th century, it would appear that words lost some of their potency – a shift, Wiener suggests, that reflected 'a decreasing fear of women and their verbal weapons, and a complementary increased fear of men and their physical threat' (2004: 177). The legal principle that words were insufficient to constitute provocation that would reduce murder to manslaughter had been established in the late 17th century. However, as Wiener notes, this principle was 'very often ignored in practice'. It was only when 'fear of the "shrew" had sufficiently faded – a point arrived at in the 19th century – that it truly became a governing principle'. Indeed, according to Wiener, the legal rule that words were insufficient a ground to raise the defence of provocation was often a point of contention between judges and juries, 'the latter often gave greater weight to a wife's provoking words than did the former'. This was particularly the case where all provocation relied on was words relating to a wife's unfaithfulness (Wiener 2004: 177–78). A discussion of these lingering legal responses to the 'nagging, shrewish, sharp-tongued woman' in one of the leading Australian cases on the law of provocation is the topic of the next section.

Legal tales; the case of *Moffa v The Queen*

> The necessity to resort to metaphor in expounding the law on this subject is disconcerting. References to supposed raising or lowering of blood temperature, reason becoming unseated, and passion mastering understanding, seem calculated to confound, rather than assist analytical processes. However, our understanding of consciousness and mental processes – as compared with our understanding of more readily observable physical phenomena – is so limited that metaphor seems generally to be regarded as essential in the expression of ideas that guide us in this area of discourse.
>
> (*R v Chhay* (1994) 72 A Crim R 1 at 9)

The Australian High Court decision in *Moffa* (138 CLR 601, 13 ALR 225) has attracted contradictory commentary on whether it affirmed or rejected the House of Lords decision in *Holmes v Director of Public Prosecutions* ([1946] AC 588) that 'a confession of adultery without more is never sufficient to reduce an offence which would otherwise be murder to manslaughter' (Morgan 1997: 238, 246–47). Morgan's consideration of the case begins with the question of why 'legal commentators can tell different legal stories about the case'. For Morgan, the answer is to 'be found in how you read "the facts"' in that there are 'many ways to tell the tale of what happened, to present "the facts", and different ways of presenting "the facts" might well lead to different (legal) conclusions'. Like Morgan, I am interested in the tales told in *Moffa*, and while my discussion of the case is in some respects similar to that of Morgan, I also aim to take account of the 'sedimented' (literary and literal) narrative history[32] of the 'nagging, shrewish, sharp-tongued' woman.

Moffa was convicted of murder for killing his wife. He claimed that after he had returned from a month's holiday in Italy, her feelings for him had changed. For more than a month, his wife had refused to have sex with him, due to poor health, and she frequently told him she no longer loved him. On the night before he killed her, he said he repeatedly pleaded with her not to leave him. The next morning he repeated his pleas for her to stay with him. According to him, she said several times that she no longer loved him. At one point, he tried to caress her. He claimed her response to him was that he was not to come near her or she would 'scratch [his] eyes out' (*Moffa* (1997) 13 ALR 225 at 235 (Gipps J)). According to his version, she then said she had been 'enjoying' herself and 'screwing with everybody on the street', called him a 'fucking bastard' and then threw some photographs of herself naked (some of which had been taken by him) for him to look at. He claimed he began to feel mad and when he began to cry she laughed at him using the words, 'get out you black bastard', which were followed by her throwing a telephone at him. He left the room, obtained a lead pipe from outside the house, returned to the bedroom and said to her: 'Is this what you want? You force me to do it'. According to him, her response was: 'I'm not scared of you, you fucking bastard'. He then beat her to death. The High Court accepted his version of the killing as not only raising the issue of provocation, but constituting sufficient provocation to reduce his conviction to manslaughter (see also *The Queen v Webb* (1977) 16 SASR 309, where the male accused claimed he had been provoked by the female deceased's words – she threatened to scream rape unless he paid her money for sex. He choked her to death. At trial, he was convicted of murder. On appeal, her words, while not considered abusive, constituted sufficient provocation to reduce the accused's conviction to manslaughter).

What interests me about the High Court judgment is the way in which the conduct of the female deceased was figured as insulting. As Morgan's rereading of the facts in this case has illustrated, the court's judges' adjectival descriptions of the deceased woman's performance enabled it/them to form the view that there was no need to re-examine the precise effect of her words on the accused (1997: 244). Having endorsed Moffa's story, it/they even added some embellishments of their own. In the discourse of the judges there were repeated proscriptions of the female deceased's conduct as 'vituperative' and 'scornful', her words as 'contemptuously expressed' and a 'contemptuous denial of any continuing affection' towards the accused/appellant, 'a proclamation of finality in the termination of their relationship coupled with an expression of pleasure in having had intercourse promiscuously with neighbouring men' (*Moffa* (1997) 13 ALR 225 at 226–32 (Barwick CJ)). In contrast, Moffa was revered for making continual 'connubial advances' toward the deceased, which she ignored (at 227). Consider Stephen J's judgment (at 237–38):

> She told him in the coarsest, and no doubt the most provocative of language that she had been having intercourse 'with everyone in the street'. . . . The deceased in this case, the jury might believe, did not simply admit to an adulterous relationship, she boasted of wholesale promiscuity.

The adjectival disavowal of her in and by the majority judgment is significant. It is *her* words that are reinscribed with adjectives such as 'sting' and 'scorn' by the judges.[33] The law reasons primarily to persuade. The belief 'that the facts of the present case can be decided according to previous patterns of resolution to similar cases' is 'always a question of selection [or] choice' as to 'which similarities and which differences are significant to the particular situation'. The analogy provides and delimits the language to be used for the present case. Not only are 'similar facts' from an earlier case used to understand the present situation, but so are a range of linguistic devices, such as metaphor and the deployment of tropes of subjectivity. Consider Gleeson CJ's comments on the role of metaphor in the epigraph section of this chapter. The language of 'sting' and 'scorn' is reminiscent of the historical literature that attributed a woman's mouth and tongue with the potential to invite and as actually inviting violence.

A final point concerns the court's use of the language of contempt ('contemptuously expressed' and so on). The doctrine of contempt and contempt in the face of the court is the official narrative of insult a magistrate or judge deploys to convey when the adjudicating tribunal feels insulted. The specific argument to be addressed here is that thinking through law's formal response to insults in the courtroom helps us to understand the performative force of insults in the context of the defence of provocation.

The doctrine of contempt in the face of the court

> You may not smoke in this Court, you may not whisper or speak or laugh. You must dress decently, and if you are a man, you may not wear your hat unless such is your religion. This is in honour of the Judge and in honour of the King whose officer he is; and in honour of the Law behind the Judge, and in honour of the People behind the Law. When the Judge enters you will stand, and you will not sit till he is seated. When the Judge leaves you will stand, and you will not move till he has left you. This is in honour of the Judge, and of the thing behind the Judge. . . . Even if there were one there greater than the Judge he would stand, for behind the Judge are things greater than any man.[34]

The common law doctrine of contempt is the formal means by which legal officials exercise their autonomy, authority and control over media reporting and other forms of criticism of the courts.[35] The powers of punishment enacted by the extant doctrine of contempt range from a fine to imprisonment and have, in extreme situations, included 'gagging' or 'shackling' the contemnor.[36] The doctrine of 'contempt in the face of the court' enables an adjudicating tribunal or member of the court to deal with situations in which they feel insulted.[37] The powers that are awarded to legal officials permit them to exercise control over the movement of bodies during court proceedings, which might take the form of a bodily gesture, a facial expression, a style of speaking and even the tone and pitch of a person's voice. As Goodrich emphasises, law compels fidelity from its subjects by exerting strict control over the protocols of courtroom speech, specifically over the dialogues that take place within its sites of office (1990: 179–209).[38]

Charges for contempt in the face of the court have been brought against 'contemnors' for using words of abuse or for gesturing with certain parts of the body, such as holding up a 'clenched fist salute' in the presence of the presiding magistrate.[39] Other types of gestures and behaviour that have caused the adjudicating tribunal to respond by charging the offending party with contempt in the face of the court include using the mouth to laugh during court proceedings (Goodrich 1990: 191). Before a person can be found guilty of contempt there must be the presence of *mens rea* or a subjective intention wilfully to insult an official of the court, but it is the 'objective appearance or effect' of the gestures, behaviour or words in question for the court that is paramount (Chesterman 1987: 33). This begs the question, in whose view and according to what image can the speaking body appear before the law?

Consider the case of *Tuckerman* involving six men who appeared in a Sydney magistrates' court to answer charges of trespass.[40] Upon each of the men raising an arm in a clenched fist salute at the magistrate, they were cited for contempt and later found guilty as charged.[41] The magistrate ruled that, collectively, their gesture took on the appearance of defying the authority of the court (which he noted could be achieved either by 'intimidation, ridicule or otherwise'). As a result, the imagined effect of the force of the insult was one that diminished the law's self-image, its autonomy and authority. The image of six men's clenched fists symbolised for the court a transgression of its autonomy, authority and control over court proceedings.[42]

A more specific example of the kinds of words and behaviour that have been attributed with the capacity to disrupt the authority and autonomy of the court can be found in the Victorian case of *Murphy* involving a barrister who, during a plea, was cited by the presiding magistrate for contempt in the face of the court.[43] Having cited the barrister for contempt in the face of the court, the magistrate stood the matter down (involving the barrister's client, Parkin) to enable the barrister to obtain legal advice to answer the charge of contempt. Following this, the barrister sought a series of adjournments to enable him to apply to the Supreme Court for an order prohibiting the magistrate from further hearing the matter involving his client on the grounds that the magistrate would be biased.[44] What interests me about the case relates to the magistrate's description of the particulars of contempt recounted verbatim at the appeal hearing and which included but were not limited to the following:

> ... talking over me and continuing to talk over me, the presiding magistrate ... repeatedly arguing the point in an unpleasant, disrespectful and disparaging manner and in a tone of apparent anger and challenge saying 'Nuh. Nah. Nah. You and I are going to resolve this matter between us here and now' and later saying 'This matter will be resolved between us' ... refusing to continue to make a plea on behalf of the accused Parkin after direction by the court to do so ... [and] ... failing to resume your seat when requested by the Court to do so.[45]

As the extract illustrates, first the barrister is taken to task for speaking back at the magistrate ('talking over me and continuing to talk over me'), which included not speaking or sitting when supposed to. Second, and relatedly, the barrister's words 'You are I are going to resolve this matter between us here and now' are described as taking the form of 'a brazen challenge to the court'.[46] However, it was not simply the barrister's 'brazen' refusal to accept the autonomy and authority of the court that was at issue. It was that a certain style and manner of speaking was held to have caused the magistrate to feel insulted and, in doing so, caused him feel he was losing control over courtroom proceedings.

A related issue for the court was whether the words issued by the barrister had caused a '[f]ragmentation of [the] criminal process'. This was implied in the dissenting judgment of Tadgell JA, who put it thus: 'To impute injustice to a justice is to insult him in respect of the very title he wears; it is like imputing blindness to a bishop'.[47] The analogy set in motion by Tadgell JA is significant as it puts into effect a causal relation between the force of the insult and judicial blindness. Of use here is the Lacanian metaphor of the mirror as it helps to understand the construction of the subject 'in the eyes of the law' or through its subjection in and to juridical practices. It is not simply the insulting trajectory of the words spoken by the barrister that is understood to have disrupted court proceedings, but that the words themselves are attributed with the very serious capacity to unmask (thwart, impair) law's image of itself. To impute a form of judicial blindness to law is to render law linguistically impotent. It is to associate law with lack, the 'passive', 'open' and 'penetrable' position usually reserved for the 'feminine'.

What is being underscored here is the idea that the use of force is a proper and justifiable response to a retrospective insult (especially between men). A specific example of the kind of retaliation (if any) that is deemed appropriate for a magistrate or judge to take in the event of feeling insulted during court proceedings can be found in *Murphy* discussed above. A section of the judgment titled 'The role of the magistrate as a sentencing tribunal' contains a passage from an earlier case detailing the function and rules binding prosecutors and judges in the event of verbal 'disputes' between them.[48] We are told that 'the foregoing rules do not oblige a sentencing judge *passively, and unquestioningly,* to accept facts as the basis for sentencing which are presented by the Crown and/or the accused' (my italics).[49] In relation to the question of whether the magistrate had exceeded his permitted function,[50] the majority of the Supreme Court ruled that ruling on such a question was impossible on the evidence before it and gave the following reasons:

> . . .the magistrate may well have feared he was losing control of his courtroom; and it would not have been surprising – or an indication of ostensible bias – if the magistrate had become annoyed, had raised his voice, and had become 'argumentative to the point of belligerence'.[51]

As the above extract indicates, the proper and justifiable response for a judge to take in the event of feeling insulted is not only one in which he must be seen to take action rather than remain passive (and by implication risk being *feminised*), but is one in which angry retaliation ('speaking back') is legitimate and justified. Indeed, Charles JA went on to say 'that arguments in court will sometimes become heated leading to sharp words and rude exchanges. Judges confronted by such exchanges may easily (and justifiably) become angered and insulted'.[52]

As the official narrative of insult a magistrate or judge deploys to convey when the adjudicating tribunal feels insulted, the common law of contempt in the face of the court awards a court power to inflict sanctions in response to words of abuse, a person's laughter in court or a refusal to accept the authority of the court. As such, it represents the authentic inscription or mark of social place and office, the true image or face of law (Goodrich 1986: 168, 197). What is at stake for law in the event of the insult concerns the question of law's masks or enunciative modalities – places from which law speaks and derives its 'legitimate source', 'point of application' and authority (Goodrich 1987: 132–57; Higgins 1997: 363). The common law doctrine of contempt in the face of the court concerns the very sovereignty of the court's jurisdiction, the right and authority to speak in its name, an authority that nonetheless derives from an elsewhere; the mouth or law of the father or the word of God or the monarch (Goodrich 1990: 301). Just as the monarch compelled allegiance from and dominion over subjects, so do those invested with the power to speak in the name of the law (legal practitioners). But the function of law is also to signify the subject to itself; it is to map the subject in its own relations, not in relation to a specific 'reality', but in inter-subjective relations with the 'other' as well as to the law (Goodrich 1990: 183). If the legal system's or court's subjectivity can be read as an effect of prior discursive formations, then power resides in its representational practices.

In the event of contempt in the face of the court, the adjudicating tribunal suffers a loss of identity, autonomy and authority. Likewise, in the event of murder by provocation, the (wrongful act or) insult is imagined as having threatened an accused's sense of self, such that he experiences a loss of self-control and claims to have killed while under that loss of self-control.[53] The insult becomes the space of culpability; the accused's position in provocation is assimilated with that of the court in contempt of court. This alliance to the value of law amounts to an endorsement by law that he who feels insulted and retaliates with violence is a legitimate subject of violence.

Women's words and the hands of men

In the case of *Gardner*,[54] the accused was convicted of manslaughter due to provocation after being charged with the murder of his ex-partner, Sylvana Marino, and convicted of murder for killing her male friend, Golly Shears. The trial judge had instructed the jury that the defence of provocation was available in relation to the killing of Marino but not of Shears. He appealed against the murder conviction on the ground that the provocation offered by the female deceased also caused him to kill Shears – who offered no provocation – who had been invited to stay at the house by Marino to give her protection from Gardner and who was asleep in another room at the time he was killed. The Victorian Court of Criminal Appeal accepted the defence narrative, that her words of abuse and her words describing past conduct (an allegation that Marino and Shears had been 'fucking all night') denigrated the accused's sexual capacity, causing him to kill them both.[55] There was evidence that the accused had informed a female companion that he intended to kill Marino up to 12 months before the killing.[56] A few nights before, while at a private function the accused had produced a knife and threatened to cut Marino's throat and burn down the house.[57] Despite his resolve to do her violence, and his gaining entry in the early hours of the morning by removing a wire screen from an open window, it was she who was positioned as 'asking for it'.

In Gardner's unsworn statement, he alleged that when he confronted Marino in her bedroom, her response was, '. . . you gutless fucking wimp . . . you cockless cunt . . . you're a gutless coward . . . leave me alone . . .'. According to him she yelled out to Shears, who was asleep in the other room, that the accused was in the house, and then to the accused, that she and the male deceased had been 'fucking all night'. He claimed that her words caused him to feel 'wild', 'angry' and 'upset' and that he 'could not control himself'. He said that he hit her with his hand. He then left her bedroom and went in search of Shears. On the way he picked up a statue of an elephant in the hallway, entered the room where Shears was sleeping and switched on the light. He saw the male deceased in bed asleep and that his upper torso was naked. '[H]e [Shears] moved, I thought he was getting up and I was shittin' myself – I just couldn't control myself and hit – I hit [the male deceased] with the elephant'. According to this account, having killed Shears, and still feeling insulted by Marino, he returned to Marino's bedroom and hit her again, presumably causing her death.[58]

It is well to remember that we have only the accused's version as to what she did or did not say or do on that night. Yet, the trial judge repeated the accused's account of what Marino said in his direction to the jury:

> You have demonstrated the love-hate relationship of a man who hated and loved, and left, but could not do without, a woman. And he [the Crown] says, that over those years of splitting and joining together . . . you have a deterioration of a man into a murderous state. . . . [O]n that . . . night, he learnt there was another man on the scene . . . This man had come between him and [the female deceased]. This man was exercising physical strength, and [the female deceased] was calling [the accused] a 'cockless wimp'. And the Crown says in the end the contempt and scorn and the mocking of [the accused], by [the female deceased], drove him to murder her . . .[59]

There was one witness, Marino's ex-husband, who corroborated the accused's allegations that Marino had used these words to abuse the accused on the telephone in the days *before the event,* including the phrase 'cockless cunt'.[60] The ideological effect of these words and their relation to each other merits consideration. Within the discourses of the courtroom, Marino's performance was reinscribed by a legal narrative of insult. Consider the phrase 'cockless cunt'. The positioning of 'cockless' next to a derogatory term for female genitals is significant in two respects. Not only does she associate him with the subject of 'lack', a castrated woman, a cunt without a cock, she also impugns his masculinity by rendering him cockless. This is suggestive of linguistic castration, she says he has no penis and no guts. She says he is not a 'real' man.

The narrative also provides a structure of identification. Throughout examination and cross-examination of witnesses, we find the deployment of a number of adjectival descriptions that are attached to the character of the female deceased. For example, words such as 'headstrong', 'bitter', 'obstinate', 'vindictive', 'abusive', 'manipulative', 'deceptive'. In one witness's view, the female deceased possessed the ability to 'suck men in'.[61] It is interesting that this same key witness testified that on numerous occasions the female deceased refused to talk to the accused on the telephone.[62] In contrast, the accused was described by a clinical psychologist as 'empathetic' toward others, 'warm', 'co-operative', 'passive', 'compliant', as a man who allowed himself to be pushed around by a woman.[63] The narrative also has a linear temporal sequence. First, he is constituted as passive in response to a woman's words, and then, as active in response to Shears's potential threat. The image of a female antagonist who dished it out verbally enables him to be positioned as a battered man, a man battered by a woman's words, and in danger of losing his masculinity.

This same narrative structure constitutes the male deceased as active. Although he was passive at the time he was killed by the accused, he was figured as a 'man of action'[64] by his hands. During cross-examination of one witness, defence counsel proposed that the male deceased, Shears, was 'a man who settled things with the fist, rather than the mouth'.[65] During a discussion between the prosecution and the judge regarding proposed jury directions on provocation, the Crown noted that in the accused's unsworn statement he gave evidence about a conversation with Marino in which she had said her relationship with Shears was one of friendship, that she had known him since school, that he would do anything for her, that he was handy with his hands.[66] In the appellate judgment, there was corroborative evidence that Marino was fearful for her safety and complained to police about her fears after being threatened by the accused at the private function a few nights before she was killed. At Marino's request, the male deceased had secured the front and rear doors of her home with locks and agreed to stay with her to provide protection.[67] For a man to be described as 'handy with his hands' implies handy around the house, an ability to carry out household repairs and maintenance. The slippage between hand and fist denotes a different order of meaning. A man who clenches his fist is a man who is prepared to fight. In contrast, women use words to complain and wound.

The preferred meaning for the court of the male deceased's character was as an antagonist. The relevance lies in the fact that if he is constituted as a 'man of action' sufficient to raise provocation, this also raises the possibility of the full defence of self-defence.[68] In relation to self-defence, the defence relied on the evidence given in the accused's unsworn statement that when he saw Shears, he 'was shittin' himself', and killed Shears to defend himself from potential violence. In relation to provocation, the defence in *Gardner* deployed the 'prototype provocation' that has always been 'where a man or woman comes home and finds the spouse in bed with someone else in a compromising position, or what appears to be'.[69] The proximity of Shears to Marino's bedroom and her allegation that they had been 'fucking all night' was sufficient to merge the two together into an image of the typical adulterous context. The Court of Criminal Appeal ruled that this image created a sufficient 'nexus' between Marino's words and the proximity of Shears in the second bedroom asleep. Marino's words implicated Shears in an imagined 'sexual orgy'.[70]

The narrative figured Shears as an innocent but potential subject of violence (handy with his fists). Moreover, he is the accused's sexual rival, an adulterer. He was figured as provocative by association with the female deceased and what she said. While he was constituted as a virile man, the accused was cast as emasculated, a fallen hero lover (in his direction to the jury, the judge said he had been in a love-hate relationship with Marino) and a coward. One could arguably rename this case, in Freudian terms, 'adultery of the tongue' (Puren 1995: 20). In the discourse of law the accused is legitimately positioned as needing to kill Shears to demonstrate and restore his masculinity.

Epilogue

The characters in Quentin Tarantino's film *Jackie Brown* have been described as 'practical people, whose needs are clear and who are not to be thwarted'; further, 'they are about action and not angst, which makes them immensely appealing' (Bauer 1998: 7). Bauer's inducement to read Louis's sudden shooting of Melanie as just a practical aspect of 'boys doing business' inscribes Louis's act of violence as straightforward and uncomplicated. The violence against Melanie, the erasure of her dead body, the disavowal of her subjectivity, was imperative to Louis getting the job done. Melanie simply got in the way. In contrast, the configuration of Louis's character, until the scene in the parking lot where he shoots Melanie, has been somewhat benign. From then on we are warned in no uncertain terms that he is capable of 'sudden' violence. The audience is invited to interpret this change in character as cathartic. Louis's decision to abandon words in favour of physical and brutal violence to resolve his problem makes him, if we follow the logic, immensely appealing.

When asked if he thought audiences had an attachment to Melanie when she died, Tarantino responded:

> No. I think the audience has a complete love-hate relationship with Melanie. Audiences applaud when Louis shoots her. It's impossible that someone could be asking for it, but she's asking for it. She's a fucking smartass, treacherous and all these things. But we also like her at the same time; she's a totally fun character
>
> (Bauer 1998: 9)

I would argue that the scene in the film demonstrates how violence is engendered in representation (de Lauretis 1984: 33). The audience is invited to identify with the violence against Melanie in such a way that it is easy to accept an all-too-familiar configuration of Melanie's sub-jectivity: the scolding woman. For the audience, perhaps her brutal death comes as a relief. If so, they are compliant about accepting this exculpatory script for men's violence against women: that, after all, she deserved what she got, didn't she? I suggest that what their applause also underscores is the success of another narrative, the 'man of action', the masculine subject who is quick with his fists and not given to words. If we miss Tarantino's invitation to view Melanie as the 'real' antagonist during this verbal exchange, we fail to acknowledge the unequal discursive investments in different and competing subject positions. Given that film narratives are the product of choice, always partly intended, created and interpreted by the producer/author, it is sometimes difficult actively to resist the dominant modes of address and read 'critically'. What escapes the gaze, what appears as 'natural', 'commonsense' or 'justified', is often overlooked or expected and can remain uncontested. In the film, the instance of insult and the gendered trope of 'she asked for it' evokes into narrative possibility the literary figure of the scold. Likewise, the deployment of a legal narrative of insult by an accused charged with murder is indelibly marked by the imperatives of gender. In the sense that we generally understand law to be retrospectively representing the lives of 'real' people and events, and film to be a conscious, but retrospective, representation of 'imagined' people and events, my reading of the intertextuality of the discourse of law and the discourse of culture disrupts the division between fact and fiction, truth and falsehood, fantasy and reality. Law emerges as a discursive site that attributes culpability by retelling a range of stories that are external to law and that betray a deep seated anxiety around (hetero)sexuality, violence and sexual difference.

Notes

1 The body of woman has long been recognised as a site on which a whole range of aspirations, fears and anxieties are projected (Brooks 1993: 5–6; see also Dijkstra 1996; Blazina 1997).

2 As Morgan notes, in focusing on the stories told about the women who 'provoked' men into killing them because they left them and/or engaged in a sexual relationship with someone else . . . '[she] . . . has not done what the editors of the book *Blood on Whose Hands* did: speak to the relatives and friends of the dead women'. Rather, she has tried to gain some of the context of these women's lives from more traditional legal storytellers . . . '[and in doing so] . . . makes no claim to truth for the stories . . . [she tells] . . .' (1997: 238).

3 I am drawing on Tyler's elaboration of 'figurative methodology' as outlined in her work on the construction of the female chav in the British media. As Tyler notes, the term 'figure' describes 'the ways in which at different historical and cultural moments specific "social types" become over determined and are publicly imagined (are figured) as excessive, distorted, and caricatured ways'. For Tyler, 'the emergence of these figures is always expressive of an underlying social crisis or anxiety: these figures are mobilised in ways that attribute superior forms of social capital to the subject positions and social groups they are implicitly or explicitly differentiated from' (2008: 18).

4 In Knox's interdisciplinary analysis of the literary and cultural conventions at work in a tale of murder in modern America, she convincingly illustrates the impossibility of there ever being a single 'truth' about the event of murder. Examining American society's preoccupation with this act of violence, Knox shows that even a single act of murder can be the subject of numerous, often competing narratives, for murder is continually told and retold in a myriad of ways: through media reportage, the confessions of murderers, psychiatric testimony, legal transcripts, the observations of courtroom spectators, cinematic productions and the literary genre of true crime. Her approach is one that makes connections between true crime books and romance narratives, and pulp murder novels of the 1930s and 1940s.

5 As such, for Young, her interest is with how 'the stories of crimino-legal justice . . . are concerned not just with the literal truth . . . but also with . . . [the] . . . allegorical truth; that is, a truth that speaks otherwise' (1996: 14). For works that characterise 'law and culture' scholarship more generally see Sarat and Kearns (1998), Sherwin (2000) and Sarat and Simon (2001).

6 As Scheppele has demonstrated, it is only 'selective narratives' that come to acquire the power of truth (1989: 2074).

7 Since the early 1990s, feminist cultural scholars have demonstrated how legal attitudes are heavily influenced by exculpatory scripts that serve to disqualify the woman victim's claims of sexual assault (Marcus 1992; Heath and Naffine 1994; Kaspiew 1995; Puren 1995; Lees 1997; Easteal 1998, Young 1998; Ehrlich 2001; Gotell 2002; Cossins 2003; Taylor 2004; Burns 2005; Comack and Peter 2005; Gavey 2005; Larcombe 2005; Temken

and Krahe 2008). They have shown that these scripts are not confined to the courtroom but are also realised in popular culture. As Gavey observes, both law and popular culture can be found to draw on 'dominant discourses of heterosexuality that positions women as relatively passive subjects who are encouraged to comply with sex with men, irrespective of their own sexual desire' (1992: 325). Indeed, for Larcombe, both 'rape law and romance fiction continue to reproduce conventionally gendered subjectivities' despite 'extensive feminist engagements with these texts over past decades' (2005: 1).

8   According to Gowing, 'descriptions of whores, queans, bawds, and cuckolds that characterised legally actionable insults added up to a whole language of gendered abuse. It was a language that differentiated persistently and profoundly between the sexual morals and sexual honour of women and men, and one in which gendered insults marked off the outlines of gender roles in sexual, marital and social relations' (1996: 59–60).

9   I note that the film has already set up Louis's incompetence independently of Melanie's opinion (see Tarantino 1997: 4).

10 The other violent scene is when Ordell shoots another ex-criminal associate, Beaumont Livingston, after Beaumont was questioned by Federal police over a job he did three years earlier for Ordell. Ordell cons Beaumont into the trunk of Ordell's car, under the guise of doing another job for him, and shoots him. During the exchange between two black men, Ordell repeatedly refers to Beaumont as a 'nigger'.

11 As Higgins writes: 'institutional discourses are never totally self-contained or self-referential. They always contain other broader social meanings and inter-relationships with other discursive formations in the hierarchy' (1997: 363).

12 For a discussion of those historians who have taken issue with Underdown's claim that scolds were seldom prosecuted until the 16th century see Bardsley (2006: 11–13).

13 Spargo observes (1944: 106) that the theme of 'the confusion of the tongue' as 'one of the great curses upon man' appears in numerous places in the Bible including the third chapter of the Epistle of St James, the ancient doctrine on the subject:

> The tongue is a fire, a world of iniquity: so is the tongue among our members, that it defileth the whole body, and setteth on fire the course of nature; and it is set on fire of hell. For every kind of beasts, and of birds, and of serpents, and of thing in the sea, is tamed, and hath been tamed of mankind; but the tongue can no man tame; it is an unruly evil, full of deadly poison.

Spargo notes that 'the twenty-first verse of the eighteenth chapter of the Book of Proverbs tells us that death and life lie in the power of the tongue'. And further that according to Quintus Septimius Florens Tertullianus, anglicised as Tertullian (c 160–c 220 AD), a prolific early Christian author, Spargo also notes that 'he includes in his list of the seven mortal sins no less than three sins of the tongue, namely, idolatry, blasphemy, and false witness' (1944: 106).

14 See for example the Dutch Renaissance humanist, Catholic priest and theologian, Desiderus Erasmus (1466–1536) *De duplici copia verborum ac rerum commentarii duo* (On Copiousness or the Copia of Words and Things 1512), translated by Betty Knott in Craig Thompson (ed) *The Collected Works of Erasmus* (Toronto: University of Toronto Press 1978) 24; and the Greek historian, Plutarch (46–120 AD) *The Governance of Good Helthe* (New York: Da Capo Press, 1968 (originally published 1530)); Plutarch 'De garrulitate' (On Talkativeness or Abundance of Speech) in *Plutarch's Moralia VI*. See also commentaries by Parker (1989: 445–65); Phillips (1981: 113–25).

15 Paster's study is of 'two dramatic occasions in city comedy which represent women needing to relieve themselves – in *Bartholomew Fair* – when the need for a chamberpot brings Win Littlewit and Mrs Overdo to Ursula's booth and in *A Chaste Maid in Cheapside* when the gossips at the Allwit christening wet the floor beneath their stools' (1987: 43–44).

16 Like many other historians, Gowing is making a reference to the Renaissance author, Joseph Swetnam, and his popular *Araignment of Lewd, Idle, Froward and Unconstant Women,* which was published in 1615.

17 For a compelling discussion of the performative force of insults see Butler *Excitable Speech: A Politics of the Performative* (1997).

18 For a discussion of the rise of a whole conduct literature devoted to disciplining the purportedly excesses and diseases of the tongue characterised as 'feminine' see Parker's analysis of Erasmus's *De Copia* (n 14) first written in 1512, and repeatedly extended until it reached its final form in 1534, to an English play performed at Cambridge, entitled *Lingua*. Parker argues that this literature reflects wider anxieties of effeminacy which attended any man whose province was the art of words (1989: 445–46). As Parker notes: '[t]hroughout The Tongue the diseases of this "wanton" bodily member are illustrated primarily by the excesses of the tongues of men'. But 'the quality itself – excess of speech or overabundance of the lingual – is repeatedly coded as "womanish" or feminine' (1989: 447). For a discussion of the ambivalent figure of the tongue as it is represented in the Jacobean play, *The Revenger's Tragedy*, see Stallybrass, who notes that 'the tongue stands in for the arts of rhetoric, which are conceptualised both in terms of female seduction and excess in terms of phallic domination' (1987: 215; see also Simmons 1977). On the theme of the discursive ambivalence shown toward the rhetorician during the Renaissance, Simmons quotes an essay by Marcel de Montaigne:

> Those that maske and paint women, commit not so foule a fault [as the rhetorician]; for it is no great losse, though a man see [women] not as they were naturally borne and unpainted: Whereas [rhetoricians] professe to deceive and beguile, not our eies, but our judgement; and to bastardize and corrupt the essence of things.
>
> (1977: 60)

19 As Kamensky notes: '[f]rom roughly 1560 and 1660, evidence ranging from drama, to theological treatises, to local court records betrays a virtual obsession with "scolding" women' (1996: 20). Snyder borrows from a 1662 Virginia statute designed to control female disruptive speech to note that 'brabbling' referred to 'a wrangling, quibbling, quarrelsome, or riotous disposition' (2003: 2). Spindel presents a contrasting view in her study of verbal abuse cases in North Carolina to 1730 where she notes that while a double standard of acceptable speech for men and women did exist, women rarely engaged in the kind of talk that would result in a lawsuit of criminal prosecution. When they did, however, it was in cases when their sexual reputation was under attack (Spindel 1995: 41). See also Bardsley on the sins of women's tongues in literature and art (2006: 45–68).

20 For a discussion of the theme of feminine silence in the writing of English dissenter and founder of the Religious Society of Friends (the Quakers) George Fox and his wife, Margaret Askew Fell Fox, see Ng's study of Quaker women 'Marriage and discipline: the place of women in early Quaker controversies' (2003: 113–140, 2007: 195–221).

See also Schofield '"Women's speaking justified": the feminine Quaker voice 1662–1797' (1987: 61–77).

21 In the *Commentaries on the Laws of England,* Blackstone writes that:

> [A] common scold, *communis rixatrix,* (for our law-latin confines it to the feminine gender) is a public nuisance to her neighbourhood. For which offence she may be indicted; and, if convicted, shall be sentenced to be placed in a certain engine of correction called the trebucket, castigatory, or cucking stool, which in the Saxon language signifies the scolding stool; though now it is frequently corrupted into ducking stool, because the residue of the judgement is, that, when she is so placed therein, she shall be plunged in the water for her punishment.
>
> (IV:13.5.8, 169)

I note that there is some disagreement among historians as to whether or not prosecutions for verbal offences peaked during the 16th and 17th centuries. Bardsley (2006), Jones (2006) and McIntosh (1998), for instance, disagree with Underdown's (1985) claim that scolding was mainly a phenomenon of the 16th century, and alongside *charivari* and witchcraft, represented a crisis in the patriarchal order and gender relations brought about by capitalism. Section 13(1)(a) of the *Criminal Law Act* 1967 (England and Wales) eventually abolished it.

22 Dobash and Dobash contend that both European and British communities used a number of direct physical punishments, such as the pillory and stocks, and symbolic chastisements, such as misrules and *charivaris.* Moreover, these practices were highly ritualised forms of shaming that were directed at both men and women who offended against the patriarchal social order. However, I am aware that tracing the actual use of the scold's bridle is problematic; as Boose observes, it 'was never legitimate'. Accordingly, Boose argues its use does not appear to be entered in the various leet court records as was the cucking stool. 'Because records are so scarce, we have no precise idea of how widespread the use of the bridle really was. What we do know', argues Boose, is that '[i]t is a device that today we would call an instrument of torture, despite the fact—as English legal history is proud to boast—that in England torture was never legal' (1991: 196; see also Spargo 1944: 257).

23 As Sheppard observes: 'And for this she is to be presented and punished in a Leet, by being put in the Cucking or Ducking-stole, or Tumbrel, an Engine appointed for that purpose, which is in the fashion of a Chair: and herein she is to sit, and to be let down in the water over her head and ears three or four times, so that no part of her be above the water, diving or ducking down, though against her will, as Ducks do under the water' (1675, cited in Spargo 1944: 122).

24 While a husband had a 'right of chastisement' over his drunken, wayward or quarrelsome wife, the chastisement had to be reasonable. For a discussion of changing attitudes towards abusive husbands in Victorian England see Weiner's *Men of Blood* (2004: 170–200).

25 It has nevertheless been adapted numerous times for stage, screen, opera, and musical theatre; the most well known adaptations include the musical *Kiss Me, Kate* (1948, music and lyrics by Cole Porter) and the film *10 Things I Hate About You* (1999, directed by Gil Junger) that was later made into an American television situation comedy series with the same name, broadcast on ABC Family in 2009. Note also the popular novel *The Scold's Bridle* written by Minette Walters and published in 1994 that was also adapted for television and aired by the BBC in 1998.

26

> I am ashamed that women are so simple
> To offer war where they should kneel for peace,
> Or seek for rule, supremacy and sway,
> When they are bound to serve, love and obey. . . .
> Come, come, you froward and unable worms,
> My mind hath been as big as one of yours,
> My heart as great, my reason haply more,
> To bandy word for word and frown for frown.
> But now I see our lances are but straws,
> Our strength as weak, our weakness past compare,
> That seeming to be most which we indeed least are.
> Then vail your stomachs, for it is no boot,
> And place your hands below your husband's foot.
>
> (5.2.161–64, 169–77)

27 As Boose states at the outset: 'for feminist scholars, the irreplaceable value if not pleasure to be realised by an historical confrontation with Shakespeare's *The Taming of the Shrew* lies in the unequivocality with which the play locates both women's abjected position in the social order of early modern England and the costs exacted for resistance. For romantic comedy to "work" normatively in *Shrew's* concluding scene and allow the audience the happy ending it demands, the cost is, simply put, the construction of women's speech that must unspeak its own resistance and reconstitute female subjectivity into the self-abnegating rhetoric of Kate's famous disquisition on obedience' (1991: 179).

28 As Boose notes: '[h]owever shrewish it may seem to assert an intertextuality that binds the obscured records of a painful women's history into a comedy that celebrates love and marriage, that history has paid for the right to speak itself, whatever the resultant incongruities' (1991: 181).

29 Boose's sources include a two-part paper entitled 'On obsolete punishments, with particular reference to those of Cheshire', by a Mr T N Brushfield, Medical Superintendent of the Cheshire Lunatic Asylum, dated 1858, and a book written by John Webster Spargo entitled *Juridical Folklore in England: Illustrated by the Cuckingstool*, published in 1944.

30 According to Bardsley: 'it was not uncommon for problematic speech to be linked with effeminacy and emasculation in poems and treatises from the late medieval and early modern period' (2006: 90–93).

31 As Boose notes, '[b]y means of the syntactical elision' of references to horses these phrases quite literally put 'the bridle on Kate rather than her horse. What this suggests is that the scold's bridle/horse bridle/scolds bridle associations were available for resonant recall through the interaction of linguistic structures and narrative ones' (1991: 199). Indeed, '[i]f the chastity belt was an earlier design to prevent entrance into one aperture of the deceitfully open female body, the scold's bridle, preventing exit from another, might be imagined as a derivative inversion of that same obsession . . . The tongue (at least in the governing assumptions about order) should always already have been possessed by the male' (Boose 1991: 204).

32 I have borrowed this term from Threadgold (1997a: 212) which is a reference to Butler (1990: 139).

33 See also Crockett J in *R v Allwood* (1975) 18 A Crim R 120 at 124, who referred to two pieces of evidence as capable of being treated by the jury as provocative:

> ... first, the statement of the deceased to the applicant that she had left him 'for sex'. Secondly, and perhaps more importantly, the words, 'Prove it', following *a contemptuous ejaculative* utterance given in reply to the applicant's expressed disbelief that the deceased had had 'sex' with Donnelly no more than four times prior to their departure together from the applicant's home. I am prepared to assume for the purposes of the present case that words alone, at least words in combination with an attitude of mockery or scorn or spoken in a sneering manner or with such truculence that they are intended to and do have the effect of belittling or deriding him to whom they are spoken, can now amount to provocation sufficient to reduce murder to manslaughter (my italics).

34 The passage quoted is from Alan Paton in *Cry; The Beloved Country, A Story of Comfort in Desolation* (1958: 136–7) and was cited in *Anissa Pty Ltd v Parsons* (on application of the prothonotary of the Supreme Court of Victoria) [1999] VSC 430 216 (Callaway JA).

35 See Arlidge and Eady for a history of the common law of contempt (1982). For an extended discussion of the scope of contempt powers, see Chesterman *Public Criticism of Judges* (Research Paper No 5 (1984)); Chesterman *Contempt* (Report No 35 (1987)).

36 According to Miller, the court physically restrained the defendant in a famous Chicago conspiracy trial; however, this did not succeed in silencing him. Moreover, Miller notes that in *Illinois v Allen* 397 US 337 (1970), the Supreme Court stated that: 'Not only is it possible that the sight of shackles and gags might have a significant effect on the jury's feelings about the defendant, but the use of this technique is itself something of an affront to the very dignity and decorum of judicial proceedings that the judge is seeking to uphold' (2000: 205).

37 For an overview of when a contempt is 'in the Face of the Court' see Miller (2000: 142–45). For a discussion of some examples of 'scandalizing a court or judge' see Miller (2000: 572–80).

38 Arlidge and Eady put it thus: 'it is a contempt to assault a judge while he is in his place doing his office' (1982: 179).

39 See the case of *Tuckerman, ex parte; Re Nash* [1970] 3 NSWLR 23. See also Walker on scurrilous abuse as a form of contempt of scandalising the court (1985).

40 For a critique of the debates raised by the case of *Tuckerman* see Chesterman (1987: 32–33).

41 The six men were sentenced according to section 152 of the *Justices Act* 1902 (NSW) to serve 14 days in prison.

42 Chesterman notes that later explanations to the presiding magistrate indicated that these gestures expressed 'solidarity' for the 'oppressed people' of the world (1987: 32).

43 *The Magistrates' Court at Prahran v Murphy* [1997] 2 VR 186. The charges of contempt against the barrister were brought under section 133 of the *Magistrates' Court Act* 1989 (No 51). The particulars of the appeal heard in the Supreme Court of Victoria are recounted in the judgment of Charles JA at 191–215. Briefly, this was an appeal from an order made by a judge of the same court prohibiting a magistrate from further hearing charges against the respondent of contempt of the Magistrates' Court at Prahran.

44 There were a number of legal issues to be determined by the court, the first of which involved the question of whether the allegation of bias by the barrister against the

presiding magistrate constituted contempt. The second issue was whether the magistrate, in his resolve to hear the proceedings involving the barrister's client, Parkin, summarily, and despite the barrister's allegation of bias against the magistrate (which caused the magistrate to feel insulted), had exceeded his permitted function as a magistrate. The question of whether the parties involved, and also the public, may have entertained a reasonable apprehension that the magistrate might not bring an impartial and unprejudiced mind to the resolution of the case before him constituted a third issue to be determined by the court (*The Magistrates' Court at Prahran v Murphy* [1997] 2 VR 186, 194 (Charles JA)).

45 ibid 198.

46 ibid 193.

47 Tadgell JA quoted a passage from 'the percipient observation of Philp J, speaking for the Full Court, in *Reece v McKenna, Ex parte Reece* [1953] St R Qd 258 at 264'.

48 *The Magistrates' Court at Prahran v Murphy* (n 43) at 201.

49 ibid.

50 Despite the barrister's allegations of bias against the primary magistrate, he was determined to hear the charges against the barrister's client summarily. The majority chose to resolve this issue by following the reasoning in the judgment of Frankfurter J in the case of *Offutt*. See *The Magistrates' Court at Prahran v Murphy* (n 43) at 212.

51 ibid 202.

52 ibid 212, citing from the judgment of Priestley JA in *Costello*.

53 Rush observes that, historically, the loss of self-control in the doctrine of provocation can be understood in terms of the seven deadly sins that emerged towards the end of the Middle Ages as 'a loss of the soul'. Whereas, 'in more modern language', it is 'the loss of the self' that is the subject of the doctrine of provocation, Rush notes that '[i]n the list of John Cassian, "the seven deadline sins are eight: *gastrimargia* (gluttony), *fornication* (lust), *philargyria* (avarice), *ira* (wrath), *tristitia* (sorrow), *acedia* (sloth), *cendoxia* (vainglory) and *superbia* (pride)"'. To this list he adds: *tristitia* which is fused with *acdedia* 'to form what would come to be called melancholia'. Moreover, '[t]he sins are deadly because they plague the soul; their perturbations induce a loss of the soul' (Rush 1997: 341).

54 *Gardner v R* (1989) 42 A Crim R 279.

55 (1989) 42 A Crim R 279, 282 (O'Bryan J). In doing so, the Victorian Court of Criminal Appeal relaxed the requirement that the provocation must be said and done by the person who was killed, ruling that provocation could emanate from a third party.

56 (1989) 42 A Crim R 279, 282. See also 233–234. See also Howe's and Morgan's retellings of 'the facts' in this case: Adrian Howe 'Provoking comment: the question of gender bias in the provocation defence – a victorian case study' in Norma Grieve and Ailsa Burns (eds) *Australian Women: Contemporary Feminist Thought* (1994) 225, 232; Jenny Morgan 'Provocation law and facts: dead women tell no tales, tales are told about them' (1997) *Melbourne University Law Review* 237–76.

57 (1989) 42 A Crim R 279 at 282.

58 At the time of the trial, the weapon, most likely a baseball bat, had not been found.

59 Trial transcript, Supreme Court of Victoria (February 1989) at 90–91a (Cummins J) (charge to jury) (*Gardner*).

60 *Gardner* trial transcript, Supreme Court of Victoria (February 1989) 315–412 (examination and cross-examination of Witness Q).

61 ibid.

62 ibid 302–316.

63 *Gardner* transcript of plea, Supreme Court of Victoria (February 1989) 42.

64 *Gardner* trial transcript, Supreme Court of Victoria (February 1989) 410.

65 The excerpt from the transcript is as follows:

> *Defence*:   Did he [the male deceased] have a reputation for being heavy handed?
>
> *Witness 'I'*: Yes, to my knowledge that sometimes was talked about.
>
> *Defence*:   A reputation for a man who settled things with the fist, rather than the mouth?
>
> *Witness 'I'*: Yes.
>
> *Defence*:   The reputation that in the event that there is a difficult situation, that he would punch something, rather than talking about it, that is what you mean, is it not?
>
> *Witness 'I'*: That's settling with the fist, instead of talking, yeah.
>
> (Gardner, Trial transcript, Supreme
Court of Victoria, February 1989, 586)

66 *Gardner* trial transcript, Supreme Court of Victoria (February 1989) 1222.

67 (1989) 42 A Crim R 279, 281 (O'Bryan J).

68 See *Parker* [1964] AC 1369; (1964) 111 CLR 665. The defence in *Gardner* relied on the facts in *Parker* where the Privy Council relaxed the requirement of suddenness, the lapse of time between the alleged trigger incident and how long the loss of self-control might continue to operate. The case involved two men, Kelly and Parker, and an argument between them, over Parker's wife. Kelly, the male deceased, and Parker's wife were having an affair. When the two men confronted each other, Kelly was held to have provoked Parker when he jeered at his adversary's lesser strength (he threatened to take the accused's wife with one hand and then beat the accused with the other). It was this image of Kelly as a virile sexual rival and as a 'man of action', that the defence in *Gardner* relied on to raise both the defence of provocation and the defence of self-defence in relation to Shears. In this narrative, Kelly and Shears are positioned as like-minded antagonists.

69 *Gardner* trial transcript, Supreme Court of Victoria (February 1989) 1291.

70 *Gardner* (1989) 42 A Crim R 279, 284 (O'Bryan J).

CHAPTER 3

Legal narratives on trial: constructions of sex, blame and culpability and the provocation defence

The Law, as that institution which most epitomises Reason, Rationality, Order, Control, is increasingly 'on trial', subject to rewriting, as the effects of poststructuralist, feminist and deconstructive theory begin to circulate within Law Schools, among those writing about the Law, and as common sense in the media and on television ... in the end, it is people and their interactions, their readings and their writings, which constitute the law. And that is why the law will never accomplish its mythical goal of truth and objectivity and universal justice.

(Threadgold 1994: 323–24)

Introduction: reading law as literature

In this chapter, I undertake a reading of the transcripts of murder trials, including reported and unreported cases and appellate judgments, in cases where an accused person charged with murder admits killing and raises the partial defence of provocation. Such a reading considers the construction and representation of subjectivity and sexual difference in legal narrations of intimate partner homicide. The primary focus of this chapter will be the Victorian case law relating to provocation, although the chapter's claims have general implications for provocation law in other jurisdictions. In examining these cases, I focus on the way the process of judgment operates discursively to construct the characters of the accused and the deceased, and to situate them within what I have termed a narrative of insult in which feminine excess (excessive speech and behaviour) is understood to drive wounded males to restore their masculinity by killing their verbal antagonist. I will further claim that the discursive process of 'plotting' events according to a familiar storyline operates not only to frame the circumstances in terms of coherence and plausibility, but to drive the narrative forward towards a conclusion – murder – with an air of inevitability.[1]

I should perhaps begin by outlining how I propose to approach my reading of these cases. I will argue in this chapter that both law and the facts are not simply what lawyers and judges find or discover; rather, that law and facts are constructed and framed in a context. In their examination of growing academic interest in treating law as narrative and rhetoric,[2] Brooks and Gewirtz describe 'law and literature' as something of a movement. For some, the 'and' means law *in* literature, the study of law and lawyers in fiction, whereas for others, the 'and' means literature *in* the law, 'the use of literary representations in the law and legal texts with a view to making the legal profession more acutely aware of its effects on human actors' (Brooks and Gewirtz 1996: 3, 15).[3] One of the main components of the reciprocity between law and literature is how law and legal texts can be examined in much the same way as a literary text might be examined. As Gewirtz explains, while the most obvious difference between law and literature is that 'law coerces people' or, more explicitly, that legal interpretation is itself a form of violence: 'both law and literature attempt to shape reality through language, use distinctive methods and forms to do so, and require interpretation' (1996a: 4). The treatment of law as 'literature' means that we should become much more 'self-conscious about the form, structure and rhetoric of legal texts, legal arguments, and other phenomena of the legal culture' (Gewirtz 1996a: 4).

The work of Goodrich (1986, 1987, 1995, 1996)[4] has focused to a considerable degree on the rhetorical tradition of textual and legal analysis as one of the oldest forms of political criticism; yet it is a method of reading the language of legal texts that is antithetical to the modern tradition dominating the legal profession today (see also Douzinas and Nead 1999: 4; Aristodemou 1999).[5] Law, as it is conventionally conceived, generates 'truth' according to internal legal principles, such as, 'neutrality', 'objectivity' and 'equality'. Moreover, it is a commonplace that lawyers and judges work in reference to an objective standard or original intention that stands outside the rhetorical system (Brooks 1996: 15). Rejecting this proposition, Threadgold suggests the 'truth' of law is one of the greatest fictions that the legal system constructs and maintains; it is a 'legal fiction' that protects its self-image as authoritative, autonomous and rational (2002: 26).[6] Similarly, Goodrich argues against the traditional method of legal analysis, which is, according to the philosophies of legal formalism or more explicitly legal positivism, 'a doctrinal faith or orthodoxy which continues to assert the rationality of law as a "system" of rules, as a "grammar" of norms or even as the "correct" expression of fundamental legal principles and rights' (1986: 215). He proposes instead that the legal text can be read in terms of a 'diversity of meanings' (1986: 206). The 1973 publication of James Boyd White's *The Legal Imagination* is considered the first text to argue that the study and practice of law should not be approached through the methods of legal formalism; rather, White argued for the inclusion of literary studies in legal education.[7] In reading the law as if it were literature, it can be seen that 'law is not merely a system of rules ... but habits of mind and expectations – what might also be called a culture' (White 1985: xiii). The greatest power of law, White suggests, lies in its language, in the coercive aspect of its rhetoric – in the way it structures sensibility and vision' (1985: viii). Goodrich's proposal of a rhetoric of law is one that requires a 're-reading of the law and the rewriting of the legal textbook in the space opened up by the concept of law as social discourse'. This methodology of law as a *social discourse* draws on Bakhtin's (1981) elaboration of a materialist theory of, or basis to, language and treatment of the discourses, discursive processes and heteroglossia generally to be found within literary language and the novel as a specific genre (1987: 143).[8] From this it follows that 'the language and text of the law must be studied not simply as a discrete logic of intradiscourse but as an accumulation and crystallisation of interdiscursive meanings' (Goodrich 1987: 208). Law can be studied, therefore, as a kind of writing, an interpretive and compositional activity, 'a technology for making worlds and selves' (Threadgold 2002: 26).

This approach to reading law and legal texts comprehends that the events described in a courtroom are not communicated in a transparent or neutral way; rather, each event requires the selection of a narrative and the choice of narrative has crucial consequences for understanding the event, the interpretation of blame, the outcome of the criminal trial, the type and severity of sentence, and the attribution of truth and authority to one version of the event (Puren and Young 1999: 8). This is how certain and preferred ideas and understandings about people's actions and behaviour in everyday life can become 'commonplace', simply accepted as the 'way things are'. It is in this way that 'the habitual connotation of one thing with or for another becomes, by convention and repetition, part of everyday knowledge and expectation, just part of the plot' (Young 1990: 4, 103). As such, the choice of which material – objects, actions, behaviours and events – is to be selected for inclusion has crucial consequences, however, for the outcome of the case. Legal narratives do not simply present the significance of events as if there is a version of the 'truth' or indeed 'reality' out there somewhere, which is somehow pure, untouched by representation and waiting to be discovered and re-presented by legal practitioners within the courtroom context.[9] Rather, narrative 'orders the facts into a storyline, and in doing so, both attributes meaning to the facts, and creates a context that makes it almost irresistible for listeners [or readers] to supply "missing facts"'(Kennedy 2002: 72).[10]

In *Reading for the Plot*, Brooks defines 'plot and plotting' as the key instruments whereby 'stories come to be ordered in significant form'. It also refers to the way we read and our need for such orderings (Brooks 1984: xi).[11] Brooks understands 'plotting' as referring to 'the dynamic aspect of narrative – that which makes a plot "move forward", and makes us read forward, seeking in the unfolding of the narrative a line of intention and a portent of design that hold the promise of the progress toward meaning' (1984: xiii). As de Lauretis also observes, the technique of plot orients the movement of desire in narrative, which is precisely a mapping of differences and specifically sexual difference into the text (1984: 121).[12] It is in this way that audiences (lawyers, judges and the jury) are made complicit with one version of events over another. The process of plotting the 'facts' of a particular case is a way of encouraging the jury to accept the force and persuasion of the arguments put forward by counsel. Depending on how the events presented are (re)ordered within a chronological sequence, the act that caused death can emerge as if having simply 'unfolded' according to this or that recognisable drama. In the previous chapter I discussed how various tropes of subjectivity (for example as illustrated by the qualifier that she 'asked for it') operate to evoke the deceased into narrative possibility. I also drew a comparison between the court's reading of the deceased's behaviour in the 1989 case of *Gardner* and the audience's reactions to the character, Melanie, in the film *Jackie Brown*, to show the implications of interpreting the event of murder as the inevitable culmination of the 'love-hate' relationship. In this chapter, I show how legal counsel exploit the conventions of romance narrative, which establishes the killer in the role of a hero beset by fate and in a tragic tale in which his ordeal is given primacy over that of the victim.[13]

The 'love triangle'

In the 1996 Victorian Supreme Court case of *Trisnadi*,[14] the jury found the accused guilty of manslaughter on the ground of provocation.[15] The jury was apparently persuaded by the accused's version of events that he killed the male deceased (A) after he discovered his girlfriend (B) and the deceased sitting together on her bed fully clothed. In his record of interview with police, it transpired that the accused and his girlfriend were due to go to breakfast (*yum cha*) together. He alleged that he was shocked at sighting the two together and, upon leaving the room, he claimed to have heard the pair laughing. The deceased then left to catch a tram. As he was leaving the house, he was confronted by the accused in the lane next to the house and an argument between the two ensued. The accused wanted to talk to the deceased about the nature of his relationship with the accused's girlfriend and they agreed to talk about it in the accused's car. While in the car, the deceased allegedly taunted the accused that the accused was stupid or blind not to know that the deceased and the accused's girlfriend were sleeping together. At this point, the accused lost his self-control and pushed hard on the neck of the deceased while they were in the front seat of the car. They struggled. The deceased's body was later discovered in the lane by passers-by, his neck and wrists having been cut by a sharp instrument.

In his opening address to the jury the prosecuting counsel told the jury that '[t]he motive for this murder . . . is one of jealousy' (*Trisnadi* 1996: 21). In contrast, the defence narrative represents the accused's version of events as follows:

> In addition to the facts as you determine them is common sense with your common experiences of life. This is particularly re-levant in this case. The facts of this case have been told a thousand times – no, a million times. The facts of this case riddle the literature. It is known in every village from ancient man through to the complex cities of the world today: it is the triangle. It is as old as time. It is something that is so familiar to you, you are nigh-on unconscious of it. It is only when the idiosyncratic facts come to you that you will understand precisely what has happened here. You will understand the classic triangle.
>
> (*Trisnadi* 1996: 33)

As legal scholars would suggest, an opening statement is 'the most valuable tool in courtroom persuasion, enabling a lawyer, through words, to "paint a picture in the mind's eye"'(Morrill 1972, cited in Snedaker 1986–1987: 15–16). Although opening statements should not, according to trial procedure, be argumentative, it is the first opportunity for legal counsel to persuade his or her audience. As Snedaker notes, '[a] persuasive opening statement is significant in producing a successful trial outcome'

(1986–1987: 16). However, equally important are the questions that are put to the jury during examination and cross-examination of witnesses.[16] As Eades observes, the structuring of a person's story begins with the police interview (2008: 210). The accused in *Trisnadi* was an Indonesian national at the time of the killing. In his tape recorded interview with the Homicide Squad he was asked to describe his relationship with B. It transpired that there was a problem with translation within a pre-dominantly Anglo-centric culture (such as Australia) that related to the phrase 'good friends' used by the accused man. When he was asked by police to indicate when his relationship with B changed from 'being boyfriend and girlfriend to just friends', he said it was 'some time in early September',[17] which was a few months prior to the killing. When cross-examined about what he told police in his record of interview by counsel for the Crown, the accused explained that he was experiencing some difficulty describing 'the relationship between a boy and a girl' from the Indonesian language to English (*Trisnadi* 1996: 450–51). The judge then intervened and asked the accused whether '[b]y using the expression "good friends"', was he 'meaning to show that you understood "good friends" to be different to "boyfriend and girlfriend"', to which he replied 'Yes' (*Trisnadi* 1996: 451).

A key component of the case for the Crown was that the accused man had not been 'overwhelmed by passion' or 'lost self-control as a result of seeing his girlfriend, his "just friend" in that room at 10 o'clock', but had acted out of 'revenge or spite' (*Trisnadi* 1996: 490, closing address to jury). In contrast, the defence narrative sought to position his ex-girlfriend (witness B) as lacking credibility by portraying her as having played two suitors off against each other. In his opening address to the jury, the defence spoke of how in the days leading up to the deceased's death, B had spent some nights at the home of the accused as well as her own. He then told them that only a few days before the deceased's death the accused was 'having dinner . . . with . . . B and her mother and others' when the deceased arrived with B's 'pet kitten' for whom he had been caring while B was overseas. He next asked the jury to put themselves 'at the table' in order to make an incriminating point about the deceased. He asked them: 'Had there been infidelity and betrayal?' Proceeding to answer the question for them, he described how there had been 'tension. Then in the following days she moves from bed to bed and on that Thursday morning, with the emotions wound up like a clock spring, . . . [the accused] . . . puts his head into his girlfriend's bedroom and he is there. . . . The emotions boil over. They meet. They fight. One dies. That is not murder' (33–34). The metaphor of a 'clock spring' threatening suddenly and without warning to 'uncoil' and presumably break the clock, works by analogy to convey to the audience (the judge, the jury and so on) that the mind of the accused man is also very close to reaching its limit.

Witness B only gave evidence at the committal hearing and not at the Supreme Court trial. This was noted by the presiding judge when delivering his charge to the jury: 'you have not, however, had the advantage of seeing her take the oath in this trial nor of answering questions in this trial' (*Trisnadi* 1996 at 534 (Eames J)). Instead, the transcript of the cross-examination of the witness by defence counsel was read out verbatim to the jury by the prosecuting counsel (*Trisnadi* 1996: 62–92). It transpired that some months prior to the death of the deceased, the witness had communicated to the accused that she wanted to end the relationship, in a letter she sent while he was in Indonesia but that he claimed he did not receive: Consider the following exchange that took place during cross-examination of the witness:

Q: You have said to the police at some stage you wrote a letter indicating to [the accused] that you wanted to break off the relationship?
B: Yes.
Q: He has indicated to you, has he, that he didn't get that letter?
B: Yes.
Q: But you say that after you had written that letter you spoke to him on the telephone about wanting to end the relationship, right?
B: Yes.
Q: But in fact the relationship did not end, did it?
B: It did.
Q: Your relationship with him continued after that?
B: No, it didn't.
Q: He in fact came to Australia in September of last year, didn't he?
B: Yes, he did.
Q: He saw you then?
B: Yes.
Q: Your relationship with him resumed during that time, didn't it?
B: No.

In this exchange, the witness is asked to answer affirmatively a series of propositional statements about her intention to end the relationship, which are also designed to convey her confusion over whether she really had finished the relationship. The cross-examination of the witness by defence counsel continued:

Q: That was a friendly letter, wasn't it?
B: Yes.
Q: You finished it with the expression, 'Love always', correct?
B: Yes.
Q: There was nothing in that letter to indicate that you didn't want to continue a friendly relationship with him, was there?
B: No.
Q: So as at September when you wrote that letter you still wanted to maintain a friendly relationship at least with [the accused], didn't you?
B: Yes.
Q: That is a letter that is written after you say you had written a letter to him ending the relationship, right?
B: Yes.

In this exchange, defence counsel is seeking to make an incriminating point about the witness, which was that by finishing the letter 'Love always', the witness was sending the accused mixed messages. It is a mainstay of all criminal trials that juries are told it is the answers given by witnesses that provide the evidence in the case and not the questions put to witnesses by legal counsel (see for example *Trisnadi* 1996 at 532(Eames J)). As Young (1998: 457) observes:

> ...[i]t is of course ludicrous to think that juries either ignore the questions and focus on the answer (a notion that denies the self-proclaimed dialogism of trial discourse), or are unaffected by the barrage of suggestions that defence counsel layout before them.

A more specific example of how trial questioning can discursively transform the character of a witness or the deceased can be found in the 1997 case of *R v N*.[18] The accused was found guilty of the murder of his girlfriend, with whom he had been in a relationship for six months. At his trial, he claimed to have killed in circumstances in which he lost self-control after a protracted argument with the deceased.[19] Earlier in his interview, the accused had told police that he punched the deceased in the mouth, causing her to fall to the ground, because 'she was trying to make [him] jealous ... [and] ... may have been speaking to another man'.[20] At his trial, counsel for the defence sought to establish that the deceased was the aggressor on the night in question. In contrast, the prosecuting counsel argued that the deceased was 'frightened' of the accused. Consider the defence narrative's representation of the argument between the accused and deceased in a sequence of questions put to witnesses who claimed to have heard the female deceased's voice on two separate occasions on the night in question. The questions were put to a witness (witness H), a neighbour claiming to have heard the accused and deceased arguing moments before the deceased was killed. Initially, the witness admitted he found it difficult to distinguish between either the voice of the deceased or that of the accused on the night of the killing. The witness was cross-examined by defence counsel as follows:

> Q: Fair enough. Except that the voices that you did hear, whoever they came from, were very – were raised?
> A: Very raised, yes.
> Q: Very raised. The next time was two o'clock, and the voice you heard was extremely loud?
> A: Yes, yeah.
> Q: Would you say that it was angry?
> A: Came across that way, yes.
> Q: Was it yelling, a yelling voice?
> A: Yes.
> Q: Was it a screaming voice?
> A: Well, screaming, yes.
>
> (*R v N* 1997: 76)

The above extract illustrates a subtle process of substitution and distortion. First, there is a shift from the plural (their voices) to the singular (the voice). Secondly and relatedly, there is a process of substituting adjectives that describe louder tones. Note that defence counsel first asks the witness if the voice he heard was 'raised'. In the next question, he asks if it was 'loud'. In the next, he asks if it was a 'yelling' voice. Finally, the witness is asked if it was a 'screaming' voice. In seeking to offer a plausible scenario as to what took place on the night in question for the jury, the defence narrative simultaneously makes an evaluation and implication as to the effect of the deceased's voice on the accused and, in doing so, escalating the pitch for the jury. In this example, the effects of the woman victim's words are auditory as well as visual.

Throughout the trial, both the Crown and the defence had repeatedly questioned witnesses about a verbal exchange that had taken place earlier in the night between the deceased and the accused were at the pub where they were drinking with friends.[21] While the prosecuting counsel was more concerned to elicit the 'content' of their verbal exchange, the narrative mobilised by defence counsel was seeking to make an incriminating point: that she 'asked for it'. By a discursive process of analogy and substitution, the replacement of one adjective for another, the effect is that the transcript literalises the effect of her words on the accused (but also on the jury in the context of the courtroom) as excessively audible, as if building up to a crescendo.

Having reminded the jury that 'it is the answer given by the witness which constitutes the evidence, and not the questions put by counsel', the trial judge chose to recount the defence narrative as follows:

> True it was, accepted [by the defence], that the accused man had struck her. But look at it in the context of the disputation, which was going back and forth and was certainly, according to his presentation, by no means one-sided. Eventually, after what must have been hours of screaming and yelling at him, as she endeavoured to deal with the situation, and in the presence of the man [witness C], who was not adding anything but difficulty to the scene, he lost control of himself and struck out.
> (*R v N* 1997 at 476 (Vincent J)).[22]

In law's auditoria, the transcript literalises the female voice into a crescendo for the purpose of positioning her within a final imagined scene or context. In *R v N*, the deceased's speech is understood to have had an incremental effect on the accused, the rising tone and pitch of her voice increasingly reinforces his perception of annoyance and aggravation, which is read as 'evidence' of her excessive aggression. As a result, her words are construed as 'adding' to her desire for autonomy, causing him not to respond with a 'punch' to her mouth this time, but with an act of force, which he does by killing her.

What the deceased reputedly said to the accused moments before he killed her was that she wanted him to leave her home, as she feared he had been physically abusive toward her children. She then lapsed into silence (*R v N* 1997 at 1–8, sentence (Vincent J)). When sentencing the accused the judge's comments reinforce the defence narrative; he said that not only was he 'regrettably familiar' with the situation in which the prisoner killed the deceased, but when the 'crime [was] considered in context', his 'personal culpability should be regarded as significantly reduced'. He concluded that: 'the factual framework' was one in which the loss of self-control was 'induced by the behaviour of the deceased' (*R v N* 1997 at 8, sentence (Vincent J)).

Similarly, in the judge's charge to the jury in *Trisnadi*, he reminded them that the acts of provocation 'which the law takes into account for the law of provocation' are 'the acts of the deceased'. Those acts 'have to be seen in the context of all the circumstances, and the extent to which an act is provocative may be influenced by the fact of it occurring in the context of there being conduct by other people as well' (*Trisnadi* 1996: 559–60). He then offered a distillation of the defence narrative, which had sought to establish that '[t]his was a case of [one woman] playing two men against each other'. He told them of defence counsel's resort to 'the analogy of it being like a watch spring tightening as the events of the week evolved and as the build up of tension increased'. He reiterated how 'during that week the accused no doubt feared increasingly the possibility that she was being unfaithful', then 'on the day he discovered that it was so and they added to it by laughing at him' (*Trisnadi* 1996: 633).

When charging the jury, the judge said that when the accused entered witness Bs bedroom, he observed both her and the male deceased sitting on her bed, and that the deceased was dressed 'possibly in shorts, and possibly in her shorts at the time, she being in pyjamas' (*Trisnadi* 1996: 561). However, by the time his representation of the defence narrative appears in his sentencing remarks, there is no 'mistake' or confusion surrounding what was to be inferred by them sitting on the bed, a move that firmly positions witness B as an antagonistic figure within the narrative and the accused man as a duped and passive victim of her duplicitous behaviour. Indeed, the judge's comments offer a clearly sympathetic (if abridged version) reading of the defence narrative. He stated that when the accused entered the bedroom and discovered the male deceased and witness B 'sitting together on the bed clothed in a fashion which unmistakenly indicated that they had been intimate', he was 'shocked and distressed at what [he] saw'. He commented on how his 'distress was increased' when he left the bedroom and 'they both laughed' at him, leading him to feel that 'they were laughing at [his] expense'. He emphasised that the accused would have 'felt a sense of humiliation and distress to discover (or more likely to have had confirmed) that [B], with whom [he was] in love was obviously having an intimate relationship' with the male deceased.[23] He said that, while he accepted that the words spoken by the male deceased were relatively minor, there was 'no doubt that the behaviour of [B] and of the deceased ... was both unwise and provocative'.[24] He also saw fit to remark that although 'the provocation said to be given by the deceased himself was relatively minor' it 'gained its force only by being coupled with the behaviour of [B]'. He reasoned that while 'members of the community understand the powerful force of love and rejections', clearly it was not something that that B understood, being a person who was not only 'immature in years' but also 'in her experience of life'. Having narrativised the accused as a jealous, vulnerable character who suffered greatly at the mercy of a young and inexperienced woman who toyed with his affections, the judge's comments serve to position her as 'asking for it': however, she was not a person who appreciated 'the potentially dangerous emotional force of jealousy'.[25]

The 1999 case of *Browne*[26] provides an interesting point of comparison and opportunity to explore further the complexity surrounding the law's construction of the romantic subject in its murder narratives. In *Browne*, letters that were written by the victim but never actually sent to the intended recipient told a kind of love story but it was not one that the court and particularly the defence were convened to hear. Browne was found guilty of the murder of his wife, Kay, and sentenced to 14 and a half years' imprisonment with a non-parole period of nine and a half years. At his trial, his claim to the defence of provocation was made on the basis of a build-up of tension within the relationship and a loss of self-control as a result of an abusive comment or comments by his wife. In his interview with police, the accused alleged that they had an argument during which she said to him: 'What the hell did I ever get married to you for?' He claimed that it was at this point he went to the kitchen and retrieved a carving knife and 'went back' to the bedroom and 'went for her'.[27] When asked what he meant when he said that he 'went for her' he explained: 'I went to get her to – just to stop her. Just to – . . .'.[28] It was also at this point that the police interviewer put the following question to the accused, which took the form of a propositional statement: 'That was the straw that broke the camel's back?', to which the accused replied '[p]robably, yes'.[29] The process of metaphor here operates on a number of different levels. On the one hand it is used to portray the state of mind of the accused as that of a man reaching his limit and as having therefore a legitimate claim to the partial defence of provocation. But on the other hand, it operates to represent the potential threat posed by the deceased's words to the accused's self-image, his sense of himself as a certain type of man. In his interview with police, the accused repeatedly referred to his wife as excessively talkative. According to him, while she was the kind of person to talk and talk about anything and everything, he was a person who would 'go into depth about things'.[30]

This portrayal of the deceased's character as excessively talkative took on particular significance in relation to the accused's discovery of two batches of letters written by the deceased, in which she fantasised about having a relationship with another man. In his interview with police, the accused claimed the relationship between himself and the deceased really began to deteriorate in the last three or four weeks after he discovered a second batch of letters.[31] Although he had confronted her about the letters in the past, he claimed that on this particular occasion, she abused him by calling him 'all sorts of things that made . . . [him] . . . feel, you know, little small. Bastardry'.

Central here is the theme of escalation; the more she talks, the more she writes, the more her words (spoken and written) are imagined as impeding the accused's capacity to remain rational, reasonable and in control. This theme of escalation was reiterated throughout the police interview[32] and continued into the trial.

A central component of the defence narrative was that the provocative conduct including words could build-up over a period of time.[33] In contrast, the prosecuting counsel submitted that the accused had become obsessed about the protection of his assets combined with his jealousy over the fantasy affair, which led to an argument. She said that 'at some stage on the day the accused had had enough': '[h]e decided to stop the abuse as he perceived it, decided to permanently prevent her from spending any more of his money, he decided to exact revenge for the shame of competing with a fantasy lover, he deceased to retaliate, he decided to kill her' (*Browne* 1999: 94). A key strategy mobilised by the defence was to show that the deceased was not only constantly critical of the accused but that she was also critical of him in public (*Browne* 1999: 189–93, cross-examination of witness E). When making his closing arguments to the jury, defence counsel reminded them that the provocative conduct could 'include words' and 'conduct' which 'builds up and goes over a period of time'. Next he reminded them that the accused had complained of being constantly criticised, denigrated, degraded constantly about feeling pathetic, about having lost his confidence'. He said that the accused was a man who had 'strict views. He would not have been happy about someone having an affair of the heart in the mind of someone else' (*Browne* 1999: 428). He then put a series of propositions to the jury in relation to the letters. First, he asked them to consider that when they read the letters, they 'will see a number of references not only to what she thinks' but that the letters are written in 'a very gushing sort of language – my darling beautiful man – and all this sort of stuff' (*Browne* 1999: 430). Next, he invited the jury 'to consider not some hypothetical man spending the day planning the execution of his wife, but a day on which there were arguments and arguments where she was adding and adding and adding – a build up to the point where he snapped' (*Browne* 1999: 461). Note that the threat posed by the deceased's words is imagined as reaching a crescendo:

> Madam Forelady and ladies and gentlemen ... [t]here is a huge amount of letters here ... they show a woman besotted with somebody, absolutely and utterly besotted with him ... They are letters besotted, of a woman besotted ... There are references to phone calls. ... Things she spoke to her friends about ... That this

was a build up of a large and who knows, I don't know, she doesn't know, who knows how many such actions of denigration occurred? . . . Don't worry about whether these letters are being sent, Madam Forelady and ladies and gentlemen. . . . It goes on, hundreds, if not thousands more. Diatribes.

(*Browne* 1999: 466–567)

As the above extract illustrates, the more she speaks, the more she writes, the more her killer is able to be positioned as an object of humiliation and ridicule, a feminised, cuckolded man. On the afternoon in question, when the deceased says to him, 'What did I ever see in you?', the accused's fears that he was losing sexual exclusivity, his voice, are realised. It is not simply that the deceased's autonomy and also her sexuality are completely disregarded in the defence narrative but that her expressions of love (the words that she used to tell her own story in which she might have emerged as a subject rather than an object of the romance narrative) are dismissed as the mere products of 'romantic fiction' – 'the stuff of women's literature – an ephemera or chimera, fantastical products of the fickle attention of the feminine mind' (Goodrich 1996: 642–43).[34] In my discussion of the next two cases, the defence narrative exploits the conventions of romance narrative and in doing so effectively repositions the killer as the 'victim' in a tragic tale of a 'romance-gone-wrong'.

The 'romance-gone-wrong'

In the 1997 case of *Richardson*,[35] the accused stabbed his fiancée 22 times to the front and back of her body thereby causing her death. Richardson was charged with the murder of his fiancée, Joanne Campbell. In his record of interview with police he claimed that on the night in question, whilst seated at the kitchen table of their home, an argument developed between them. They shouted at each other over whether or not they could afford a honeymoon. During the course of the argument he further claimed the deceased uttered words to the effect that if there was to be no honeymoon there would be no wedding. He said she then picked up a box containing wedding invitations and threw it across the room, hitting him on the shoulder. He grabbed her, asking what she was doing. She screamed and he released her. The deceased again picked up the box and threw it. He became angry and moved towards her with the purpose of scaring her. He said that she grabbed a knife from the kitchen area and told him to 'back off'. However, he continued to advance. Although he stated he was uncertain how he sustained the injury, at some stage he sustained a cut to the little finger of his left hand. He stated that he had no recollection of what occurred after that time until he found himself on the floor covered in blood and the deceased lying naked nearby. There was blood everywhere and the knife was beside him. He was convicted of murder and sentenced to 15 years' imprisonment with a non-parole period of 10 years.

In *Richardson*, evidence of the history of the relationship was admitted into the trial, as was evidence of a prior incident that had taken place six months earlier. On this occasion the accused had been drinking and had held the deceased in a headlock causing her to fall to the ground. A key component of the argument put forward by the defence was that the relationship between the accused and deceased was fraught with problems about finances, particularly as it related to the wedding and the honeymoon. In addition, the defence sought to convince the jury that since 'the headlock incident', the accused had become increasingly fearful that the deceased would leave him. In contrast, the Crown argued that the accused was a somewhat 'immature' person who 'simply lost his temper' on the night he killed the deceased, but that it was not an act done in sufficient provocation to avail himself of the partial defence. In *Richardson*, the following exchange took place during cross-examination between the defence counsel and a witness who was the mother of the deceased:

Q: [Witness's name] is the position this, that [the deceased] was a bright, intelligent woman?
A: Yes.
Q: She was a determined young woman?
A: Not determined, no, if she was – I wouldn't say determined, she liked sort of achieving things.
Q: She had in mind things that she wanted to do and she set out to achieve them?
A: That's right.
Q: For instance, like buying a block of land and building a home, those were thoughts that she wanted to implement?
A: That's right.

(1997: 35)

In the above exchange, the witness is asked whether she thought the deceased was a 'bright' and 'intelligent' person, adjectives that travel with positive connotations of character. Next, she is asked whether she thought the deceased was a 'determined' person, a proposition the witness sought to clarify: 'Not determined, no . . . she liked . . . achieving things'. It is not clear at this point whether the line of questioning demarcated above can be taken as insinuating that the deceased was financially demanding and therefore was 'emasculating' him.

An important part of the defence argument was that since the accused was regularly unemployed, he worked from time to time as a sub-contractor, the relationship between the accused and the deceased was fraught with tensions and problems arising from financial difficulties. A few moments later in *Richardson*, another exchange took place during cross-examination between the defence counsel and the same witness:

> Q: When he visited you, that is [the accused], he would come there with your daughter and he really played a very small role in what was happening in household discussions; he just sat virtually in the background?
>
>   . . .
>
> A: He never joined in much at all, he kept in the background, yes.
> Q: So he was, if not shy, retiring at least, he didn't come forward with any sort of outward signs of involvement?
>
>   . . .
>
> Q: So he would virtually sit there and say very little?
> A: He would just talk, like normal talking, like a normal – we would include him in everything. . .
> Q: I am not suggesting you didn't but you say he was in the background in the sense he played very little part in the active conversation that was going on at various times he was there?
> A: That's right, yes.
> Q: [Deceased's name] was the assertive person, is that right?
>
> (1997: 37–38)

In this exchange, the witness is encouraged to represent the accused through recourse to the relatively innocuous stereotype of the 'shy', 'retiring' male. At the same time, the questions asked by the defence juxtapose two types of character: one, the deceased, who is represented as the 'active' one in the relationship and the other, the accused, who is represented as 'passive' and 'quietist' (the more she talked the more he just sat 'in the background'). In the above exchange, what is being presented for the jury is an image of the deceased as someone who sought to usurp the position of the male in the relationship ('she had in mind things she wanted to do'; 'she was determined'; she was 'active' in conversation and so on). This strategy of inviting witnesses to affirm that the deceased had a 'stronger' personality than the accused (was the more 'assertive', 'determined' and 'focused' person) persisted throughout the trial. At one level, this line of questioning is a tactic deployed by the defence to enable the jury better to understand the situation between the parties involved in the case, at least as the defence sees it. At another level, however, it is an example of the kind of strategy Young has described as working through 'implication' and 'insinuation' (1998: 456–57); in this instance, one that enables a causal link between the deceased's words and behaviour on the night and the accused's reaction to be established. I suggest that the witnesses may be quite unaware that their responses to trial questioning are assisting the defence narrative to make an incriminating point about the deceased's character. The questions asked by the defence are designed to portray the deceased as a 'strong', 'determined' woman who exhibited all the signs of normal femininity ('she had a regular job', she was 'bright', 'hoped to get married' and so on). It is in this way that the narrative mobilised by the defence enables an accumulation of culpability to be attached to the deceased and is what gives the accused 'relief' in the form of a defence (Hachamovitch 1997).

In *Richardson* Hampel J's charge to the jury offers a highly abridged version of the history of the relationship as narrated by the defence. This is done in the manner of simply cataloguing the 'facts'. A number of devices figure in his direction to the jury, which reveal the genre to which the law's narration of the death of the deceased ultimately becomes attached. In his opening remarks, Hampel J reminds the members of the jury of their obligation to consider the evidence of the history of the relationship as 'part of the circumstances' between the accused and deceased 'up to and on the night' (*Richardson* 1997: 485). This is followed by a rehearsal of the history of that relationship, which included an assemblage of matters that were focused upon during the trial that sought, according to him, 'first of all' to emphasise 'the good quality of their relationship as a whole' (*Richardson* 1997: 495). In a series of paragraphs linked in logical succession, Hampel J delivers a narrative in which various incidents – one involving violence described as 'the headlock incident' and 'a general argument' between the pair six months earlier – are linked with later ones – the purchase of 'the block of land', that they 'built a house and moved in' and planned 'to get married' – and which render the psychological impact of what the murdered woman allegedly said and did on the night in question as significant. Indeed, this discursive device figures in Hampel J's subsequent representation of events leading up to the accused's act of killing and the conclusion that he was prepared to accept the accused's account of the event. Hampel J systematically distils the details and phases of the relationship between the accused and deceased in a way that reveals his acceptance that they were brought together by voluntary romantic choice. According to his account of the 'evidence of a number of witnesses' – which included some who observed how, on the day before the accused's act of killing they were 'lovey-dovey', 'getting on well' and 'being affectionate' (496) and others who saw them 'driving' together and 'walking the dog' (496–98) — Hampel J invites the jury to concur that these images confirmed the romantic context in which the killing ultimately took place (he told them the relationship was 'on the whole ... a good one, right up to the evening Joanne died': 504). By privileging and imputing significance to the accused's version of events, an account which sought to establish that right up until he killed her, 'they were close and affectionate' and were 'both excited' about his purchase of 'two rings' (504), despite the 'residual tensions' between them about the 'question of the money, the honeymoon and the wedding' (497), the jury is invited to accept one version of events over another.

The jury in *Richardson* returned a verdict of murder. However, the outcome of the trial is of less consequence than are the implications of the law's use and production of a narrative of insult with its key trope of a woman 'asking for it'. It is significant that the same sequencing of events that shaped the defence narrative and drove it forward with an air of inevitability throughout the trial was redeployed during the plea in mitigation of sentence. Here, counsel for the defence submitted that the judge impose a sentence at the lower range for murder. In his representation of the details of the history of the relationship between the accused and the deceased, familiar phrases and events are again subsumed within a chronological sequence in the defence counsel's plea. In *Richardson*, the plea begins:

> In ... 1992 ... they started to live together at premises ... he wasn't working ... they decided, nevertheless, to purchase the block of land and build a house. In a sense that decision indelibly impressed upon the relationship with a commitment which ultimately led to the tragic result in many ways.
>
> (1997: 564)

There are a number of devices of narrative at work here. First, events that occurred in 'real' time are recounted in 'narrative' time with the effect that they are assumed to follow a neat formulaic structure. Once events have been reorganised within a linear temporal sequence – a beginning, a middle and an end – a sequence of events or actions take on familiarity and become time-dependent as if they have a 'natural' or 'true' order (Martin 1986). As Culler points out, a tendency is to substitute (or confuse) chronology with causation ('this' is assumed to cause 'that' and so on) (1981: 183). To that extent, the end of the narrative is accepted as implicit in past events all along. Moreover, any variations in character or in the imagined motivations of the accused do not affect the overall generic structure and movement of the narrative, which takes on additional significance in the plea:

> They were looking to a happy future . . . the debts kept piling up . . . They [were] seen by all and sundry as happy, caring young people . . . one, [the deceased] with ambitions and hopes for the future set upon a home, a family; the other, [the prisoner], who [was] financially . . . way behind the eight ball.
>
> (*Richardson* 1997: 566)

In the above extract, the audience (the sentencing judge) is encouraged to identify with both characters ('they were looking to a happy future') and to share their worldview ('they were seen by all and sundry as happy, caring young people'). A second narrative device also at work has to do with the genre of the romance narrative. The plot that drives the romance narrative towards its conclusion is the developing romance between the hero and heroine despite the heroine's misgivings about her choice of love object.

In the above extract, note the reference to the deceased as someone who was 'set upon a home, a family'. This image of her as financially demanding and its effect on the accused lends an air of legitimacy to the defence narrative that the accused's fear that he was losing control over their finances was increasing. A few moments later, his defence counsel submitted:

> In the last six months he worked on and off. The financial problems were increasing . . . the bills were growing and the arguments grew, doors were slammed and voices raised, but never resort to violence . . . They lived together. They had been as man and wife. . . . The desire by my client to marry seems to grow . . . The arguments became more frequent as the funds seemed to grow less.
>
> (*Richardson* 1997: 567)

What is being put into effect here takes place through a discursive process of distortion. The transcript literalises the accused's fear of rising debt in order to make an incriminating point about the effect of the deceased's words on the night in question. This is done through a process of analogy and the juxtaposition of images designed to give the impression that the situation between the two of them was building up into a crescendo (the 'bills were growing' as were the 'arguments' and the volume of their 'voices'). Once the various phases of the relationship and events have been reordered within a discrete chronological series, the causal logic gains momentum and the deceased's words on the night are understood as the calcifying moment in the narrative. In a final move that invests the defence narrative with a degree of legitimacy, Hampel J's sentencing remarks culminate in a succinct reconstruction of the romantic context in which the event of murder is understood to have taken place:

> It is not only a tragic case, but it is a bizarre case in many respects. It is one which is unusual in my experience. Most cases have a background of violence, hate, jealousy, and misplaced possessiveness. This does not appear to have any of those features. What occurred, therefore, is very difficult to understand. That does not excuse it, but it places it in an unusual category of cases. . . . [this was] basically a good, loving relationship.
>
> (*Richardson* 1997: 591)

The above passage illustrates that the contexts of violence that come before the courts do not simply reflect a given state of affairs. Rather, they are produced. In shifting the literary frame to the genre of tragedy ('It is not only a tragic case, but it is a bizarre case in many respects ... [this was] basically a good, loving relationship'), Hampel J activates a range of positive attributes of character that include chivalry and honour and that become attached to the accused and which constitute his act as a legitimate attempt to defend against loss (of his self-image and also his masculinity). It is the discursive proximity between the law's narrative and the romantic narrative, with the latter's entwined themes of tragedy and fate that the event of murder in *Richardson* ends up rewritten as the inevitable culmination of a 'romance-gone-wrong.'

The case of *Leonboyer*[36] involved a man who stabbed his 19-year-old girlfriend, Sandra Morales, 25 times in her head, back, groin and shoulder, after she allegedly told him she did not love him, that she had been have an affair with someone else, which she followed with a taunt in Spanish to the effect that 'he did it better than you did'. At his first trial, the accused raised both the defence of automatism and the partial defence of provocation.[37] In doctrinal terms, the mentality that is the concern of the defence of automatism is one that generally refers to 'involuntary conduct resulting from some form of impaired consciousness'. If successfully argued, the accused is acquitted of the crime of murder. Discussing the Australian legal context, McSherry observes that the defence of automatism has been relied on where the accused has claimed to have suffered 'a blow to the head', 'sleep disorders', 'the consumption of alcohol or other drugs', 'neurological disorders', 'hypoglycaemia', 'epilepsy' and 'dissociation arising from extraordinary external stress' (2005: 920–21). In *Leonboyer* the Crown case against the accused was that he knew what he was doing on the night he killed the deceased and stabbed the deceased 'in a fit of anger and jealousy ... [and] ... to inflict the ultimate punishment' (May 1999: 104, opening address to the jury). In contrast, the defence narrative sought to persuade the jury that the words spoken by the deceased delivered 'a psychological blow' causing the accused's mind to dissociate ('split'). According to defence counsel, this was 'not just a confession of infidelity' but a 'confession operating on whatever stresses were already operating on his mind' (*Leonboyer* May 1999: 114, opening address to jury).

From the very beginning of the trial in *Leonboyer*, the jury was told things that are crucial to the subsequent formulaic structure of the defence narrative:

> [T]hese two were apparently a happy couple as far as [he] was concerned. ... they met, they went to sign a lease and put the bond down on a flat that they were going to occupy together and live as man and wife ... they intended to have a full relationship, as far as this man was concerned ... they went home, had a meal and watched television in each other's arms ... what appeared to be a happy, joyous couple, 10 minutes later there were over 20 stab wounds ... something happened to his mind that resulted in what can only be described as a frenzied act.
>
> (May 1999: 115, opening address to jury)

In the above extract, the defence narrative locates the cause of the death of the deceased within the context or circumstances of the relationship. They were a 'happy, joyous couple' who had a history together and one that importantly had a future: 'they went to sign a lease ... live together as man and wife'. As in *Richardson*, discussed above, it is significant that the accused and female deceased are depicted as having been brought together by voluntary romantic choice. Note also how the deceased's desire is consumed within and according to the accused's point of view: 'these two were apparently a happy couple ... they intended to have a full relationship, as far as this man was concerned'. As in the case of *Richardson*, the defence narrative in *Leonboyer* maintains a discursive proximity to the discourse of romance, which gives primacy to the male subject's progression through the narrative. However, in the masculine economy of romance, the female subject's utterances and desire do not figure in quite the same way (Puren 1995: 21).

In his opening remarks to the jury, defence counsel submitted that, although the 'confession of adultery' was 'stressful, traumatic and dramatic, by itself it did not cause the state of automatism' (*Leonboyer* May 1999: 114–115). A crucial aspect to the defence narrative was that despite its 'happy' outward appearance, the relationship between the accused and the deceased was fraught with tension and anxiety arising from the deceased's sexually indifferent behaviour. The narrative mobilised by the defence also sought to represent the accused's act of killing the deceased as culturally specific. An example can be found during cross-examination between the defence counsel and a witness who was the mother of the deceased. The defence asked the witness to confirm whether she and her boyfriend regularly attended the same nightclubs as her daughter. The witness replied in the affirmative. Next he invited the witness to clarify her age, which she did (she was 39), and that of her daughter (who was 18 at the time). A few moments later, this exchange was followed with a proposition: '[The accused] said to you, did he not, that he didn't like [the deceased] dancing with those older Colombians?', to which the witness responded 'Yes' (*Leonboyer* May 1999: 341). At this point in the defence narrative, the witness was no doubt quite unaware the defence's suggestion that she somehow failed to cite the norms of motherhood because she regularly socialised with her daughter and 'those older Columbians' would later underwrite the manner in which her daughter's words on the night she was killed became imputed with ideological significance. Some further examples from the transcript of *Leonboyer* serve to highlight how the defence narrative sought to render the psychological impact of the wound from the deceased's words on the night as culturally significant.

Throughout the trial, both counsel repeatedly emphasised for the jury how in the months leading up to the killing, the accused was under considerable stress as he was in the final stages of a law degree. In a further move designed to lend plausibility and coherence and, more importantly, the weight of authority and objectivity to the sequencing of events as represented by the defence narrative, counsel led evidence from a number of expert witnesses. In one exchange during cross-examination between the defence and a medical practitioner who was also a psychiatrist, the expert witness was asked whether he accepted 'the proposition that a mind can be made more vulnerable by pre-existing stresses, psychological stresses, so that one final blow will break the camel's back' (*Leonboyer* May 1999: 528). A few moments later, this same witness was invited to reflect whether he could 'conceive of situations where, if someone was sufficiently vulnerable and had been under sufficient stress . . . the revelation of sexual infidelity . . . may cause that person to dissociate' (*Leonboyer* May 1999: 532)? The witness conceded: 'In an automatic manner, yes'.

In another exchange during the making of his unsworn statement, the accused was asked by his counsel whether he spoke Spanish at home to which he replied, 'always . . . with his mother' (*Leonboyer* May 1999: 612). He was then asked whether as a child he had played a Spanish flamenco instrument, whereupon he replied that he did, and explained that it was 'played by beating a drum' (*Leonboyer* May 1999: 612). In a manner similar to that in *Richardson*, we can see the deployment of key tropes of masculine loss that enable the event to be rewritten in a way that sets up the accused's reaction as caused by a build-up of stresses and anxieties over a period of time. An example to illustrate this can be found during examination of an expert witness for the defence, who was a practising psychiatrist, medical practitioner and professor of psychiatry at a leading Australian university. The following exchange took place between the prosecuting counsel and the expert witness:

> Q: But the going and getting and the using of the knife in the context of this case has but one purpose, doesn't it?
> A: Well, the knife was used for one purpose, yes.
> Q: In circumstances where there existed a very powerful motive to want to hurt?
> A: Yes.
> . . .
> Q: That his reaction to that, I'm putting to you, isn't particularly unusual or out of the ordinary; we don't know how people respond in those situations.
> A: We weren't there, that is why it is a high probability, but I was interested in the stab movements because he actually plays a percussion drum and that involves a rapid movement (indicating), and I mean this is just theoretical because I wasn't there. . .
> . . .
> Q: You see, at the very least, it is well directed violence, isn't it?
> A: Well, we don't know what else it was directed at, but yes, it would appear to be well directed violence, isn't it.
>
> (*Leonboyer* May 1999: 689–90)

In the above exchange, the expert witness is seeking to convince the jury that the accused was in a dissociated state when he killed the deceased by suggesting the accused's 'stab movements' mimicked the 'rapid movement' the accused man would make when playing 'a percussion drum' (as he was a percussionist). Earlier, during the giving of his unsworn statement, a series of propositional statements was put to the accused by his counsel, those being designed to convey the importance of his Chilean background;

for example, he was asked 'In your upbringing how many of the traditions and cultures ... were taught to you?', 'Did you speak Spanish?', 'Spanish music?', 'did you play an instrument?', 'Which is played by beating the drum?', 'You were watching Spanish movies, then what happened?' (*Leonboyer* May 1999: 574).[38] Note the sudden shift in topic in the final question and also the connective 'then what happened?'. It is clear from this line of questioning that the defence is seeking to imply that the accused was so overcome by what the deceased said on the night that his mental state was not one in which his actions in killing the deceased could be understood as those of a person who was acting 'consciously' and 'voluntarily'. Rather, he had been so subjected to trauma (by the words of the deceased) that his mind had dissociated to the extent that 'the body will perform quite complex manoeuvres, far more complex than stabbing' (*Leonboyer* May 1999: 113, opening address to jury).

In his charge to the jury, Hampel J's rehearsal of the evidence summed up the case for the defence in a manner that lends the defence narrative an air of legitimacy. On the issue of provocation, he told them that, although the prosecuting counsel had argued that the law in this area was 'contradictory or inconsistent', he did not find this to be the case (*Leonboyer* May 1999: 783). He said that when the evidence was looked at as a whole, 'there is not very much in dispute about the background and the circumstances of the relationship. There may be a slight difference in emphasis but generally the issues are fairly clear' (*Leonboyer* May 1999: 785). When considering the 'ultimate question' they were to decide in the case, 'What was the state of mind of the accused?', he told them they were to have regard for the:

> ... longitudinal picture ... [including] ... the background mani-
> festations, incidents, relationship, comings and goings, tensions,
> stressors, all those matters ... starting from the childhood events
> to the other incident I've already mentioned.
>
> (*Leonboyer* May 1999: 785)

In a final move Hampel J offers the jury a succinct version of the defence narrative. Recounting the narrative for the defence, which 'talked about their relationship in the context of their culture', he next invited the jury to consider:

> ... the operation of factors such as the change in their relationship,
> the intensity of his studies, the final confrontation with the father,
> the 'new vision' as he called it with Sandra, and it is in that context,
> he argued, that you should look at the degree of the psychological

blow produced before he stabbed her. He asked you to consider it was much more than just a mere admission of infidelity, it was a breakdown of his whole structure.

(Leonboyer May 1999: 787)

My point here is not to focus on the legal outcome of the case, even though it was one in which the jury was unable to reach a verdict and led to Leonboyer's first trial being aborted. What is important is the salience of the narrative of insult with its key trope of a woman 'asking for it' for legal decision-making. At Leonboyer's second trial, a different judge (Cummins J) ruled that the defence of provocation was *not* open for the jury. Significantly, however, he also noted that:

> ... the door is not fully closed to words alone being sufficient in appropriate circumstances to constitute provocation. Brabianto surely was wrong when he said to Othello:
>
> But words are words: I never did hear
> That the bruis'd heart was pierced through the ear.
> *(Othello* I, 3, 218-219).[39]

In agreement with McSherry, at one level Cummins J's decision can be understood as one in which he 'played a gatekeeping role in preventing the defence of provocation going to the jury in circumstances where an accused had killed his estranged partner' (2005: 912). However, at another level it is one in which the 'reauthoring of the tale' of murder is not accomplished by a single author but by the multiple voices of legal authority and literature (Knox 1998: 81; Philadelphoff-Puren and Rush 2003: 193). Moreover, although Leonboyer's claim to the defence of automatism was unsuccessful, the plot of the 'romance-gone-wrong', including its key character (a sexually indifferent woman who taunted the accused by insulting his sexual prowess) was what enabled law to conduct its own reasoning (Philadelphoff-Puren 2005). It is in this sense that I understand the standard provocation tale of a woman 'asking for it' can be retold in a way that assists defence counsel to raise different questions of legal doctrine (the defence of automatism), while at the same time articulating sexual difference according to the values of law.

Conclusion

What I have offered here is a (re)reading of a number of legal texts in order to highlight that the event of murder is first and foremost a story. By focusing on the literary and narrative conventions at work in law's stories, we can see the cultural impulses that drive the narrator of the tale of murder to tell a particular story. Moreover, plot and plotting are the key instruments whereby stories are ordered in significant form. This insight becomes especially important when we are talking about murder because it helps to see the way in which the deceased is made to perform in a cultural script that is not her own. Obviously the cultural script of a woman 'asking for it' is not set in stone, but when it is mobilised in a criminal trial, it is clear where the advantage lies. The moment of homicide law reform and, particularly the decision to abolish the partial defence of provocation, raises the question of whether, and to what extent, the same old exculpatory cultural script for male violence against women will simply be redeployed (by different authors) at the sentencing stage (in different discursive contexts). When announcing the 2005 amendments to the laws of homicide in Victoria in 2005, former Victorian Attorney-General Rob Hulls said the law regarding provocation had 'not kept pace with changing social values'. The defence of provocation, he said, 'was developed from times past when it was acceptable, especially for men, to have a violent response to an alleged breach of a person's honour'. Hulls stated that a defence that reduces a charge of murder to manslaughter would no longer be available to '[p]eople who kill in circumstances where they lose self-control', such as a killing committed 'in anger at discovering a spouse has been unfaithful'. Taking specific issue with that part of the doctrine that was found to involve the promotion of a 'culture of blaming the victim', Hulls resolved that it no longer was reflected in the values of modern society (Office of the Attorney-General Media Release (2005)). My creative reading of what Hulls is, in effect, saying here is that it is no longer appropriate to tell this tale of murder (although I note that his gender-neutral reference to 'people who kill in circumstances where they lose self-control' masks the empirical reality that it is typically men who kill in such circumstances). However, since the 2005 reforms to the laws of homicide in Victoria, emerging developments in Victorian case law would appear to suggest that, despite the abolition of the provocation defence, the same old tale of a woman 'asking for it' is being used by men who have killed their intimate or former partners to avoid a conviction for murder. A discussion of the claim that provocation-type arguments are being made in the guise of other defences to homicide is explored more fully in the next chapter.

Notes

1 McQuillan explains that Brooks (1984) is here referring to 'the desiring dynamic in narrative which moves the reader and story towards the end, while simultaneously delaying that end' (2000: 325).

2 While most scholars credit James Boyd White as the founder of the law-and-literature movement, others such as Richard Weisberg, Robert Weisberg, Ronald Dworkin, Robin West and Patricia Williams are proponents of seemingly separate genres of theorizing that have sparked much debate. Other notable examples of the legal storytelling approach include the Special Issue of the *Michigan Law Review* 87 (1989). On the theme of the narrative construction of the 'facts' in legal decision-making see Jackson (1990: 23–50) and Papke (1991).

3 In the Introduction to *Law and Literature*, Julius describes the project of relating law to literature as 'commonly taken to have four elements. There is the study of the law relating to literature (the law of literature). There is the study of the literary properties of legal texts (law as literature – as a "branch of literature"). There is the study of the methods of interpretation of legal and literary texts (legal and literary hermeneutics). Last, there is the study of the representation of law and legal processes in literature (law in literature)' (1999: xiii). The approach taken in this book falls within the last approach.

4 In *Legal Discourse: Studies in Linguistics, Rhetoric and Legal Analysis* (1987) and *Reading the Law* (1986) Goodrich argues against the traditional philosophical view of law as a hermeneutically sealed or unitary discourse and proposes that the study of law should instead see law and legal language as a social and powerful discourse that is connected to other disciplines and discourses but is also an instrument in pursuit of control over meaning. Goodrich has also written two historical analyses of the institutions of the common law: *Law in the Courts of Love* highlights law's repression of minor jurisprudences and forgotten jurisdictions and institutions such as the 12th century courts of love, a jurisdiction presided over by women (1996) and *Oedipus Lex: Psychoanalysis, History, Law*, which describes the early theory and history of images that were not recognised by law and were therefore repressed only to erupt in law's unconscious, in 'symptoms' and 'slips of the tongue' – in short, its 'competing jurisdictions' (1995).

5 As Gewirtz argues: 'law is all about human life', yet it constantly 'struggles to keep life at bay'. This idealised vision of law, as one that proclaims law must be seen to be separate from and unfettered by 'politics, passion, and public resistance', is what the legal process is all about: '[d]istinctive legal rules of procedure, jurisdiction, and evidence insist upon and define law's autonomous character – indeed constitute the very basis of the court's authority' (1996b: 863).

6 Goodrich contends that the courts of love, whether real or imagined, produced judgments as jurisprudentially relevant and useful as more traditional legal fictions. From this it follows that '[f]iction is the figure of truth. Law has always produced and promoted legal fictions' (1996: 636).

7 See the Preface to the abridged edition of the book (1985: xi–xvi).

8 In terms of the study of law, Goodrich observes that Bakhtin's perspective upon discursive processes focuses on two principles. The first is that linguistic practices be viewed in terms of their 'historicity'. This is the idea that language 'bears with it the weight of its own past': '[t]he words we use are already imbued – both in their singularity and in their combination – with multiple meanings or ideological accents'. The second is that linguistic practices are ideologically saturated and can thus be explained sociologically. Accordingly, Goodrich argues that '[t]he word is dialogic, "its specificity consists precisely in its being located between organised individuals, in its being the medium of their communication"' (1987: 143). Meaning is therefore 'to be viewed or understood as an effect of the social hierarchical organisation of communication, and to be explained in terms of the constraints and conditions of that interaction itself' (Goodrich 1987: 143–44).

9   In her discussion of legal and media representations of the English case of *Thornton* [1992] 1 All ER 306, Young observes that: 'when the narrative appears in its legal form, subtle mutations, manipulations and metamorphoses occur. This is not to suggest that the above-mentioned media accounts of the event, or indeed any version of it, have any purchase on the "Truth" (whatever that might be, and from which the legal account could be claimed to deviate). The "Truth", if such a thing could exist, may be known only to the participants of the event; even then, I would argue that the accounts of the victim and assailant would be dramatically different' (1994: 137–38). Accordingly, Young argues that if an event 'is to exist for us', it must first 'be articulated' and, like any and all events, will already 'have been articulated in numerous contexts and in a variety of ways' (1997: 129).

10 Taking up the insights of Brooks (1996) and Clover (1998), Kennedy argues that 'a narrative is not simply produced by stringing facts together; rather, narrative archetypes pre-exist any given set of facts, and the facts are plotted in accordance with a given archetype' (2002: 79). In this sense, she is using the term narrative 'to mean the textual process of plot-making' (Kennedy 2002: 72).

11 Borrowing from the work of the novelist E. M. Forster, Martin observes that 'the statement "the king died and then the queen died" is a story, while the statement "the king died, and then the queen died of grief" is a plot' (1986: 87).

12 Considering 'by what means desire works along with narrativity', de Lauretis believes that '[t]he problem ... is that many of the current formulations of narrative process fail to see that subjectivity is engaged in the cogs of narrative and indeed constituted in the relation of narrative, meaning, and desire; so that the very work of narrativity is the engagement of the subject in certain positionalities of meaning and desire. Or else they fail to locate the relation of narrative and desire where it takes place, where that relation is materially inscribed – in a field of textual practices. Thus, finally, they fail to envisage a materially, historically, and experientially constituted subject, a subject engendered, we might say, precisely by the process of its engagement in the narrative genres' (1984: 106).

13 I am loosely drawing on Knox's discussion of 'the cultural impulses that drive the narrator of the tale of murder – whatever its medium, form, or ostensible genre – to tell a story that will encompass and address questions ancillary to the actual subject'. Like Knox, I am 'preoccupied' with issues of how murder is always culturally mediated and 'the structure of authority in the murder narrative' (1998: 4). Moreover, Knox demonstrates that the victim does not play much of a role in the tale of murder; rather, it is primarily concerned with the murderer and the ordeals that she/he faces such as the trial and execution (1998: 93).

14 *Trisnadi* trial transcript, Supreme Court of Victoria (November–December 1996) (Eames J).

15 This is illustrated by the headline accompanying one newspaper report, which read: 'Judge's racial fears for love triangle killer' (Anonymous 1996).

16 Some feminist researchers have explored the way in which the type of questions asked during the police interview has a bearing on the answers given. Bacon and Lansdowne have argued that the techniques deployed in police interviews in cases involving women who have been killed by their husbands are 'limited by a concentration on the issues that will be relevant at the trial, specifically intention, and by the policeman's own personal prejudices and preconceptions' (1982: 87-88). According to one study carried out by the Women's Coalition Against Family Violence, they argue that the questions asked by interviewing officers reflect a judgment they have often already made as to the circumstances of the killing and the accused person's motive. Moreover, they find that

'[m]otives such as jealousy, arguments, separation or finances are suggested.' Thus, '[t]here is a disproportionate focus by police on the woman's behaviour or on other events, rather than the offender's past behaviour' (1994:101). Young has also written on this topic in relation to the disingenuous cross-examination of the 'complainant' in rape trials (1998) as has Taylor in relation to child victims of sexual abuse (2004).

17 *Trisnadi*, transcript of interview with police and Budianto Trisnadi (answer to question 188).

18 *R v N* trial transcript, Supreme Court of Victoria (October 1997) (Vincent J).

19 In his interview with police, the accused said he could not remember the content of the argument, only that he and the deceased were 'rowing' because earlier he had punched her in the mouth. At one point during his interview, the police interviewer tried to establish whether the 'row' had been 'continuous' (Interview with Police (March 1996) question 182). The accused said he did not know. The police interviewer then asked him whether he and the deceased were 'rowing' or having a 'more serious form of arguing', like a 'heated argument?' Interview with police (March 1996 questions 309, 310, 311). The metaphoric distinction the police interviewer is seeking to make here is significant. The use of 'row' as a term to describe and convey the sense of an argument draws upon the common-sense understanding that all marriages involve 'spats'. It is a way of saying what everyone knows, which is that most people have normal arguments, most couples argue about relatively normal things some if not most of the time. The use of 'heated' to describe and convey the sense of an argument is a conventional metaphor that is used to imply one that is marked by emotional intensity, vehemence or even violence. The implicative effects of the metaphorical representations of the argument that allegedly took place between the accused and deceased on the night in question can also be seen during the process of the examination and cross-examination of witnesses at the trial.

20 *R v N* interview with police (March 1996 answer to question 189).

21 *R v N* trial transcript, Supreme Court of Victoria (October 1997examination of witness B at 58, cross-examination of witness H at 76, examination of witness A at 86, cross-examination of witness A at 89–90, examination of witness E at 98, cross-examination of witness G at 114).

22 And a few moments later:

There was ample evidence from the neighbours on this aspect, which [the defence] submitted showed that the deceased was screaming and yelling over a number of hours. . . . In contradistinction to the female voice, that of the male voice as heard by the various witnesses was considerably softer
(*R v N* trial transcript, Supreme Court of Victoria
(October 1997 (Vincent J) at 545 (charge to jury)).

23 *R v Budianto Trisnadi*, unreported judgment, Supreme Court of Victoria (18 December 1996) (Eames J) at 6 (sentence).

24 ibid at 8 (sentence).

25 ibid at 12 (sentence).

26 *R v Browne* [1999] VSC 282, trial transcript, Supreme Court of Victoria (June 1999) (Hampel J).

27 ibid transcript of interview with police and Ian Leslie Brown (answer to question 414).

28 ibid transcript of interview with police and Ian Leslie Brown (answer to question 415). Having picked up the carving knife from the kitchen, he returned to the bedroom where

his wife was brushing her hair. He then inflicted two deep fatal stab wounds to her chest and other more superficial injuries (ibid at 3).

29 ibid transcript of interview with police and Ian Leslie Brown (answer to question 385).

30 ibid (answer to ibid 255).

31 In his statement to police, the accused described his relationship with the deceased as 'beautiful' up until the discovery by him of the first batch of letters she had written and in which she fantasised about having a relationship with another man (who was the de facto partner of the accused's daughter from a previous relationship). As it turned out the letters were never sent (see *Browne* trial transcript, Supreme Court of Victoria (June 1999) at 42 (opening address by prosecuting counsel). When asked what he did when he discovered the letters, the accused told police that he photocopied them and sent them to his solicitor. He explained that this was because things had deteriorated between them so much that he had 'already cut her out of [his] will' (*Browne* transcript of interview with police and Ian Leslie Brown, answer to question 142). He also explained how he believed the letters were based on a fantasy and were therefore 'ridiculously silly'.

32 According to him, when he confronted the deceased about the first batch of letters, she told him 'she didn't love' the other man, '[i]t wasn't the real thing' (*Browne* transcript of interview with police and Ian Leslie Brown, answer to question 161). She apparently described how they 'got on so beautifully' and 'that she had had four and a half hour conversations' with him on the phone (*Browne* transcript of interview with police and Ian Leslie Brown, answer to question 165). When asked by police to describe the deceased's character, the accused offered that '[s]he had absolute personality with everyone. Absolute personality'. He was then asked if this aspect of her character upset him to which he replied: '[n]ot particularly, unless it – we went out to do something or whatever and she kept on talking and talking and talking and it was – it held me up for whatever reason it was. Not from jealousy. It might've been, but I don't think so. She – she'd keep on talking and talking and talking and talking, but she had this ability, which is the opposite from myself – because I'd go into depth about things, you know, she'd talk about anything'.

33 *Browne* trial transcript, Supreme Court of Victoria (June 1989) at 105 (opening address to jury).

34 In Goodrich's account of the 12th century courts of love, a jurisdiction that was associated with the emotions, questions of fidelity and the amorous space of affective exchange between lovers, he observes that '[t]he love letter was the trope or writ of law in the courts of love and it was in the form of letters, through correspondence, that the *précieuses* would map the most profound domain of human relations or interactions, that of the heart or *carte de tendre*' (1997: 246). Goodrich's work highlights that the courts of love were highly threatening (1997: 250). Among the reasons he gives for this is that 'the object of their regulation, the affectivity of relationship and of amorous exchange, belonged to a patriarchally governed private sphere' (1997: 247). In the jurisdiction of the courts of love, 'love and marriage' were 'combinations of a different species of love' (Goodrich 1996: 653). Accordingly, legal history has tended only to recognise love as 'a negative incident of marriage'. The Ecclesiastical tradition 'predictably considered feminine sexuality and lust threats'. The ideal of femininity was that it should be 'veiled' or 'shamefaced'. The 'self-effacing' virgin should 'look down or look away so as neither to tempt nor to fascinate the eyes of men' (Goodrich 1996: 651). Goodrich observes that critics of the courts of love depicted them as 'the work of the imagination' and their 'decisions . . . amusing fantasies'. Goodrich is here making an observation about the 'domestic code' highlighted in a '16th century instruction book for Christian women

[that] depicted silence as the "noblest ornament of a woman" adding, curiously: "Thou arte none attourney of lawe ... nor pleadeste not in courte ... Holde thou thy peace as bowdly as other speake in courte"' (1996: 652). It is in this sense, according to Goodrich, that the love letter and the writ of law 'share a comparable yet distinct concern with authenticity and truth. . . . More specifically . . . the love letter institutes the domain or space in which relationships of love can occur in the same way that historically the writ instigated the space of a legal form of exchange' (1997: 253). See Seuffert (1999) for a particularly compelling application of Goodrich's insights to domestic violence.

35 *Richardson* trial transcript, Supreme Court of Victoria (May 1997) (Hampel J).

36 *DPP v Leonboyer* [1999] VSC 450.

37 *Leonboyer* trial transcript, Supreme Court of Victoria (May 1999) (Cummins J)(").

38 Counsel for the defence also sought to lead evidence of a senior lecturer in sociology at the University of New South Wales whose area of expertise was with how second generation migrants 'invest and, indeed, over-invest in relationships that they have between, or with their family and with others'. However, the judge ruled the evidence inadmissible; *Leonboyer* (May 1999) at 639–44.

39 *R v Leonboyer* [1999] VSC 450 (20 October 1999)(Cummins J) at 5. The accused was sentenced to 18 years' imprisonment and a minimum non-parole period of 14 years. *DPP v Leonboyer* [1999] VSC 422 unreported (5 November 1999) (Cummins J). On appeal, the majority (Phillips CJ and Charles JA) held that the trial judge had correctly withdrawn the provocation defence from the jury. *DPP v Leonboyer* [2001] VSCA 149 unreported (Phillips CJ, Charles and Callaway JJA) (7 September 2001).

CHAPTER **4**

Victoria's new homicide laws: provocative reforms or more stories of women 'asking for it'?

Introduction: the demise of provocation

In 2008, Western Australia became the third Australian state to pass legislation repealing the controversial rule of law that provocation reduces murder to manslaughter (*Criminal Law Amendment (Homicide) Act* 2008 (WA). Tasmania abolished the provocation defence in 2003 (*Criminal Code Amendment (Abolition of Defence of Provocation) Act* 2003 (Tas) as did Victoria in 2005 (*Crimes (Homicide) Act* 2005 (Vic)). The partial defence of provocation has also been abolished in a small number of overseas jurisdictions. In 2009, the New Zealand parliament passed legislation repealing the partial defence of provocation (*Crimes (Provocation Repeal) Amendment Bill*). In 2009 in England and Wales, the *Coroners and Justice Act* 2009 was introduced.[1] The latter Act significantly revised the law of diminished responsibility, and also introduced a revamped partial defence of 'loss of control', which replaces the partial defence of provocation and creates a defence akin to the plea of 'excessive self-defence' (Yeo 2010).[2] While it remains to be seen what the impact of the various and specific reforms to the laws of homicide in these different international jurisdictions will be on the prosecution and punishment of people who kill a current or former partner in future cases, the 2005 amendments to Victoria's homicide laws have been heralded as among the most 'radical' ever to have been implemented (see for example Coss 2006). American homicide law has been slow to respond to feminists' concerns about the gender bias of

121

criminal law, yet has led the way in allowing expert testimony on battered woman syndrome. In comparison, as Ramsey has recently observed, the decision taken in the Australian states of Tasmania, Victoria and Western Australia to abolish the provocation defence are among 'the boldest strides towards a feminist transformation of homicide law' (2010: 34).[3] While there is some evidence to suggest the reforms have produced some positive outcomes for women defendants who kill their abusive partners, it is too soon to tell if the intent behind the Victorian legislature is being realised. However, recent developments in Victorian case law – where men have killed a current or former intimate partner since the 2005 amendments – have raised concerns about the apparent continuation of provocation-type arguments that 'excuse' male violence and construct the woman victim as deserving of her fate.

In May 2010, a case involving Luke John Middendorp made headlines in the Victorian newspapers (Anderson 2010c; Capper and Crooks 2010; Howe 2010; Murphy 2010). Middendorp fatally stabbed his former female partner, Jade Bownds, four times in the back after she allegedly 'came at him with a knife in her right hand'. Moments after he stabbed her, Luke Middendorp was heard by witnesses to have said that she was a 'filthy slut' who 'had it coming' and 'got' what she 'deserved' (Murphy 2010). According to the accused at trial, he had stabbed his ex-partner because he was acting in 'self-defence' (R v Middendorp [2010] VSC 202). In contrast, the prosecution contended that the jury should reject this account that she attacked him with a knife and that the stabbing was in response to a threat to his life or physical safety. According to evidence adduced at the trial, nine months prior to killing his ex-partner, Luke Middendorp had a Family Violence Order recorded against him (Anderson 2010c). There was also evidence of the relationship that showed that both parties had previously been violent towards one another and engaged in frequent fights and arguments (R v Middendorp [2010] VSC 147). Finding in favour of the accused, the jury convicted him of defensive homicide (R v Middendorp [2010] VSC 202).[4]

The victim's mother expressed outrage at the verdict and said that she was 'truly disgusted with the system' (Anderson 2010a). She said her daughter was 'scared of him' and that her daughter's killer 'was facing other charges of assaulting her' (Murphy 2010). She asked: '[h]ow can a man who is twice her size have to stab her four times in the back because he was in fear of his life?' (Wilson 2010). According to media reports, there was a huge disparity in their sizes. Luke Middendorp was more than 'twice her size' (eg 186cm tall) and weighed a 'hulking' 90kg, whereas Jade Bownds was a 'tiny', pint sized woman' who weighed just 50kg

(Murphy 2010; Anderson 2010a, Anderson 2010b, Anderson 2010c). Others expressed outrage at the verdict and felt this was yet another case that 'excused' the male defendant's violence against the deceased by putting her character on trial (Capper and Crooks 2010; Howe 2010).[5] As a result of the publicity this case received, there were calls for the new laws of homicide in Victoria to be overhauled. A specific concern raised by the *Middendorp* case was whether, in the absence of the partial defence of provocation, defensive homicide was becoming its replacement (Capper and Crooks 2010).

In response to this criticism, in August 2010, the Victorian Department of Justice (DOJ) published a discussion paper entitled *Review of the Offence of Defensive Homicide*, inviting legal professionals, experts in the field of family violence and the wider community to comment and give feedback on the operation of the new laws (DOJ 2010). When announcing the release of the discussion paper, the then Victorian Attorney-General, Rob Hulls, revealed that the Department of Justice had always intended to adopt the Victorian Law Reform Commission's (VLRC) recommendation to review the new laws within five years, and said the review of 'the controversial law of defensive homicide' was already underway (Hulls 2010b). He said that 'family violence remains a complex epidemic and it may be that there is further reform that can occur in time to better respond to its realities' (Hulls 2010a). There is little doubt that the discussion paper is an important first step in assisting law reformers to determine whether further changes to Victoria's homicide laws are necessary. In its opening pages, the discussion paper states the reforms explicitly recognised that change was required 'to the law and *to the culture*' of the criminal justice system (DOJ 2010: 3, my italics). However, as decades of feminist legal scholarship have demonstrated, the (masculinist) internal culture(s) of the legal profession can be slow and sometimes resistant to change (Thornton 1991; Merry 1992; Hunter 1996; Schneider 2000; Armstrong 2004; Graycar and Morgan 2005; Hunter 2006a, 2008). While the re-emergence of concerns about the apparent continuation of 'excuses' for male violence and the problem of victim-blame in post-abolitionist jurisdictions (such as Victoria) are of concern, it is equally important, this chapter argues, to reflect critically on the emerging developments that have taken place in Victorian case law (since the 2005 amendments) so we can more effectively target future interventions and strategies.

The 2005 Victorian amendments: a feminist success story?

In the Victorian legal context, the decision leading to the abolition of the provocation defence was only in part designed to redress the problem of victim-blame.[6] The decision was accompanied by other key changes introduced into the *Crimes Act* 1958 (Vic) through the *Crimes (Homicide) Act* 2005 to make it easier for women who kill in the context of family violence successfully to claim self-defence and 'excessive self-defence' (defensive homicide). For many commentators, the 2005 reforms to the laws of homicide in Victoria, Australia, represent the success of feminists' efforts to ensure legal categories are as responsive to the complexities of women's experiences and values as they are to men's experiences and values – a project focused on the concept of substantive rather than formal equality (Hunter 2008: 6; see also Graycar and Morgan 2006, discussing the VLRC's report; see also Forell 2006 and Ramsey 2010). Commenting on the Victorian legislature's decision to allow social context evidence or what is otherwise referred to as evidence of 'social framework' in cases of homicide involving family violence, Douglas describes it as a promising legal development that represents an attempt to 'ensure that women's experiences of violence inform the analysis of the question of the necessity of the self-defence response ... [and] ... also specifically recognise the potentially cumulative effect of family violence on an individual and the particular dynamics of relationships' (2008: 55). In her comparison of developments in provocation law in the Australian legal context and those that have taken place within the United States and Canada, Forell has observed that while substantive equality is protected under Canadian constitutional law it 'has not resulted in the kind of woman-friendly provocation rules in Canada' that have been implemented in Australia.[7] For Forell, the key reason that explains why Australia 'is the leader in incorporating substantive equality into its provocation doctrine' is that, unlike Australia and the United States, Canada has a single nationwide provocation statute and murder carries a mandatory life sentence (2006: 30). Although various criticisms of the Canadian defence of provocation have been widely canvassed in feminist legal debates, as have a number of options for reform (eg the Canadian Association of Elizabeth Fry Societies 2000; Nova Scotia Advisory Council on Status of Women 1998; Côté et al 2000),[8] many are in the camp that the defence of provocation should be abolished, but only if and when mandatory minimum sentences for murder are also abolished (see for example Sheehy 2001; Forell 2006; Holland 2007). Others have been more sceptical of the capacity of feminists' claims of equality to bring about social and legal change for women.

The limits of feminists' claims for equality

Since the advent of second-wave feminism, there now exists a sophisticated discourse of equality in feminist and other critical scholarly literature

(Easteal 2001). While many forms of prejudice against women, gender stereotyping and direct sex discrimination have been named and challenged as forms of unequal treatment, some of which have been addressed and even eliminated, many would concede that the concept of equality has been highly productive for feminist legal activism. Despite the fact that appeals to, and claims of, equality as a way of organising feminist legal activism have been a useful and often vital rhetorical strategy, what is also clear is that many have become '[d]isenchanted' with both the liberal notion of formal equality,[9] and its main rival in feminist legal scholarship, substantive equality (Hunter 2008: 4).

In her discussion of the use of equality concepts in the context of reform of the partial defence of provocation, Douglas has recently argued that while this has allowed some recognition and contextualisation of women's experiences, it has produced a range of ambivalent results (2008: 43).[10] One practical effect has been to direct battered women away from the complete defence of self-defence to the provocation defence instead (Douglas 2008: 44; see also Tolmie 1991; Kirkwood 2000; Bradfield 2002). To the extent that law has sought to accommodate women's 'difference', this has tended to be in the form of expert evidence about 'battered woman syndrome' (BWS). Although the acceptance of evidence of BWS has created a legal space from which these women have been better able to tell their stories, these stories still need to be mediated by an expert, an outcome that Douglas believes has proven to be disempowering, essentialising and stigmatising for women (2008: 52; see also Nicolson 1995: 188–89).[11] These failings have led Douglas, among others, to remain sceptical about the capacity of the 2005 Victorian amendments to make the criminal law as responsive to women's experiences as it is to men's experiences in the self-defence context (2008: 56–57; see also Morgan 1997; Carline 2005). For some critics, the failure of equality concepts to advance women's interests means it is time to move on (Boyd 2008: 59–80; Hunter 2008: 81–104). Others are clearly more supportive of the concept (eg Graycar and Morgan 2008: 105–24). Others still are of the view that there is a 'need for a fresh approach' (Hunter 2008: 4).

Feminist scholars have long demonstrated that laws relating to domestic violence are always going to be dogged by 'the implementation problem', that is, by lawyers and judges who do not necessarily share, or are often resistant to accepting, those feminist understandings. As Hunter observes, it is important not to take 'implementation for granted'; nor should we 'ignore the importance of existing legal cultures' (2006a: 734, 773). Indeed, feminist legal scholars are very much aware and have even come to expect that any attempt to engage with the criminal justice system runs the risk of producing a range of negative, indeed dismal, results for women (Smart 1989; Thornton 1991; Armstrong 2004; Graycar and Morgan 2005; Hunter 2006a; Douglas 2008; Hunter 2008). Hunter (2008: 8) explains that this is because:

> [l]aw transforms elements of experience (such as being subjected to domestic violence) into fixed, objectified, and disempowering categories (such as those of 'victim', or 'battered woman'), and decisions as to whether individual women fit into these categories and therefore qualify for protection are made by unsympathetic law enforcers.[12]

As highlighted above, a key concern for many of provocation's critics is whether, and to what extent, in post-abolitionist jurisdictions such as Victoria, the problems with provocation will simply be shifted to the sentencing stage.[13]

Provocation in sentencing

The VLRC was of the view that a key benefit of shifting claims of provocation to the realm of sentencing is that it gives greater flexibility to judges about which sentence to impose (2004: 33). However, many have remained worried that shifting claims of provocation to the realm of sentencing will do little to put an end to exculpatory narratives of excuse for male violence – the narrative of a woman 'asking for it' – from being mobilised in mitigation at sentencing (Morgan 1997; Côté, Sheehy and Majury 2000; Burton 2003; Howe 2002, 2004b; Maher et al 2005; Coss 2005, 2006; Douglas 2008). As Morgan (1997: 275–76) argues, leaving 'provocative' facts to the discretion of a judge in sentencing 'will do nothing to remove the gendered assumptions embodied in the current use of the provocation defence by men in situations of "sexual jealousy"'. Victorian barrister, Dr Jocelynn Scutt, has said that: '[a]bolishing provocation, yet retaining its principles so that judges could apply them in sentencing [will] not correct the wrongs of provocation law. It simply transfers these problems from the trial to the sentencing stage of the court process' (2005: 29). Howe has worried that it is likely that in a 'post-provocation' climate these same 'ill-considered arguments will continue to masquerade as objective, value free assessments' of men's excuses for their anger and violence towards women and other men (2002: 46; see also Howe 1999: 128). Former Federal MP and anti-violence against women campaigner, Phil Cleary, also observed that: '[t]here is nothing in the legislation to say a woman's infidelity, alleged or otherwise, won't be dissected in a murder trial. Certainly, it will not be excluded when a judge calculates a sentence' (2006: 21). These expressions of apprehension are justified, given the tendency for sentencing in cases of domestic homicide to undermine legal developments that potentially benefit women (Horder 1989; Easteal 1993b, 1994; Graycar 1996; Nourse 1997; Côté et al 2000; Burton 2003; Dinovitzer and Dawson 2007; Stubbs and Tolmie 2008).

These concerns regarding the shifting of claims of provocation to the sentencing phase were recently discussed in a research report entitled *Provocation in Sentencing*, published in 2008 by chair of the Victorian Sentencing Advisory Council (SAC), Professor Arie Freiberg and the SAC's senior legal policy officer, Felicity Stewart (2008a: 2, 2009: vii). The report, which is not an official endorsement of the views of the SAC, adopted the Victorian Law Reform Commission's option of incorporating 'an equality analysis into the substantive test for provocation "to attempt to ensure that legal rules operate without reinforcing systemic or historically discriminative perspectives"' (Stewart and Freiberg 2009: 50; VLRC 2003: 95–96). Although the VLRC did not specifically canvass the equality rights approach in relation to provocation mitigation in sentencing, the authors of the report argued that:

> ... an equality analysis of potentially mitigating provocation would disqualify behavior that arose out of the victim exercising his or her equality rights such as the right to personal autonomy (including conduct associated with leaving an intimate relationship, commencing a new relationship with a new partner, choosing to work gain an education or forming social relationships).
> (Stewart and Freiberg 2009: 50; see also Stewart and Freiberg 2008a: 4, 52, 2008b: 301)

Indeed, the problem driving debates about reform of the defences to homicide in Australia, as in the United Kingdom, was that 31.5 per cent of all homicides involved a situation where a person killed his or her partner, or a former partner, or a sexual rival. The overwhelming majority of these killings were committed by men who tended to be 'motivated by jealousy or a desire to control their partner' (over three-quarters or 78.6 per cent). About half the homicide incidents in the context of sexual intimacy involved allegations of family violence against the accused (95.5 per cent of these involved a woman victim) (VLRC 2004: 15; VLRC 2003; Morgan 2002).

Related to this, the report endorses the reasons based approach to sentencing canvassed by the VLRC 'as a framework for understanding what types of conduct should, and should not, reduce an offender's culpability' (Stewart and Freiberg 2009: 38). This approach represents a return to assessing 'the original rationale for provocation insofar as it is focused on the *wrongfulness* of the victim's actions and the justifiability of the offender's aggrievement, rather than on whether the offender lost self-control as a result of something done by the victim' (Stewart and Freiberg 2009: 42).[14] While there is obvious merit behind the reasons based framework for sentencing, which 'is intended to provide an appropriate framework in which the moral or social dimensions of culpability can be considered' (Stewart and Freiberg 2009: 41; for an appraisal of the proposed approach to sentencing in the Victorian context see Ramsey 2010), the guidelines are not mandatory (Kissane 2008); thus it is up to individual judges to give effect to the spirit of the reforms, an issue that is considered below.

Some emerging developments in Victorian case law

Since the *Crimes (Homicide) Act* 2005 was implemented, there have been some developments in case law that suggest the reforms in Victoria have led to positive outcomes for women defendants who kill their violent abusers. However, the recent public outcry over the verdicts reached in a number of cases involving men who have killed their current or former female partners would also appear to suggest a continuation of 'excuses' for male anger and violence towards women. It is worth briefly restating the nature of the reforms to Victoria's homicide laws before exploring some emerging developments in case law since the 2005 amendments.

After a lengthy process of consultation undertaken by the Victorian Law Reform Commission, the Victorian legislature repealed the controversial partial defence of provocation and implemented a comprehensive package of reforms through the *Crimes (Homicide) Act* 2005 which were aimed at tackling entrenched gender bias in the criminal law (Office of the Attorney-General Victoria 2005).[15] The amendments included clarification of the law of self-defence in relation to murder and manslaughter.[16] The reforms confirmed that in order for self-defence to succeed, the accused person must have held a subjective belief that the actions taken in self-defence were necessary (section 9AC of the *Crimes Act* 1958 (Vic)), and that belief must have been based on reasonable grounds (section 9AE of the *Crimes Act* 1958 (Vic)). The 2005 amendments also make it clear that even if the accused person is responding to a harm that is not immediate, or his or her response involves the use of force in excess of the force involved in the harm or threatened harm, that self-defence may be raised (see section 9AH(1) of the *Crimes Act* 1958 (Vic)). The most specific reform made to the law of self-defence concerns a new section added to the *Crimes Act* regarding the laws of evidence such that evidence highlighting the relationship and social context of family violence can be admitted in cases of homicide (section 9AH(3)(a)–(f) *Crimes Act* 1958 (Vic)).[17] In addition to allowing such evidence, statutory recognition was also given to the VLRC's recommendation to reintroduce 'excessive self-defence' through the introduction of the new offence of 'defensive homicide' (section 9AC and 9AD *Crimes Act* 1958 (Vic)). According to the then Attorney-General, Rob Hulls, the new offence will apply to situations where 'a killing occurs in the context of family violence' and where the accused person genuinely held the subjective belief that the actions taken in self-defence were necessary, but that belief was ultimately unreasonable (Office of the Attorney-General 2005). The offence of defensive homicide operates as an alternative charge to the charge of murder and, if successfully argued, carries a maximum term of imprisonment of 20 years.

During the consultation process conducted by the VLRC, some critics expressed concerns about the capacity of law reform to be of direct benefit to women who kill their violent abusers (VLRC 2004: xxx, 94, 99). For example, concerns were raised in relation to the VLRC's recommendation to reintroduce 'excessive self-defence' (defensive homicide) as a 'safety-net' for women who kill violent partners. According to one submission cited in the VLRC's final report, it was alleged that should the defence of excessive self-defence be reintroduced, juries would automatically decide women's actions were 'excessive', without properly considering the reasonableness of their actions. As a result, women might be convicted of manslaughter, while men could continue to argue self-defence successfully and be acquitted (VLRC 2004: xxx, 94, 99). A second and related concern was that women offenders may be 'encouraged' away from proceeding to trial (by their defence lawyers or the Office of Public Prosecutions, for instance) and instead seek to rely on the full defence of self-defence, with a real chance of acquittal.

Since the *Crimes (Homicide) Act* 2005 was implemented, the decisions not to proceed to trial in two cases involving women defendants who killed a male victim after a prolonged history of family violence have been cautiously interpreted as a sign that the reforms are working (Tyson et al 2010; DVRCV 2010). On 27 March 2009, the then Director of the Victorian Office of Public Prosecutions, Jeremy Rapke QC, dropped a murder charge against a young woman from Shepparton accused of murdering her stepfather, who sexually abused her. He said there was no reasonable prospect that a jury would convict her and outside the court her lawyer, Brian Birrell, said: '[t]he legal defences in this case have always taken the view that a jury would find this to be a legally justifiable homicide' (Johnson 2009b).[18]

On 6 May 2009 a magistrate dismissed the murder charges against Freda Dimitrovski, accused of killing her husband, Sava Dimitrovski, after a three day committal hearing. Freda Dimitrovski's lawyer, Ian Hill QC, said: 'recent changes to the Crimes Act made self-defence in family violence cases acceptable under law' (Anonymous 2009a; Stevens 2009).[19] Arguably, the reason these two cases did not proceed to trial is because they fit into traditional notions of self-defence (with respect to imminence and proportionality) (Tyson et al 2010; DVRCV 2010). Furthermore, it has not necessarily followed that other women defendants who have killed their violent abusers have obtained similar (positive) outcomes.[20]

It is interesting that a plea of defensive homicide has been accepted by the Victorian Office of Public Prosecutions in a large number of cases involving a male defendant who has killed a male victim in what appear to be situations that would have previously supported a plea of provocation (eg in what are largely one-on-one, 'spontaneous' violent encounters) (DOJ 2010). Since the *Crimes (Homicide) Act* 2005 came into effect, 17 male defendants have been sentenced on the basis of defensive homicide;[21] 13 of these have been the result of a decision by the Office of Public Prosecutions to accept a plea of guilty.[22] This development is not all that surprising if we consider that during its consultation phase, the VLRC anticipated that the reintroduction of excessive self-defence (defensive homicide) may provide an additional basis for a plea of manslaughter to be negotiated, without resulting in any substantial change in how these cases are managed.[23] Furthermore, the VLRC acknowledged that, in some cases, it may also provide an additional basis on which an accused person might be charged with manslaughter (2004: 98). There has been some public criticism of the decisions of the Director of Public Prosecutions in Victoria to accept a plea of guilty to defensive homicide in many of these cases, particularly those involving a male defendant who killed a male victim (eg Evans 2010; Fyfe 2010; MacDonald 2010), although the arguments have not been put as strongly as those made about the legal outcome in *Middendorp*. But it does beg the question as to whether the Victorian legislature should adopt the VLRC's recommendation that all plea negotiations (written and verbal) be made transparent and officially recorded (as is the case in some other Australian states) (2004: 106). Such a move stands to increase public understanding about, and awareness of, the plea bargaining process.[24]

Another more positive development (on the face of it at least) is that in the majority of cases where women have been killed by their intimate partner or ex-partner after 2005 when the *Crimes (Homicide) Act* 2005 came into effect, most of these male defendants have not successfully relied on a 'sexed excuse' for their crime. Since 2005, 27 male defendants have been charged with murder for killing an intimate female partner or ex-partner. Of these, 21 have been sentenced on the basis of murder; 12 were the result of a plea of guilty to murder[25] and another nine were convicted of murder after a trial.[26] There have only been six cases involving men who killed their intimate partner or ex-partner who have had their culpability reduced to manslaughter after a trial.[27] The case of *Middendorp* is the only case involving a man who killed his ex-partner and who has been convicted of the offence of defensive homicide after a trial.[28] However, it would certainly appear that in some of these cases, provocation-type arguments are being mobilised in the guise of defensive homicide. In at least five cases, the presiding judge sentenced the male defendant on the basis that he was satisfied that some argument or altercation had developed between the parties that escalated to such a point that this was what induced an intention in the offender to cause death or really serious injury.[29] And in some of these cases, the presiding judge said he accepted that the male defendant's response to the alleged argument or altercation between him and the deceased was not planned or premeditated; rather, his response was 'sudden', 'unplanned', 'a spontaneous outburst of anger-related violence', one in which he 'lost it' or 'severely overreacted' or 'occurred in consequence of the final argument and confrontation' that the defendant had with the deceased.[30] There have only been a few cases where the presiding judge was clearly unsympathetic to the male defendant's claim that he 'snapped' or momentarily lost self-control in response to something said or done by the deceased, and saw fit to issue a strong condemnation that the use of violence as a response to the termination of a relationship was inappropriate. In the case of *R v Azizi* [2010] VSC 1112, which I will discuss in more detail, there was also clear evidence of a long history of violence and abuse perpetrated by the defendant towards the deceased.[31]

According to the authors of the *Provocation in Sentencing* report, while 'the full impact on sentencing outcomes of the reforms initiated by the Victorian Law Reform Commission . . . will only become apparent in years to come', it was anticipated that 'offenders who otherwise might have been convicted of provocation manslaughter' may 'now face sentencing for murder' (2009: vii). If we accept that a murder conviction sends a more appropriate condemnatory message to the wider community that stigmatises this type of killing (intimate partner homicide), then it would appear that the Victorian reforms have yielded some positive results in terms of case outcomes. It was predicted that those offenders, who otherwise might have claimed provocation prior to the legislative reforms in Victoria, may be convicted of defensive homicide (Stewart and Freiberg 2009: vii). Accordingly, this positive assessment of legal outcomes is provisional and needs to be considered alongside recent claims about provocation-type arguments being made in the guise of other defences, in this instance, the offence of defensive homicide.

Is this the end of cultures of 'excuse' for male violence?

It is noteworthy that throughout the trial of Luke Middendorp there was little or no media present until the victim's mother, Shaye Beck, consulted with Jane Ashton, Communications Coordinator for the Women's Domestic Violence Crisis Service, Melbourne, Victoria after she was contacted by Channel Nine's *A Current Affair* programme.[32] Phil Cleary also saw fit to comment on this initial lack of media attention given to the case. He said: 'When Luke Middendorp, who stabbed his ex-girlfriend four times in the back, was found guilty only of defensive homicide, not murder, there wasn't a word of indignation on talkback radio or a word of sympathy for his victim's grieving mother from one of our high profile human rights lawyers' (Cleary 2010). In an article published immediately following the jury's decision in the *Middendorp* case (to find the male accused not guilty of murder but guilty of the offence of defensive homicide), Sarah Capper, a policy officer with the Victorian Women's Trust, and Mary Crooks, the Trust's Executive Director, raised questions about the capacity of the reforms to homicide law in Victoria to contend 'with the grim, gendered realities of family violence' (2010: 21; see also Howe 2010).[33] The article by Capper and Crooks issues a stark reminder about the intent of the reforms: the 'removal of provocation' was so that violent men who used the partial defence 'as an excuse for jealous rage and anger' could no longer do so 'and have what should have been murder convictions downgraded to manslaughter, with a lesser sentence'. Attorney-General Rob Hulls, when announcing the reforms, said that: '[t]he common law has slowly changed to take into account other circumstances where a person may kill to protect themselves – for example, where a person kills in response to long-term family violence'. As Capper and Crooks remind us: '[t]he key point here is that much of this reform was designed to take account of family violence ... Shaye Beck's call for a review is understandable. Family members will want intentional killing to be labelled for what it is – murder'. Thus, they asked: what is required for 'the legal system to uphold the original intent of these law reforms, particularly where there is a history of violence towards the woman and where the woman killed is a victim blamed?'

In response to these criticisms, in August 2010 the Victorian Department of Justice published a discussion paper entitled *Review of the Offence of Defensive Homicide*, inviting legal professionals, experts in the field of family violence and the wider community to comment and give feedback on how the new offence is being used (Hulls 2010b). According to a joint submission to the Department of Justice in September 2010 on behalf of the Victorian Women's Trust (VWT), the Domestic Violence Resource Centre Victoria (DVRCV), Domestic Violence Victoria (DV Vic) Inc, the Federation of Community Legal Centres (FCLC), Koorie Women Mean Business (KWMB), and Women's Health Victoria (WHV) (Tyson et al 2010), a key problem with the jury's decision to convict Luke Middendorp of defensive homicide lay in its failure to have regard for the empirical literature on the gendered dynamics of family violence. Specifically, the authors took issue with the way in which the killing was represented in court as the inevitable culmination of a 'tempestuous, even violent' relationship:

> ... while both parties were involved in frequent fights and arguments, on the day in question, Jade Bownds had arrived at the house with a male companion (possibly for protection, the companion was 'chased away' by Middendorp), and that witnesses heard Middendorp threaten to stab her.

The authors also note that in contrast to the empirical literature documenting the prevalence of separation assaults on women, men, by contrast:

> ... do not live in such fear of their own lives, especially in the process of leaving a relationship (and homicide statistics support this).
>
> (Tyson et al 2010: 11–12)

> 'In a significant number of cases when women have killed in the context of an intimate relationship, there is a history of violence used against the women'.
>
> (VLRC, quoted in the discussion paper: 16)

Thus, the authors remain concerned that there is a real possibility that the outcome reached in this particular case may open the door for other male defendants who have killed women in the context of family violence to claim that their culpability should be reduced from murder to defensive homicide or manslaughter (2010: 6–7). The submission concludes by outlining a number of proposals for ongoing and further reform for the Victorian Government to consider, including the recommendation that a specialist domestic homicide unit be housed within the Office of Public Prosecutions along the lines of the specialist sexual offences unit that is already in operation in Victoria (Tyson et al 2010: 17).

Clearly, the jury's determination that it could not rule out Luke Middendorp's subjectively held, but ultimately unreasonable, belief that what he did was necessary to protect himself from his ex-partner has raised some grave concerns. In particular, it raises concerns about the continuation of 'cultures of excuse' for male violence in post-provocation jurisdictions. While a specific rationale for the abolition of the partial defence of provocation concerned the problem of how these cases construct the woman victim as to blame for her own death, the abolition of provocation was brought about at the same time as new legislative provisions to facilitate evidence being admitted in support of an argument of self-defence or 'excessive self-defence' (defensive homicide) in the context of a family violence situation. To this end, section 9AH of the *Crimes Act* 1958 facilitates blame being ascribed to the victim where the victim has perpetrated family violence and the killing is in response to this. In short, the *Middendorp* case is one that clearly involves victim-blame in the context of self-defence. Thus, there is an urgent need for future research that focuses explicitly on the ways in which the murder event is read as an inevitable culmination of the relationship's history. In *Middendorp* the defence narrative sought to locate the circumstances of the killing within the discursive frame of the 'tempestuous' relationship. By representing the history of the relationship between the parties as similar to the elements of a storm, culpability for the deceased's death can be distributed to both parties. Just as 'angry' or 'dark' clouds on the horizon convey the likelihood of a storm, describing the relationship between the parties as 'tempestuous' implies that both parties were displaying violent anger. If we recall the discussion in the previous chapter, once events and details of the 'history' of that relationship have been reordered within a linear, temporal sequence (such as the 'love-hate' relationship or the 'romance-gone-wrong'), that sequence of events and actions takes on an air of familiarity – particularly a sense of foreboding – and as a result appears as if it is a coherent and plausible account of what took place. However, as Culler reminds us by his reference to the semiotic theory of framing in art, 'framing is something we do; it hints of the frame-up (falsifying evidence beforehand in order to make someone appear guilty)' (1988: ix).[34]

At this point it is necessary briefly to consider the earlier case of *Sherna*,[35] which also attracted significant public criticism. In that case, a Victorian jury found the male defendant, Anthony Sherna, guilty of manslaughter by an unlawful and dangerous act (rather than guilty of murder or of defensive homicide) after he fatally strangled his de facto partner, Susanne Wild, with the cord of his dressing gown. According to the defendant at trial, on the night in question Susanne had come 'storming' into the laundry 'yelling and screaming' about a mobile phone bill upsetting both him and his dog, Hubble, which Anthony had been 'rocking to sleep'. Susanne then left the laundry and walked towards the kitchen. Anthony put the dog to bed and followed Susanne into the kitchen. On the way, he said he grabbed the cord from his dressing gown, which was hanging on the back of the laundry door. When asked by police what was going through his mind at the time he grabbed the cord, he said: 'I was just so angry. I just – because I was drunk I grabbed the cord to kill her. I was so angry'. He maintained that Susanne was on one side of the kitchen bench and he was on the other. He recalled that the dressing gown cord was out of sight because he was holding it in his hands, which were hanging down by his side. He said he then tried to regain his composure and calm himself down, but then she said something about the mobile phone bill, which got him fired up again. It was at this point he lost his temper and strangled her with the dressing gown cord until she could no longer breathe. When asked whether she said anything when he approached her with the dressing gown cord, his response was, she said: 'Tony, no, don't do it', but he just ignored her.[36]

According to counsel for the defendant, the killing of Susanne Wild was not 'pre-planned'. 'Quite to the contrary', she submitted to the jury in her opening address, 'it was entirely spontaneous. It was a sudden eruption as a result of the cumulative effect of many, many years of abuse'.[37] Throughout the trial, the defence narrative sought to position the woman victim as a thoroughly unlikeable woman who sought to dominate and control the male defendant through her verbally abusive behaviour. This construction of the woman victim's character is partly due to evidence adduced at the trial by Anthony Sherna that told of how 'Susie was a mouth – really mouthy, none of the neighbours liked us at all. None of the neighbours would talk to us because she was always mouthing off at them . . . So for me, it was – just every day was pressure-cooker day' (*DPP v Sherna* [2009] VSC 494: 2). Citing some of this evidence, the defence narrative's construction of the deceased as a scolding wife who was killed by her 'cuckolded' de facto partner was echoed in media reports that featured the following headline: 'henpecked hubby "snapped" over upset dog' (Hunt 2008; Anderson 2009; Anonymous 2009b).[38] In her closing address, Ms Dixon told the jury Anthony Sherna had been trapped within what she described as 'a grossly dysfunctional relationship with Susanne Wild who dominated and controlled him to a pathological extent'. She said he was a man who 'had reached the threshold of his horrible life with Susie Wild. He was always defending himself from daily abuse and put-downs'.[39] Clearly, the jury's sympathy lay with the defendant, as indicated by the decision to find him not guilty of murder or defensive homicide but guilty of manslaughter by an unlawful and dangerous act. However, if we accept the evidence that was also adduced at the trial in this case and obviously lent support to the plausibility of the defence narrative, this case needs to be understood as an unusual case of intimate partner homicide committed in the context of family violence, with the victim being the de facto male partner (for a discussion of the rare instance of a case involving a claim of 'battered husband syndrome' see Schwartz and DeKeseredy 1993; Straton 1994; Simone 1997).

When making her plea, it is interesting that counsel for the defendant sought to distinguish the current situation from those more 'typical' provocation manslaughter cases involving sexual jealousy and infidelity:

> Your Honour, we are really entering into new and uncharted territory here as a result of the new changes to the Crimes Act . . . it must be borne in mind that whatever Your Honour does in this case is going to have to sit well against cases where the accused is a female and has been subjected to psychological domination or abuse and may have been convicted of manslaughter, for example, where there is no present threat. So it is not a simple sentencing exercise in this case . . . It is very different from those provocation manslaughter cases where the issue is about some sense, and I suppose Ramage might be one of these, where there is a sense of the wife was having it off with the boyfriend and there is a kind of sexual jealousy kind of an overtone.
>
> (*Sherna* trial transcript, Supreme Court of Victoria
> (October 2009) at 1007–1008, plea)

It would appear that in a post-provocation context, feminist arguments about the propensity for defence narratives to mobilise gendered stereotypes about unruly female victims who provoke the rage of their tragic cuckolded partners, in an effort to elicit sympathy from juries and judges are being realised (see for example Howe 2002: 42). However, the claim that provocation's narratives are being used in the guise of other defences – in this instance – manslaughter, needs further consideration.

If we consider that in his closing address to the jury in the *Sherna* case, the prosecuting counsel saw fit to comment on how the accused had either 'personally or through his counsel . . . complained mercilessly about

Susanne Wild'. He said the court had 'been absolutely awash with criticisms of her'. He intimated this was a tactic on the part of the accused and/or his lawyer, who deliberately sought to say 'something, anything, however small, [but] negative about Susanne Wild'. Thus, the prosecuting counsel was critical that this had been 'quite a one-sided process'. While he conceded the practice of resorting to defence tactics that blame the victim was linked to the nature of the adversarial process, he said it was not one in which the victim was the one on 'trial as to her character'. This led him to conclude the process 'may have had a tendency to obscure the reality of what it actually was that this man did to his wife'.[40] Although the jury determined that it did not accept the male defendant's subjective but unreasonable belief that he did what was necessary to defend himself (thus, they found him not guilty of defensive homicide), their decision to return a conviction of manslaughter by an unlawful and dangerous act shows how provocation-type arguments are being mobilised in the guise of other offences (eg the problem of victim-blame in the context of provocation ends up being a problem in another context, which is manslaughter), an area that, to date, has not received much critical attention from provocation's critics (on this point see Stewart and Freiberg 2009: vii).

Challenging legal culture(s)

As indicated above, the discussion paper *Review of the Offence of Defensive Homicide*, states in its opening pages that the 2005 reforms to the law of homicide in Victoria explicitly recognised change was required both to the law and *to the culture* of the criminal justice system (DOJ 2010: 3). However, as decades of feminist legal scholarship reminds us, often the (masculinist) internal culture(s) of the legal profession can be slow, and sometimes resistant, to change (Kaspiew 1995; Hunter 1996, 2006a, 2008). To provide a brief illustration, consider the comments made by the (now retired) Deputy Chief Justice David Byrne QC,[41] who presided over the *Middendorp* case. When sentencing the defendant, he described the defendant's act in killing his ex-partner a 'foolish act' committed against a 'troubled young woman' (*R v Middendorp* [2010] VSC 202 paragraph 17(Byrne J)). Although also noting that the defendant's history had 'been a history of violence towards a woman less strong than' him (paragraph 27), describing the act of killing as 'foolish' only serves to minimise that prior history of domestic violence which included numerous death threats. As Busch has observed, there is little or no sense that threats of this kind may represent criminal behaviour and the implicit assumption is that she is an unworthy victim (1994: 110). One could conclude from this that the judge's comments represent an 'isolated instance' of gender bias on the part of the legal profession (or even a foolish lapse?). However, there is also much contrary evidence suggesting that masculinist bias is a '"real, significant but largely unconscious" systemic problem' (Kaspiew 1995: 351). If we compare the above comments with those made in the case of *Azizi* (discussed below), it would appear that some members of the judiciary are seeking to implement normative change by adopting an 'equality approach' to sentencing in cases of domestic homicide as recommended in the *Provocation in Sentencing* report.

Soltan Azizi was charged with murder after he strangled his wife to death with her scarf.[42] He claimed he did not intend to kill, or do really serious injury to his wife when he pulled on the scarf. Rather, he maintained that her death was an accident and that he pulled on the scarf to stop her from biting him on the leg after he bent down to pick up their 18-month-old child, Hamsa, whom she had allegedly thrown onto the floor. According to the defendant, when he asked his wife why she was doing this to the baby, he alleged that she said: 'in Australia that is her right, that the mum has the right to do those things' to which he responded 'it may be your right but the baby might die'.[43] When sentencing Soltan Azizi, King J determined that she was in agreement with the decision of the jury to return a verdict of murder, that she did not find Azizi to be 'a witness of truth' and that she was 'not prepared to act upon the material [he] gave under oath'. Rather, King J was of the view that:

> . . . over the 14 years of your marriage, [you] subjected your wife to ill-treatment both of an emotional and physical nature. I find that you have treated her as a person lacking in individual rights, and a person that must do what she was told to do by you.
>
> (*R v Azizi* [2010] VSC 112 at para 18 (King J))

Whereas Middendorp's act of killing his ex-partner is not understood by the judge who presided over that case as specific to Anglo-Australian culture, Soltan Azizi's act is characterised as conflicting with current Australian values. This point can be illustrated by King J's remark that Soltan Azizi's treatment of his wife 'was not what would be normally acceptable in this country':

> It is clear that you were unable to accept that your wife had rights, which rights included the ability to leave you if that was what she desired, to seek an intervention order against you, if that was what she required and to be supported to live separately and apart, if that was what was required.
>
> (*R v Azizi* [2010] VSC 112 at 7–8 (King J)).

Justice Betty King's comments in the case of *Azizi* above issue a strong condemnation of the violence and control that took place within the relationship leading up to the murder, whereas Byrne J's description of the relationship in *Middendorp* is one that sees it as the inevitable culmination of a 'tempestuous, even violent' relationship. What this also reveals is a tendency on the part of the legal system to misrepresent 'partner violence' as 'equally harmful to both parties' (Howe 2010).

Finally, the above comments need to be interpreted in light of feminists' criticism of how the provocation defence is just another aspect of the legal system's production of racist stereotypes, especially when it relates to male anger and violence against women (Volpp 1994; Yeo 1996; Sing 1999; Nelson 2002; Phillips 2003; Maher et al 2005; Dick 2009). According to Maher et al, the Australian legal system's tendency to narrate men's 'excuses' for their anger and violence towards women differently when violent masculinity is practised by white middle-class men, compared with those identified as 'culturally "other"' means that these same 'underlying assumptions and ideologies about masculinity ... are likely to continue to affect the arguments and judgments made in sentencing men who have perpetrated intimate homicides' in post-abolition of provocation jurisdictions (2005: 148, 151–52).

A specific example of a non-critical (non-feminist) assessment of men's excuses for anger and violence against women can be found in a speech given at a Social Justice Forum organised by the University of New South Wales's Law Faculty. New South Wales Chief Justice Jim Spigelman warned that Australia's changing demographic means courts increasingly have to deal with cultural traditions that involve violence against women. He said that throughout Europe significant issues have arisen with respect to Islamic and South Asian communities extending to honour crimes and forced marriages. In a colonising gesture, he offered that 'we' in Australia are 'not able to compromise on key issues like violence against women', and cited the 'winding back' of the partial defence of provocation as evidence that Australian courts had made 'great progress ... in bringing about gender equity before the law' (Hall 2010).

Spigelman's insistence that it is mainly those men from 'other' (Islamic and South Asian) communities, who hold sexist cultural traditions involving violence against women, who threaten to clog up 'our' Australian courts (Hall 2010) is worrying indeed. As Howe has recently remarked, comments such as these illustrate how racialised excuses for male anger and violence towards women are able to persist in 'the new "post"-provocation judgments of abolitionist judges' (2002: 46). This is because it is not only the body of the woman victim that is put on trial but also those men who have failed to approximate the norms of appropriate masculinity. As discussed above, it is apparent that some judges have issued condemnations of behaviour they deem to be 'unmanly' or inappropriate since the 2005 amendments to the laws of homicide in Victoria. However, it would appear we still have a way to go in the process of educating not only society, but equally, if not more importantly, lawyers and judges, about their complicity in reproducing hegemonic tales about women who 'ask for it' when they appear to sympathise with defence narratives constructing the circumstances of such killings as 'foolish acts' or 'tragedies'.

Conclusion

This chapter has argued that, although it seems the beneficiaries of the new offence of defensive homicide are overwhelmingly men who have killed other men, there is also some emerging evidence to suggest it is operating to advance the interests of some women who kill their violent abusers. What the discussion of the *Middendorp* and *Sherna* decisions has also shown is that the characters of dead women who have been killed by their intimate partners or ex-partners are still being put on trial. Many feminist scholars (including many of those within the Victorian legislature) remain optimistic that the decision to abolish the partial defence of provocation will put an end to the (legal) culture of blaming the woman victim for male anger and violence. It is the particular inscription of male rage as a normal characteristic of masculinity that shores up the cultural commonplace narrative that the woman victim 'asked for it' and hence, is deserving of what she gets. It is constructions such as these that have quite literally come to set the limits of law's understanding. In acknowledging, however, that the 'law is very much a two-edged sword for women, which can end up doing more harm than good', Hunter observes that feminist law reformers need to be attuned to the ways in which '[l]aw transforms elements of experience (such as being subjected to domestic violence) into fixed, objectified, and disempowering categories (such as those of "victim", or "battered woman")' (2008: 7, 8).[44] For Hunter:

> ... the real problem for women may turn out to be not lack of legal recognition, but hostile social discourses of which law is only a part. Thus, rather than accepting law's claims to be a powerful instrument for justice, feminists should focus their attack on those wider discourses as they are manifested in law and elsewhere.

Law reformers have not necessarily engaged explicitly with discourses of masculinity in their debates around whether or not to abolish the partial defence of provocation; however, a dominant ideal of masculinity clearly informs the provocation defence and has operated to condone some men's violence against women (and other men).[45] Law has manifestly failed to ask, much less address, its own 'sex question'. In seeking to address law's failure to adequately account for and respond to the different circumstances of women's offending vis-à-vis men's offending and the enduring problem of men's violence against women, the authors of the *Provocation in Sentencing* report noted that:

> [i]n the transformation of the law of provocation, the past should not continue to influence the present in undesirable ways and the partial defence should not re-emerge in a new guise as a particular variety of murder. Many of the old assumptions will need to be discarded and a new normative framework must be developed.
> (Stewart and Freiberg 2009: vii; see also 2008a: 2)[46]

When discussing its recommendation to abolish provocation, the VLRC reiterated that: 'one of the recognised roles of the criminal law is to set appropriate standards of behaviour and to punish those who breach them' (2004: 56). As noted by Stewart and Freiberg, 'where public policy requires normative changes in behaviour' it is also important that sufficient weight is given in sentencing to punishment, general deterrence and denunciation (2009: 20). However, as Threadgold insightfully observes, if legal practitioners are serious about achieving normative change, then this requires continued scrutiny of the legal system's 'textual practices and its relations to other social bodies, both institutional and individual – using all the resources that critical theory, literary theory, discourse analysis, rhetoric and feminism and sociology can offer'. However, Threadgold also points out that '[l]egal fictions are *not* the same as literary fictions. They have real and devastating and immediate social and personal effects, which must be explored in their specificity and difference as well as in their complex intersections with the literary and other institutions'. Moreover, she argues that rewriting these legal fictions needs to be an explicit agenda if we are to see real and lasting change (Threadgold 1994: 340–41, original emphasis).[47]

If the standard provocation tale of a man's uncontrollable rage and anger at his nagging, unfaithful and departing wife is to be subverted, we need to be ever vigilant that it does not simply end up rewritten as yet another narrative of excuse that can be used in the guise of other defences to homicide. As the discussion of *Middendorp* showed, the story that is now being told in some cases involving a man who kills his current or former partner (and underwrites the new offence of defensive homicide) is one where male violence is read as a subjective, but unreasonable, response to a woman of whom he is not only 'fearful', but who is also the victim of his violence. In the final chapter, I consider some of the implications of and limitations with the narrative turn in studies of the relationship between men, masculinities and male violence in the area of crime and criminology. The next chapter discusses how a particular version of psychoanalytic theory, combined with the individual biography or life history, is seen as necessary to understand the particular experiences and motivations of violent men. However, it seems that it is only the academic expert who is able to ascertain the meaning behind (the emotional) 'truth' of these experiences. Moreover, it is not simply that the psychosocial approach is one in which its authors are telling *more stories* about violent men; there are also some disturbing similarities between their stories and those we find mobilised in provocation cases.

Notes

1 In August 2004, the UK Law Reform Commission published its report on the defences to homicide (*Partial Defences to Murder: Final Report*). It recommended retaining the use of the provocation defence but that it is legislatively redrawn to redefine and narrow the circumstances in which it can be raised. The UK Law Commission also recommended it undertake a more substantial review of the law of murder, and in November 2006 published its report, *Murder, Manslaughter and Infanticide*, in which it revealed that the Home Office would be taking over the review of the law and would be consulting on broader public policy issues such as sentencing (Law Commission, 'Bringing the law of homicide into the 21st century' *press release* (29 November 2006, cited in Roth 2007: 35).

2 According to Carolyn Ramsey, this policy shift is away from condoning men's anger, and there still needs to be a 'qualifying trigger', namely fear of serious violence or circumstances of an extremely grave character giving rise to a justifiable sense of being seriously wronged. Anger in such a situation may be sudden, such as might occur in the case of a man, or the steadily mounting anger, such as the 'slow burning fuse' or the 'straw that broke the camel's back' such as might occur in the case of a woman subject to continuous beating or abuse by her husband. It is assumed the defence will not succeed where the accused person is simply very angry, or motivated by revenge, or responding to sexual infidelity. Some have argued that this is unfortunate. As Ramsey has observed, 'the *Coroners and Justice Act* retains the possibility that mere words – things "done or *said (or both)*" – *might rise to* that level' (2010: 99, original emphasis).

3 According to Lee's (2003) examination of the criminal law defences of provocation and self-defence in the United States, she argues that what is ultimately needed to address the problem of bias and undue leniency is a change in social attitudes.

4 For a recent discussion of the use of relationship evidence in the Australian legal context see Hamer (2008: 351–67).

5 According to Jane Ashton, whose brother-in-law was the last man in Victoria to be convicted of provocation manslaughter for the 2003 killing of her sister, Julie Ramage, the new law of defensive homicide was 'being used as an excuse by men to murder women. The woman is dead. She can't give evidence, yet she has been smeared' (Murphy 2010).

6   According to the VLRC, claims of provocation that successfully result in a conviction for manslaughter can often be upsetting for the families of victims, particularly in cases involving a prior history of domestic violence (2004: 32). The VLRC further notes that often this leave many families of victims with a sense of injustice 'that the accused has "got away" with manslaughter' (VLRC 2003: 70, 2004: 32). Furthermore, 'continued existence of provocation can be seen as promoting a culture of blaming the victim and sending a message to the wider community that some victims' lives are less valuable than others' (VLRC 2004: 32). Thus, it recommended that the provocation defence be abolished and that considerations of provocation mitigation could more appropriately be dealt with at the sentencing phase (VLRC 2004: 32).

7   It should be noted that it has been more than 10 years since the Federal Department of Justice Canada (FDJC) published its consultation paper on the defences to homicide, *Reforming Criminal Code Defences: Provocation, Self-Defence of Property, a Consultation Paper* (FDJC 1998), in which it recommended the abolition of provocation, and significant reforms to the law of self-defence for battered women. However, the defence is still available and governed by s 232 of the Canadian *Criminal Code* (R.S.C. 1985).

8   In 1998, the Federal Department of Justice Canada published its consultation paper on the defences to homicide *Reforming Criminal Code Defences* (n 7) and recommended the abolition of provocation and significant reforms to the law of self-defence for battered women. In Canada there have been a number of high profile cases where men have relied on the provocation defence out of anger and jealousy (see Klineberg 2002: 37–73) for a discussion of *R v Parent* ([2001] 1 SCR 761) and McDonald and Smith (1999) for a discussion of *R v Klassen* ((1997) CAN lii 4705 (YK CA). It is significant that in 2004 a conservative government campaign led by Stephen Harper implemented key changes to federal funding guidelines for women's organisations such as the National Association of Women and the Law (NAWL) and the Status of Women Canada (SWC). These changes resulted in the closure of NAWL in September 2007 and 12 regional offices of SWC. The Harper government also saw fit to remove the issue of equality from the SWC's mandate, which leads me to speculate that these issues are unlikely to be on the political agenda in the near future (Côté 2006).

9   Graycar and Morgan, for instance, have demonstrated the persistence in law 'in viewing equality as meaning only formal equality, that is, the Aristotelian belief that all people should be treated the same, regardless of circumstances'. They have argued that it is one that has for too long meant a more fruitful concept of equality has remained hidden. Accordingly, Graycar and Morgan argue that the failure to recognise social context – that 'women who are killed and the women who kill are, in effect, the same women, and the contexts in which women and men kill are not commensurate' – has often led to a further failure on the part of law reform bodies to accept, rather than persistently ignore, that the provocation defence is gender-biased (2006: 399). Thus, they argue that the concept, substantive equality, is one that recognises the disparate circumstances in which men and women kill (Graycar and Morgan 2006: 405–406).

10 The first example outlined by Douglas refers to the shift away from the strict requirement of the need for a discrete act or specific triggering incident toward greater acceptance that it did not reflect the experiences of many battered women. Citing the cases of *Chhay v R* ((1994) 72 A Crim R 1) and *R v R* ((1981) 28 SASR 321) as examples Douglas notes that, in both cases, the courts accepted 'that the loss of self-control in relation to provocation could develop after lengthy abuse' (Douglas 2008: 47; see also Tarrant 1990). The second change was the shift away from anger as being the only kind of emotion assumed to underlie the defence towards acceptance of the idea that the underlying emotion

experienced by battered women was fear and/or panic. While this development was an important and significant one, in practice, expanding the range of circumstances in which the provocation defence can be raised to make it more available to woman defendants, for example, increased its availability for men as well (Douglas 2008: 46–47; see also Morgan 1997: 253). The third change, related to the relaxing of the requirement that the specific trigger or provocation be 'sudden' and towards recognition that the provocation could accumulate over a period of time has, in its practical application, extended the timeframe for men who kill as well – particularly in situations where they kill for reasons of sexual jealousy and perceived infidelity (Douglas 2008: 49; see also Morgan 1997). The fourth and last example provided by Douglas concerned the relaxing or expanding of the rules of evidence in relation to battered women's experiences of violence so that they could come within the concept of the 'ordinary person' (Douglas 2008: 50). Although admitting evidence of 'battered women syndrome' (BWS) was aimed at demonstrating the different kinds of responses that might be made in circumstances where women had suffered abuse over a prolonged period, it is one that still requires medical or other experts to tell their story. As a result, this approach has tended both to essentialise and further typecast battered women (Douglas 2008: 50–52). Indeed, Douglas notes that for some critics the defence was ultimately 'beyond redemption' and they argued that it should be abolished (see eg Howe 2002: 43).

11   Despite these failings, Douglas's discussion of recent decisions is one in which she notes a growing reluctance on the part of some members of the judiciary 'to accept that adultery or verbal taunts about sexual ineptitude are provocation for the purposes of the defence' (2008: 53). However, she also observes how 'these examples are merely discrete instances relying on the discretion of individual judges and juries. These developments do not necessarily follow any coherent principle' (2008: 54).

12   According to Hunter (2008: 8):

> . . . the real problem for women may turn out to be not lack of legal recognition, but hostile social discourses of which law is only a part. Thus, rather than accepting law's claims to be a powerful instrument for justice, feminists should focus their attack on those wider discourses as they are manifested in law and elsewhere.

13   Prior to its abolition in Victoria in 2005, the partial defence of provocation was available to an accused person charged with murder. Unlike the full defence of self-defence, which results in an acquittal, a successful defence of provocation reduced the crime of murder to the lesser crime of manslaughter. The elements that were to be proven in order for the defence of provocation to succeed were as follows: the deceased must have said something and/or acted in a way that was provocative; the accused must have lost self-control as a result of the provocation and killed the deceased while experiencing that loss of self-control; and overriding both of these legal requirements is the further demand that the accused must have acted as an ordinary hypothetical person would have acted (the common law test for provocation is stated in *Masciantonio v The Queen* (1995) 183 CLR 58 at 67).

14   According to the report: 'the crucial questions for a court will not relate to the defendant's loss of self-control' because, following the insights made by Coss, among others, 'the real "loss of control" is that men have lost control of their women' (2006: 52, cited in Stewart and Freiberg 2009).

15   Tasmania was the first Australian state to pass legislation repealing the partial provocation defence in 2003 (*Criminal Code Amendment (Abolition of Defence of Provocation) Act*

2003 (Tas)). Interestingly, Tasmania is the only Australian state to abolish the partial defence of provocation as a stand-alone decision. As Ramsey has emphasised, '[n]o evidentiary changes were introduced to make it easier for battered women charged with murder to convince the jury that they had acted in self-defence, and no substitute for provocation was enacted.. This had led her to reiterate concerns made by Bradfield, who has noted that '[f]or some Australian feminists, Tasmania's surgical strike raised a grave concern that eliminating the provocation doctrine would actually "worsen the legal position of battered women who kill"' (2003: 324, cited in Ramsey 2010: 69).

16 Judicial practice in terms of directing on the common law of self-defence and statutory self-defence has recently been clarified by the Victorian Court of Appeal in *Babic v The Queen* [2010] VSCA 198.

17 Evidence of the history of the relationship between the person and a family member, including violence by the family member towards the person or by the person towards the family member or by the family member or the person in relation to any other family member can include the: cumulative effect, including the psychological effect, on the person or a family member of that violence; social, cultural or economic factors that impact on the person or a family member who has been affected by family violence; the general nature and dynamics of relationships affected by family violence, including the possible consequences of separation from the abuser; the psychological effect of violence on people who are or have been in a relationship affected by family violence; social or economic factors that impact on people who are, or have been, in a relationship affected by family violence. For a full discussion of the reforms to the law of self-defence in Victoria see Hopkins and Easteal (2010).

18 Robert Richter, a prominent QC, had also agreed to represent her without fee, 'partly because of the case's strong relevance to Victoria's new defences to homicide legislation' (Johnson 2009a).

19 The more recent acquittal of Susan Falls, who shot and killed her violent husband in Queensland in May 2006, has been described as sending 'a message to all battered women and victims of serious violence that there is justice in the legal system' (Swanwick 2010).

20 Since writing this chapter, there have been a number of other Victorian cases involving women who have killed a male victim. Although it is beyond the scope of this chapter to discuss these cases in any depth here, it should be noted that a young indigenous woman, Melissa Anne Kulla Kulla, pleaded guilty to one count of manslaughter after she was charged with the stabbing murder of Hussein Mumin on 10 September 2008 (*R v Kulla Kulla* [2010] VSC 60). On 3 March 2011, Eileen Creamer was found guilty of the offence of defensive homicide after she killed her husband, David, with a South African weapon known as a knobkerrie (*R v Creamer* [2011] VSC 196). The jury accepted the evidence led in Ms Creamer's defence, which was that she was repeatedly forced to take part in group sex with men other than her husband. On 12 April 2011, the Victorian Office of Public Prosecutions accepted a plea of guilty to defensive homicide in the case of Karen Black, who killed her de facto husband, Wayne Clark. The judge accepted that the killing took place in the context of a long history of drunken verbal abuse by the deceased towards the defendant and which also involved threats, intimidation, harassment, jabbing and prodding, as it did on the night in question (*R v Black* [2011] VSC 152).

21 *R v Smith* [2008] VSC 87; *R v Edwards* [2008] VSC 297; *R v Giammona* [2008] VSC 376; *R v Smith* [2008] VSC 617; *R v Taiba* [2008] VSC 589; *R v Baxter* [2009] VSC 178; *R v Treziese* [2009] VSC 520; *R v Spark* [2009] VSC 374; *R v Wilson* [2009] VSC 431; *R v Parr* [2009] VSC 468; *R v Croxford & Doubleday* [2009] VSC 516; *R v Evans* [2009]

VSC 593; *R v Middendorp* [2010] VSC 202; *R v Ghazlan* [2011] VSC 178; *R v Svetina* [2011] VSC 392; *R v Martin* [2011] VSC 217; *R v Jewell* [2011] VSC 483.

22 *R v Smith* [2008] VSC 87; *R v Edwards* [2008] VSC 297; *R v Giammona* [2008] VSC 376; *R v Smith* [2008] VSC 617; *R v Taiba* [2008] VSC 589; *R v Baxter* [2009] VSC 178; *R v Treziese* [2009] VSC 520; *R v Spark* [2009] VSC 374; *R v Wilson* [2009] VSC 431; *R v Evans* [2009] VSC 593; *R v Ghazlan* [2011] VSC 178; *R v Martin* [2011] VSC 217; *R v Jewell* [2011] VSC 483.

23 Other Australian states such as Western Australia have implemented changes to the laws of homicide with the explicit aim that these will 'result in more guilty pleas, fewer trials, and more convictions – saving court resources and reducing stress for victims' families' (Office of the Attorney-General Western Australia 2008).

24 For a discussion of the plea bargaining process in the Australian context see Flynn (2007, 2009).

25 *DPP v Lam* [2007] VSC 307; *R v Diver* [2008] VSC 399; *R v Piper* [2008] VSC 569; *R v Foster* [2009] VSC 124; *R v Dutton* [2010] VSC 107; *R v Felicite* [2010] VSC 245; *R v Singh* [2010] VSC 299; *R v Bayram* [2011] VSC 10; *R v Mamour* [2011] VSC 113; *R v Penglase* [2011] VSC 356; *R v Hopkins* [2011] VSC 517; *R v Carolus* [2011] VSC 583.

26 *R v Brooks* [2008] VSC 70; *R v Ellis* [2008] VSC 372; *R v Baxter* [2009] VSC 180; *R v Chalmers* [2009] VSC 251; *R v Robinson* [2010] VSC 10; *R v Azizi* [2010] VSC 112; *R v Caruso* [2010] VSC 354; *R v McDonald* [2011] VSC 235; *R v Weaven* [2011] VSC 508.

27 *DPP v Pennisi* [2008] VSC 498; *R v Smart* [2008] VSC 155; *DPP v Sherna* [2009] VSC 494; *R v Reid* [2009] VSC 326; *R v Lubik* [2011] VSC 137; *R v Grimmett* [2011] VSC 506.

28 *R v Borthwick* involved a man who was convicted of manslaughter by criminal negligence after he killed his 'love rival', Mark Zimmer, who had formed a relationship with his ex-girlfriend, Nicola Martin, in the previous three months by driving his van into him. Although the sentencing judge described Borthwick's actions in killing the deceased as 'a serious example of the crime of manslaughter by criminal negligence', she said that the killing was committed in the context of a 'breakdown' of his 'two-year-relationship with his girlfriend' and commented how he had become 'jealous of Mark Zimmer and persistently sought details of their contact and had threatened to harm and kill him with guns and knives'. She also noted that Mark Zimmer had tried to calm him down and had reported Borthwick's behaviour to the police ([2010] VSC 613 at 2 (Williams J)).

29 *R v Brooks* [2008] VSC 70; *R v Ellis* [2008] VSC 372; *R v Diver* [2008] VSC 399; *R v Foster* [2009] VSC 124; *R v Felicite* [2010] VSC 245; *R v Bayram* [2011] VSC 10.

30 *R v Diver* [2008] VSC 399; *R v Foster* [2009] VSC 124; *R v Piper* [2008] VSC 569; *R v Felicite* [2010] VSC 245; *R v Bayram* [2011] VSC 10.

31 In the case of *R v Singh* [2010] VSC 299 the defendant pleaded guilty to the murder of his wife, whom he had beaten to death. Both were Indian citizens and had recently settled in Australia. When sentencing the defendant the judge said he was 'completely satisfied' that the defendant's wife 'was not having any illicit affairs' and that his 'allegations were the product of his fevered imagination'. While he accepted that the killing was 'unplanned', he said that 'the background of family violence could not be ignored: It cannot be overlooked that this murder was the culmination of a long history of brutality towards . . . [his] . . . wife' (paragraph 20) (see also Petrie 2010a, 2010b).

32 Private communication between the author and Jane Ashton.

33 There was also a public outcry following an earlier decision by a Victorian jury to find Anthony Sherna not guilty of murder but guilty of manslaughter by an unlawful and dangerous act after he strangled his de facto wife, Susanne Wild, with the cord of his dressing gown. Former federal MP and law reform campaigner, Phil Cleary, whose sister,

Vicky, was killed by her ex-boyfriend, Peter Keogh, in 1987 outside the kindergarten where she worked, and who was convicted of manslaughter after he claimed that Vicky provoked him, declared the jury's decision to acquit Anthony Sherna 'of murder after he admitted to strangling his de facto wife . . . a scandal and a disgrace'. He urged Attorney-General Rob Hulls to 'revisit his homicide law changes that four years ago abolished the defence of provocation'. He reasoned that the manslaughter verdict not only 'indicates that men are entitled to kill women in such circumstances', stating that 'the *Sherna* case fitted provocation's "blame the victim" template' (Munro 2009b). On his website, Cleary asks: 'Why was the old-fashioned and dangerous idea about Sherna being "hen-pecked" allowed to run almost unchallenged?' (2009).

34 The full quote (1988: ix) reads:

> . . . 'framing' is something we do; it hints of the frame-up ('falsifying evidence beforehand in order to make someone appear guilty'), a major use of context; and it eludes the incipient positivism of 'context' by alluding to the semiotic function of framing in art, where the frame is determining, setting off the object or event as art, and yet the frame itself may be nothing tangible, pure articulation.

Culler also observes that narratives could not function without this idea of putative causation. However, this is due to the 'double logic' of narrative. What he means by this is that meaning is contingent on a process of reading backwards (knowing an effect we go back and search for its cause). At the same time, the narrative suggests 'by its implicit claims to significance that these events are justified by their appropriateness to a thematic structure' (Culler 1981: 178). When meaning is assumed to 'speak for itself' there is a resulting tendency to assume it requires no further justification.

35 *DPP v Sherna* [2009] VSC 494. This was the second trial involving this accused person following the failure of the jury to reach a verdict at his first trial (Munro 2009a).

36 *Sherna* trial transcript, Supreme Court of Victoria (October 2009) 26–28 (opening address to jury). After Anthony Sherna strangled Susanne Wild, he dragged her body to her bedroom and left her lying face down on her bed for three days while he went out to play the slot machines and visit a brothel. But after the smell of decomposition became so bad that he overheard a neighbour complaining about it, he proceeded to dig a grave in which to bury her body in their back yard (Hagan and Russell 2009).

37 ibid 42 (opening address to jury).

38 Witnesses who gave evidence at the trial were asked to give an opinion as to what sort of person Anthony Sherna was. One witness, a colleague of Anthony's, said: 'I thought he was a pretty nice guy. He was just a little bit, seemed to be nervous a lot and a little bit timid . . . when it came to speaking in a group' (*Sherna* trial transcript, Supreme Court of Victoria (October 2009) 62 (cross-examination by prosecuting counsel). Media reports also commented on how Anthony Sherna considered his dog a 'child substitute' because he rocked it to sleep every night (Iaria 2009; Anonymous 2009b).

39 ibid 830. Anthony Sherna claimed he was in a very controlling and verbally abusive relationship with the deceased, Susanne Wild. There was evidence adduced at the trial to show that the relationship was one in which they had no children, were isolated from family and friends, did not go out to restaurants, slept in separate bedrooms, how the defendant's toilet access was restricted (she did not permit him to defecate at home) by his de facto partner and that he was made to sleep in the laundry with his dog, Hubble. Counsel for the defendant (Ms Jane Dixon) also relied on the evidence from a consulting clinical and forensic psychologist, Jeffery Cummins, who was of the opinion that the

defendant was suffering from 'battered woman syndrome'. Mr Cummins testified that Anthony Sherna exhibited key symptoms, including social isolation arising from 'an extremely symbiotic relationship' in which they were 'inappropriately dependent on each other'. He said that this led to Anthony 'feeling powerless', 'helpless and worthless'. His self-esteem deteriorated to such an extent that 'he became significantly depressed'. He further diagnosed that Anthony was suffering from 'a chronic depressive condition' known as 'a dysthymic disorder'. He also assessed him 'as having an adjustment disorder' (ibid 638–39).

40 ibid 766 (closing address to jury).

41 The judge who presided over the *Middendorp* case, Deputy Chief Justice David Byrne, has since retired (Wood 2010).

42 *R v Azizi* [2010] VSC 112.

43 ibid at 5 (King J).

44 Burman, for example, has recently observed that the inability of criminal law to produce gender equality is primarily linked to how the female victim is constructed and offered criminal legal protection in cases involving men's violence against women in heterosexual relationships, a problem she traces to the well known opposition between victimisation and agency (2010: 174).

45 The VLRC endorsed the approach taken to the study of the relationship between men, crime and masculinities as outlined by Polk in his book *When Men Kill: Scenarios of Masculine Violence*, published in 1994. However, this discussion took place only in relation to the historical development of the doctrine of provocation in which references to 'honour' but not 'masculinity' are made (eg VLRC 2003: 82) and debates surrounding the use of the provocation defence by men who claim they killed another man after a non-violent 'homosexual' advance in which references to 'male honour' and 'masculinity' are also made (eg VLRC 2003: 67).

46 As Forell notes, the Victorian reforms recognised that it is no longer appropriate that the legal system should be seen to endorse the emotions that motivate men who commit domestic homicide (eg rage and jealousy) over and against the emotions that motivate women who commit domestic homicide (fear) (2006: 54–55).

47 For an equally compelling discussion of a poststructuralist poetics of law reform see Golder (2004b: 53–65).

CHAPTER 5

Critical fictions: masculinities theory and challenges to men's violence against women

Introduction

Since the emergence of the first wave of feminism four decades ago, debates about men, gender and masculinities have formed a thread of continuity within a diverse body of work that has recently been characterised as masculinities research (Dowd 2008, 2010). While feminist legal scholarship has long recognised the fundamentally misconceived concept of the universal category 'Woman' (Smart 1989, 1992; Naffine 1990), these developments have paved the way for work that explores the relationship between men, violence and crime by foregrounding the concept of masculinity and/or masculinities (Collier 1998). Indeed, critical attention to the 'man question' has become a hot topic within criminology (Messerschmidt 1993; Newburn and Stanko 1994; Carlen and Jefferson 1996). As some critics have argued, much of this work is fraught with a number of epistemological and methodological difficulties, not the least of which concern a profound uncertainty about what exactly is meant by masculinity in the first place (Hearn 1996: 213; see also Collier 1998: 16–23, 2004: 285). While it is not the purpose of this chapter to provide a detailed review of this criticism, it is necessary to draw attention to key aspects of, and developments within, this masculinities research in order to demonstrate some inadequacies of a number of ways in which the relationship between men, masculinities and violence against women (and other men) is currently being understood. In the discussion below, I begin by outlining how masculinity and its connection to men's violence has become a pressing issue for criminology – and indeed criminologists – to discover. In doing so, I pay particular attention to some of the criticisms currently being made of one strand of this work in the area of crime and criminology – the so-called 'third stage' in thinking about masculinities that developed as a 'corrective' not only to earlier masculinity studies but, more importantly, to the poststructuralist and postmodern turn within feminist theory over the past 20 or so years. Here, I outline some problems with the current use being made of the 'narrative interview method' and/or 'life history approach' that characterises this third stage – the 'psychosocial approach' – of thinking about the relationship between masculinities and men's violence against women and some men. I do this by outlining some of the criticisms that have been made in relation to this third stage of thinking about masculinities and crime. Collier, for instance, is far from convinced that by 'seeking to "take masculinity seriously"', the 'veil of ignorance' has now been lifted and we can all sit back and leave the hard work to pro-feminist identified academic men (rather than feminists) to enlighten us about the problem of men's violence against women (1998: 177). Nor is Howe convinced by what critical criminologists have had to say about violent men (Howe 2004a, 2008). Like Collier, Howe offers a range of criticisms of the work of critical criminologists and their engagements (or lack thereof) with the postmodern turn in criminology and feminist theory – particularly, the psychosocial approach – which promised to 'shift thinking about the relationship between masculinities and crime to "a different level"' (2008: 136). Let us now consider what these and other writers have had to say about the different approaches to reading the relationship between masculinities and men's violence.

The men's movement and the idea of masculine 'crisis'

Many have now documented how critical men's studies emerged as a reaction to second-wave feminism (Buchbinder 1994; Whitehead 2002; Edwards 2006). Initial responses to feminism and feminists gave rise to small networks of men's consciousness-raising groups that sought to address some of these issues (Edwards 2006: 25). The men's liberation movement (incorporating mythopoetic men's groups and anti-sexist or pro-feminist men's groups), developed primarily in Britain in the 1970s and 1980s, but also in the United States and Australia. The challenging of gender norms that characterised the women's movement of the 1970s led to examining men 'as gendered beings', rather than as 'non-gendered objects of study' (Dowd 2008: 206). As Buchbinder observes, a common response by many women throughout the 1960s and 1970s was a sadness and anger to the idea that their history under patriarchy had been a tale of oppression by men (1994: 15). Moreover, a key reaction shared by many men at the time was that they felt 'unfairly blamed by women and feminism' had portrayed 'women inappropriately as victims and men as perpetrators' (Pease 2000: 94–95). Men's reactions ranged from 'variously puzzlement' to 'a reciprocal rage', part of what feminists writing at the time have called 'the male backlash against feminism' (Buchbinder 1994: 15).[1] Accordingly, Buchbinder argues that the various challenges that were allegedly 'flung at men by modern feminism' at this time proved 'something of a conundrum for men'. Not only did it 'force' many men 'to willy-nilly review their own position and assumptions', it required them to 'justify' themselves in the face of '[a]ccusations by women of chauvinism, of injustice, of sexism on the part of men with whom they come into daily contact – fathers, brothers, partners, sons, bosses, colleagues and friends', to develop strategies and 'measures to rectify injustices against women perpetrated on the basis of sex alone and to ameliorate women's lot' (Buchbinder 1994: 15–16).

Most often, although not always, the argument in the men's movement that women and feminism had unfairly blamed men either suggested or implied that this had somehow caused a widespread 'crisis' of masculinity (Collier 1996; Clare 2000), yet to this day what this actually means in populist and academic circles remains unclear (Edwards 2006: 7). Although it is almost impossible to synthesise the key factors and concerns that characterise the entire masculinity in crisis thesis, two levels of crisis can be identified. The first was 'a reaction of anger and violence ... A more elaborated version of this kind of response has been the call issued by some men to all other men to rediscover their inner, primitive masculinity' (Buchbinder 1994: 16–17).[2] A key work that inspired many men's involvement in what researchers have since described as a disavowedly 'anti-feminist' and 'misogynist men's movement' was Robert Bly's *Iron John: A Book About Men* (1991). In this work, Bly contends that feminism had caused many men to 'lose' their masculinity (and also their voice), which he characterises as an essential, universal essence. In order to overcome this masculine 'crisis',[3] Bly encouraged men to bond with each other in order to rediscover their core sense of self (Dowd 2008: 207, fn 16).[4] Mirroring developments within the women's movement,[5] the main discursive activity many men were engaged in at this time was 'located in small consciousness-raising groups' in which they sought fundamentally to explore what it meant to be a man (Edwards 2006: 25; see for example Kimmel and Kaufman 1995). What men were essentially doing here took the form of storytelling, or in terms expressed by Rush, the 'narrativization' of masculinity (1992: 5). While not all of the stories being told at this time were tinged with an anti-feminist rhetoric (Edwards 2006: 34–36), many began to emerge in magazines specifically dedicated to exploring men's responses to this broader 'masculine' or 'gender crisis' such as *Achilles Heel*, a magazine published in Britain (see Seidler 1991, *The Achilles Heel Reader*), the *Men's Anti-Sexist Newsletter* or MAN and *Changing Men*, both published in the United States, and *X/Y: Men, Sex, Politics*, in Australia.

The other class of response to this idea of masculine 'crisis' was somewhat more affirming of women's claims and led to a critical re-examination of masculinity that developed in conjunction with the emergence of feminist scholarship of the 1970s, and also mirrored developments within the gay liberation movement (Buchbinder 1994: 19).[6] In a parallel development to the establishment of women's studies courses in universities, the late 1980s saw the emergence of a relatively new field of study, the theory of masculinity – also sometimes called the new men's studies – being taught in universities in the United States, Britain and, much later, in Australia (Buchbinder 1994: 23–24). While the study of men and masculinities was already being explored in a number of books – for instance, in the United States, *Men and Masculinity*, edited by Joseph Pleck and Jack Sawyer, in 1974; in Britain, *The Limits of Masculinity*, by Andrew Tolson in 1977 and *Rediscovering Masculinity: Reason, Language and Sexuality*, by Victor Seidler, in 1989 – the shift of the study of men, away from the more private domain of the consciousness-raising activity of men's groups and into the more public domain of universities, was an important one. As Buchbinder explains, '[t]he academicizing of men's issues has generally been led by several disciplines, chief among them sociology and psychology . . . [i]n recent years, the theory of masculinity has also been taken up by cultural studies' (1994: 24). While many of the pro-feminist and politically-motivated attempts to amalgamate the critique of masculinity with feminism within universities are to be applauded, for some critics the attempt to weld men's studies and feminism is fundamentally 'flawed by the very diversity of feminisms and indeed feminist projects' (Edwards 2006: 36). As Edwards observes, if feminist theory remains limited in its own applications to the study of men and masculinity, the critical studies of masculinity may offer a more successful alternative, particularly in relation to questions of violence (2006: 57).

However, as Dowd notes, this early work in men's studies was focused on men's disadvantages or the limits of their gender role, which was very controversial for some feminists (2008: 207). Indeed, the whole notion of focusing on men grew out of the insistence that men (rather than feminists) 'narrate' masculinity in all its diversity. It is not surprising therefore that a certain defensiveness on the part of some academic men characterised responses to developments within second-wave feminist scholarship; indeed, the call being made from within universities was for *academic men* to talk and write about other men's masculinities including their experiences of crisis. This point has been made by Collier (1998: xi), who observes how:

> ... the much heralded 'crisis' of masculinity, far from constituting a moment of 'truth' about particular changes taking place in the lives of men and women (be it in relation to their criminality, their family roles, their work, economic status, sexuality or emotional lives, and so forth), is in fact ... emblematic of broader tensions surrounding ideas of heterosexuality, family and social (dis)order ...

Thus, for Collier, what appeared 'to be conversations about "masculinity" ... can usefully be seen as attempts to tell other stories, to give voice and bear witness to other subjects and to speak of broader concerns, anxieties and tensions' (1998: xi). In the section that follows I explore several critical insights that have come to characterise masculinities scholarship that largely developed from the discipline of sociology and the work of R. W. Connell and whose agenda for contesting men's privilege under patriarchy has been far reaching.

Hegemonic masculinity

Connell has been one of the leading theorists of masculinity (1987, 1994, 1995, 2000). Connell's 'social theory of gender' and, more particularly, the concept of 'hegemonic masculinity' was developed in an attempt to extend the insights of sex roles theory (1985: 262–64, 1987: 47–54).[7] As Jefferson observes, this thesis began by considering how to conceptualise 'masculinities' in the everyday interactions and settings within which men live their lives, 'especially when power inequalities of class, race, and other social relations are included' (1994: 15). Connell's answer to this question reflected developments in sociological thinking around sex and gender since the 1980s and lay with the reworked Gramscian concept of 'hegemony'. According to Connell, 'there is no one pattern of masculinity that is found everywhere'; rather, there are different masculinities in the sense that '[d]ifferent cultures, and different periods of history, construct gender differently'. Moreover, 'masculinities do not sit side-by-side like dishes on a smorgasbord ... there are definite social relations between them' and they are arranged according to 'relations of hierarchy' (1998: 3–4). Hegemonic masculinity is thus taken to refer 'to a selective range of categories culturally associated with the masculine: specifically, such qualities as aggression, "macho", pride, competitiveness, duty, feelings of insecurity, failure and so forth' (Collier 1998: 19).

Gender relations, for Connell, are constructed in terms of three interrelated structures: labour, power and cathexis (1987: 91–118). Connell's concept of social structure represents a departure from Giddens's formulation (1987: 94–95, 140–41), which, as Maharaj explains, has enjoyed enormous currency but 'does not meet the requirements of a social theory of gender whose aim is transformative' (1995: 52). According to Connell (1987: 92, original emphasis):

> [T]he concept of structure is more than another term for 'pattern' and refers to intractability of the social world. It reflects the experience of being up against something, of limits on freedom; and also the experience of being able to operate by proxy, to produce results one's own capacities would not allow. The concept of *social* structure expresses the constraints that lie in a given form of social organization (rather than, say, physical facts about the world).... the constraints on social practice operate through a complex interplay of powers and through an array of social institutions.

For Connell, the notion of 'structure' is inseparable from 'practice' (1987: 93). The important point here, and one that Giddens has missed, is that 'being constituted by everyday practice, structure is vulnerable to major changes in practice' (Maharaj 1995: 53). It is in this sense that Connell's 'gender regime is, at any historical moment, always in a dynamic process of constitution' or contestation (1987: 184–85; see also Collier 1998: 18).

Central to Connell's question of how gender relations are organised as an ongoing concern is the more difficult question of how individuals are to break out of the current gender order or regime (Maharaj 1995: 57). Key here is Connell's idea that while most men are the recipients of the 'patriarchal dividend' (the economic and social advantage that extends to all men in the overall gender order which guarantees, or is taken to guarantee, the dominant position of men and the subordination of women), not all men actually accord with, or live out, the hegemonic (heterosexual) masculine ideal (1987, 1995: 77–79). Indeed, the importance in coming to grips with men's relationships with other men is brought home particularly as 'one's standing and place is never secure' in the competition for hierarchy. Masculinity is something that is never attained but is something which must be constantly tested. It is somewhat ironic, as Dowd points out, that 'men, although powerful and empowered as a group, feel powerless; thus, they must strive to be a man everyday' (2008: 210; see for example Kaufman 1994). As Connell explains, the most emotionally powerful line of demarcation in the hierarchy of masculinities, although by no means the only one, is between heterosexual and homosexual masculinities (1998: 4).[8]

For Connell, the task facing many 'pro-feminist' men was that of instructing other men how to 'separate themselves from the mainstream masculinity with which they were familiar, and to reconstruct their personality to produce a new, non-sexist self' (1995: 130).[9] As Connell (2000: 3) put it:

> The new feminism of the 1970s not only gave a voice to women's concerns, it challenged all assumptions about the gender system and raised a series of problems about men. Over the decades since, the disturbance in the gender system caused by the women's movement has been felt by very large numbers of men.[10]

Although Connell was attempting to theorise the transformative potential of this 'crisis' in gender relations, it was acknowledged that even though some men may be 'committed to a real and far reaching politics of personality' (and are therefore 'serious' at 'being the Sensitive New Age Man'), they may be put in a 'double bind . . . with the men pressed on one principle to express emotions and on another to suppress them' (1995: 134). Accordingly, Connell argued that many men's attempts to reconstruct their relationships with women in their lives 'could easily be seen as acquiring a kind of femininity'. As Connell explains, 'the moment of separation from hegemonic masculinity' was both a 'goal' and a 'fear' because it basically 'involves choosing passivity' (1995: 132).

For Connell, the project of 'annihilating masculinity' was all the more difficult for those men who had 'formed a relationship with a strong woman who takes the initiative and supplies the energy'. Indeed, Connell offers that some men who may be very much attached to their masculinity (the 'intractability of emotional attachment' or the 'stickiness of cathexis'), may react by choosing to be aggressive and violent. According to Connell, these feelings of anger and aggression are understandable because they evoke 'emotional undercurrents from pre-Oedipal relationships . . . the primary relationship with the mother'. Connell explains that these feelings of anxiety are reminiscent of the 'primary scene' between mother and child during the Oedipal phase of separation. Thus, for Connell, the cause of men's desire for violence toward women cannot be separated from the way that this energy 'has unmistakable overtones of early relations with a mother'. In Connell's account, the 'project of having an open, non-assertive self' (when 'undo[ing] Oedipal masculinity') is to risk having no self at all; 'it courts annihilation' (1995: 136, 179). According to Connell (1995: 137):

> Oedipal masculinization structured the world and the self for them in gendered terms, as it does for most men. To undo masculinity is to court a loss of personality structure that may be quite terrifying: a kind of gender vertigo.

These passages raise some issues of concern about how the feminine figures and is figured by Connell's own reading of men's violence against women (or feminised men). In Connell's account, the experience of 'gender vertigo' manifests itself in the same way as a drama of 'hopeless love'. Accordingly, Connell argues that this is because passivity is 'a fact of our emotional lives', 'not because we cannot choose other attachments but because we cannot walk away from the consequences of past ones'. Thus, for Connell (1987: 212–13):

> [o]ne can only switch them off at a cost that for many people is intolerable, the cost of making a great void in every aspect of life. We know what this feels like for people who have suffered it involuntarily – the abandoned lover, the bereaved.

While it could be argued that Connell's thesis involves a significant degree of projection, what is also clear is that while there is abundant evidence to suggest masculinities are able to change, there is also evidence to suggest the contrary. But what is problematic about Connell's reading of men's desire for violence against women – a reading borrowed from the mythical structure of the story and text of Oedipus – can be seen as a problem with representations of violence more generally.

In her work on how 'representations of violence are inseparable from the notion of gender', that even when violence is 'deconstructed' as 'ideology' or according to Connell's thesis, 'myth', Italian feminist Teresa de Lauretis has shown that it follows that violence is always, already 'engendered in representation' (1984: 33). In her (re)reading of the story of Oedipus, de Lauretis observes that 'inscriptions of violence (and family violence) at that' are already woven into its representation of violence (1984: 44). Accordingly, she argued (de Lauretis 1984: 43) that all representations of violence draw on the same mythical structure (as Juri Lotman demonstrated with his theory of plot typology):

There are only two characters, the hero and the obstacle or
boundary. The first is the mythical subject, who moves through the
plot-space establishing differences and norms. The second is but a
function of that space, a marker of boundary, and therefore
inanimate even when anthropomorphized.

For de Lauretis (1984: 43–44), in the mythical text, there are two
predetermined speaking positions: one for '[t]he hero [who] must be male
regardless of the gender of the character' and the other for 'the obstacle'
who, 'whatever its personification (sphinx or dragon, sorceress or villain), is
morphologically female – and indeed, simply, the womb, the earth, the
space of his movement':

> As he crosses the boundary and "penetrates" the other space, the
> mythical subject is constructed as human being and as male; he is
> the active principle of culture, the establisher of distinction, the
> creator of differences. Female is what is not susceptible to
> transformation, to life or death; she (it) is an element of plot-space,
> a topos, a resistance, matrix and matter.

When Connell's thesis is read in light of this feminist work, we can see that it
is the narrative that sets up the structure of identification and that orders the
relation between the subject and object of that narrative; that is, *it is the
narrative* that discovers the cause of male anger and violence towards women
as the latent (if attenuated) result of a past history of childhood 'crisis'.

Over the past decade, masculinities scholars have debated the usefulness
of the concept of hegemony in theorising men's violence against women
(Hearn 1998, 2004) and, particularly, in the context of globalisation
and gender relations (Connell and Messerschmidt 2005; Beasley 2008;
Messerschmidt 2008) and the place of masculinities in international
politics and/or corporations (see for example Special Issue on 'Hegemonic
Masculinities in International Politics' in the June 2008 issue of *Men and
Masculinities*), but much of this discussion has taken place outside criminology. In the next section I begin with an overview of some of this
criticism in light of the 'masculinity turn' in the area of crime and criminology. This is intended to set the scene for the discussion that follows in the
next section, where I explore what is ostensibly the 'third stage' in thinking
about men and masculinities: the psychosocial approach.[11] This 'third stage'
integrates the 'narrative interview method' with a reading of some men's
violent behaviour as motivated by an array of unconscious 'anxieties and
desires producing psychological defences which are not only produced [eg

originate in childhood] but are necessary . . . but not without contradiction' (Collier 2004: 295).

The 'man question' in criminology

The question of how men and their masculinities are connected to crime and criminality has become a pressing issue for criminology – and indeed criminologists – to discover. As Collier has observed: '[t]he relationship between men, masculinities and crime is a now well-established feature of the criminological landscape' (2004: 285; see also Collier 1997, 1998, 2010a).[12] Indeed, the 'man question' has not only become a pressing issue within academic circles (Naffine 2003; Collier 2004, 2010a; Dowd 2008, 2010; Howe 2008), it has also informed a range of concerns and debates bearing on the substance and development of criminal justice policy and practice; ranging from work seeking to examine the relationship between separated fathers, family violence and family law reform (Collier 1995, Kaye and Tolmie 1998; Seuffert 1999; Collier and Sheldon 2006, 2008; Collier 2010b: 197–202) to the vastly growing literature calling for men to become involved in changing and/or challenging their own and other men's violence against women (and other men) through the facilitation of pro-feminist attitudes and violence prevention (Flood 2004, 2011; Flood et al 2010; Flood and Pease 2006, 2008, 2009; Pease 2002, 2003; Tarrant 2009). While it is not my intention to canvass this diverse body of scholarship here, in this section I wish to revisit some of the criticisms that have been made of other work or studies on men's violence that come from within criminology. Of particular importance here is the influence of two books, James Messerschmidt's *Masculinities and Crime* (1993) and Tim Newburn and Elizabeth Stanko's edited collection *Just Boys Doing Business* (1994), both of which strongly endorse the concept of hegemonic masculinity,[13] and which have foregrounded developments since the 1990s in criminology's debates about 'masculinities and crime' (Collier 1998: 18, 2004: 287).

Crime as a 'mantle' for manhood? Messerschmidt's structured action theory

James Messerschmidt's 'structured action' framework (1993, 1997, 2000) has been highly influenced by the work of Connell (1987, 1995) and the concept of hegemonic masculinity. Messerschmidt was also influenced by Giddens's structuration theory (1991, 1976) and the 'doing gender' approach, which emphasises the idea of gender as a situated social and interactional accomplishment (Goffman 1979; West and Zimmerman 1987; West and

Fenstermaker 1993; Fenstermaker and West 2002). Although Messerschmidt is not overly sympathetic towards feminist scholarship, his work nonetheless took up a number of key insights from feminist research since the 1970s (eg Smart 1978; Heidensohn 1985; Stanko 1994) that had successfully begun to address the 'masculinity' of crime and also to explore the failure of criminology to adequately theorise women's offending (Edwards 2006: 58–60). Messerschmidt was interested in 'the way social action is linked to structured possibilities/constraints' and 'how the class, race, and gendered relations in society constrain and enable the social activity of young men' in the schoolyard and how this 'activity' in turn relates to crime (1994: 81–82). Following Katz (1988), Messerschmidt (1993, 1997) cites robbery as the crime that epitomises the criminal activity *par excellence* through which working-class men attempt to assert their masculinity. Proceeding from the position that crime is a 'mantle' for manhood, Messerschmidt argues that '"[b]oys will be boys" depending upon their position in social structures and, therefore, upon their access to power and resources' (1994: 82). Moreover, just as schoolboys who are unable to prove themselves physically and sexually by conventional means sometimes do so abusively (Messerschmidt 2000), 'wife-beating can serve as a situational resource for constructing a "damaged" patriarchal masculinity through which a man's right to dominate his wife and sexually possess her can be reaffirmed'. In Messerschmidt's account, men experiencing powerlessness in the labour market sometimes choose marital rape as a suitable resource for asserting themselves as 'real men'. Accordingly, Messerschmidt investigates how both sexual and assaultive violence by adolescent males against women and other young men 'may be accountable practices for "doing masculinity"' (1999: 199). The net result was a criminological theory that focuses on how crime serves as a 'suitable resource' for doing (accomplishing) masculinities 'when other resources' that 'are determined by social structures' are unavailable (Messerschmidt 1993: 143–50).

There is little doubt that Messerschmidt's attempt 'to integrate the complexities of race, class, gender and sexuality, and to take structural patterns of inequality seriously' has had a major impact on the criminological literature on masculinities and crime (Collier 2004: 291; see for example Kersten 1996; Polk 1994). But as some critics have explained, Messerschmidt's theory is limited by being both 'tautological' and methodologically 'flawed' (Walklate 1995: 181; Jefferson 1997a; Hood-Williams 2001; Edwards 2006: 60). These criticisms aside, Messerschmidt's account 'that men choose violence against women as a means of achieving a positive masculine identity, albeit in circumstances limited by the structures of labour, power and cathexis' has provided a particularly useful tool for theorising men's crime and violence. As Collier discusses, Messerschmidt's theory of men 'accomplishing' masculinity through their involvement in crime, has been applied to 'diverse crimes [such] as burglary, rape, the sexual abuse of children, the taking of motor vehicles without consent, corporate crime, football "hooliganism", state terrorism, traffic offences, "road rage", violence towards other men, and so forth' (1998: 20). For Collier, however, the sheer breadth and diversity of accounts of men 'accomplishing' masculinity through their involvement in crime is 'asking a great deal of the concept masculinity'. Accordingly, Collier argues that '[w]hat men are not seen as "doing" is a masculinity which might in any sense be interpreted as "positive"' (1998: 20; see also Edwards 2006: 60–62). Indeed, there is 'a certain rigidity in how men are seen to accomplish the attributes of dominant masculinity' (Collier 2004: 292).

The limitations that inhere in the work of the 'leading exponent of "second stage" thinking on masculinities in criminology' (Hood-Williams 2001: 39), and 'that enabled Messerschmidt to infer that the majority of western men consider violence against female partners to be a socially acceptable, even celebrated, way of "doing gender"' (Gadd 2002: 63), have led some critics to question whether his work has done little more than provide violent men with a selection of discourses through which to deny, excuse, rationalise or justify their behaviour (Hearn 1998; Gadd 2000: 430, 2002: 63). This has led to a further questioning of whether the term 'masculinities' adds anything to the analysis of criminal events.

The argument that Messerschmidt's account of the concept of masculinity has primarily been 'deployed as an empty tautology signifying nothing more than (some of) the things that men and boys do' has been explored by Hood-Williams (2001: 39). Hood-Williams stresses that the idea that particular types of crime can provide an alternative resource for accomplishing gender when other masculine resources are available 'is implausible and logically flawed' (2001: 39). What is left unexplored, for Hood-Williams, is why it is that this only occurs on 'certain occasions' and in 'certain contexts' (Messerschmidt 1993: 84). Hood-Williams demonstrates that 'he cannot say *which* men or why it is that only *particular* men reach for this resource'. Moreover, it is not entirely clear 'what defines these occasions'. Why, for instance, 'do only a minority of men summon crime when their masculinity is threatened? Should we suppose that the majority of non-criminal men have never had the essential nature of their masculinity questioned and so have never needed recourse to crime?' Accordingly, Hood-Williams argues that 'the basic assumption here, that crime is explicable as an expression of masculinity, is implausible' (2001: 44). Indeed, as other critics have demonstrated, it would appear that, on the one hand, 'hegemonic masculinity is an unambiguously positive attribute for men in the sense that it is, for a host of (unexplored) psychological imperatives, something which is desired, to be achieved, to be accomplished'. On the other hand, 'the cultural valorization of hegemonic masculinity would appear to correlate strongly with – if it is not inherently interlinked to – various destructive, violent ways of "being a man"' (Collier 2004: 293). As such, the possibility of a more complex model of masculinity tends to be effaced in Messerschmidt's criminological theory.

In contrast, and applauding Messerschmidt's analysis as 'a significant advance on early radical feminist explanations, without in any way letting masculinity off the hook', Tony Jefferson has suggested, in his interpretation of the life and times of Mike Tyson (1996b, 1997b), that masculinity may not be explained only by reference to the sociological categories of race, class and sex conceived of as divisions within a social structure (1996a: 340–41). Accordingly, Jefferson argues, through an engagement with what he describes as 'the third stage in thinking about masculinities and crime' – a body of work I discuss in more detail below – that there is a need to move beyond a focus on the 'social' toward recognition of a psychologically complex subject for whom the meanings of masculinity cannot be confined to generally oppressive and negative lists of traits or characteristics (1997a: 542–44). In contrast to Messerschmidt's deployment of 'a rational, unitary but self-interested subject operating in a structurally unequal society' (Jefferson 1994, 1997a: 543; Gadd 2000: 430), Jefferson's work signals a significant departure from this 'social psychological notion of "identity", i.e. accomplished, coherent and unified' to one that gives attention to 'the complexities of men's experiences' by foregrounding the tensions between the social and psychic dimensions of masculinity (1994, 1997a: 544–47) without which 'it is not possible to *explain* why most men do not accomplish masculinity through violence' (Gadd 2002: 65, original emphasis).

The psychosocial approach

What has been characterised as 'third stage' thinking about the relationship between masculinities and crime promises to be a 'highly sophisticated alternative to second stage thinking' (Hood-Williams 2001: 38) and is illustrated by the work of Tony Jefferson writing alone (1994, 1996a, 1996b, 1997a, 1997b, 1998, 2002a, 2002b, 2004) and with Wendy Hollway (Hollway and Jefferson 1997, 1998, 1999, 2000a, 2000b), and more recently with David Gadd (Gadd and Jefferson 2007a, 2007b). Focusing on the individual violent offender, Jefferson's work represents an effort to (re)create a sociologically literate psychoanalytic or psychosocial approach to men's violence and, in doing so, effect a shift in thinking to a different level. It is, first and foremost, intended as a 'corrective' to early feminist thinking since the 1970s that, according to Jefferson, has failed to account adequately for the complex relationship that exists between masculinities and violence. If the 'one-dimensional' or 'Hyde-like' portraits of 'normal masculinity' offered up by radical feminism – read as oppressive, violent, powerful, controlling: the evil male 'other' to the female's essential goodness – failed to be challenged by second wave feminists (socialist feminists and women of colour), then the problem for 'straight' and 'pro-feminist' and 'gay' men who were also taking up 'the challenge to "do something" about the problem of male violence', by taking 'masculinity seriously', was that these portraits were ones in which many men 'struggled to recognize themselves' (Jefferson 1996a: 338–39). Accordingly, Jefferson argued that while Connell's notion of hegemonic masculinity – a range of masculinities structured in dominance to an ideal against which a series of alternative, subordinate masculinities competed – provided part of the answer,[14] it was Messerschmidt's attempt to rethink the relationship between 'masculinities and crime' that can be counted as the most 'sophisticated' and 'significant advance on early radical feminist explanations'. By identifying the points at which 'class and race relations combine to reduce conventional opportunities for the accomplishment of hegemonic masculinity, crime offers a ready replacement', Messerschmidt's approach constituted an 'original and imaginative attempt to come to grips with some very difficult theoretical issues'; it did not, however, provide 'the whole explanation' (Jefferson 1996a: 340).

Advocating a shift in emphasis from 'structure' to 'discourse' (Gadd and Jefferson 2007b: 42–43), the psychosocial approach to masculinities and crime can also be understood as a corrective to early masculinities theory that seeks to explain why most men accomplish masculinity without being violent. Here Jefferson makes use of 'developments in social theory outside criminology ... principally those associated with the term poststructuralism and with contemporary psychoanalysis, especially the work of Lacan, Klein and Object Relations theory'. Once again, however, we are told that while feminists have been foregrounding questions of feminine subjectivity they have failed adequately to theorise masculine subjectivity and, in doing so, remained caught within what is for Jefferson the 'deterministic impasse' that characterises Foucauldian discourse analysis more generally. Accordingly, Jefferson proposes to 'avoid reducing subjects to an effect of discourse',[15] necessitating a '(re)turn to psychoanalysis' (Jefferson 1996a: 341, 1997a: 540). In Jefferson's account, the seeds of the psychosocial approach are to be found in the work of Henriques and colleagues in *Changing the Subject*, published in 1984, and the work of one of the authors, Wendy Hollway's *Subjectivity and Method in Psychology* (1989) (Jefferson 1994: 24–28). Building on their critique of the 'rational unitary subject', which for Jefferson is implicit within Messerschmidt's determinist structured action model (Collier 2004: 294), Jefferson is keen to develop a more complex understanding of what motivates particular men to commit crime. The focus of analysis shifts from an emphasis on individual subjects as simply the products of discourse to the way that individuals are 'located within a variety of discursive relations . . . "the subject is composed of, or exists as, a set of multiple and contradictory positioning or subjectivities"' (Henriques et al 1984: 204, cited in Jefferson 1994: 25).

The key question for Jefferson is 'what motivates people to "choose" to invest in or identify with one discursive position rather than another' (1994: 25; see also Gadd and Jefferson 2007b: 43–46)? Borrowing from Henriques et al's reworking of Lacanian psychoanalysis and Hollway's more social reading of Klein, which shows 'how the defence mechanisms of splitting and projection are constantly implicated in the inter-subjective management of anxiety; and finally by illustrating how "the continuous, attempt to manage anxiety, to protect oneself . . . provides a continuous, more or less driven, motive for the negotiation of power relations"' (Hollway 1989: 85, cited in Jefferson 1994: 26), Jefferson's answer lies in his theorising of masculine subjectivity which takes place 'via the notion of a dynamic unconscious with hidden desires'. As such, this approach promises to 'prise open the possibility of making sense of the contradictions and difficulties that particular men experience in becoming masculine' (1994: 28–29). Accordingly, Jefferson argues: '[w]ithout this sensitivity to the difficulties of uniting social and psychic processes – often pulling in different directions – it is not possible to theorize masculinity in a way that men will recognize' (1994: 29). By integrating the 'biographical interpretive' or 'life history' or 'narrative interview' method (Hollway and Jefferson 1997, 2000a, 2000b; Gadd 2000; Jefferson 2002a; Gadd and Jefferson 2007b: 61–68), the net result is a more sophisticated and methodologically advanced account of the anxious defended subject who facilitates violence in a way that makes 'subjectivity and the role of the unconscious central, but without losing grip on the social' (Jefferson 1996b: 154, 1997a: 539, 2002b: 73–74).

For Jefferson, 'identifications of "individuals" with certain discursive positions defend against feelings of anxiety or lack, and are hence *empowering*' (Hollway 1989, cited in Gadd 2002: 65, original emphasis). In his work on Mike Tyson, for instance, by deploying the psychoanalytic presumption of a defended, fragmented subject, anxiously managing (repressing, splitting and projecting) thoughts, feelings and memories that threaten the integrity of the self' (Gadd 2000: 43), Jefferson offers 'a more complex plurality of aggressor and victim positions' (Gadd 2002: 65). In the next section I discuss Jefferson's depiction of the 'emotional truth' of the life and times of the infamous individual, Mike Tyson, who was so overwhelmed by his unconscious attempts to ward off a whole host of childhood anxieties that he ended up being sentenced to 10 years' imprisonment for one charge of rape and two charges of criminal deviatory conduct involving a woman victim in 1992 (Jefferson 1996b, 1997b). In doing so, I pause to reflect on some disingenuous effects of Jefferson's own narrative.

The anxious, defended male: a search for the emotional 'truth'

The aim of Jefferson's psychoanalytic reading is to move towards 'a more definitive' biographical account of the life of boxing champion, Mike Tyson, that can account for the ways in which 'psychic processes are not unique to each individual, but are shared and therefore socially underpinned' (1996b: 154). Jefferson begins his account by promising to deliver 'a particular understanding of subjectivity and its transformations' (1996b: 153) and, in doing so, explain Tyson's conviction for rape in 1992, a crime for which he was sentenced to 10 years' imprisonment. Accordingly, Jefferson argues that the rape can be (re)read as motivated by 'an attempt to master' his 'own anxieties and fears', which he 'projected' onto a another person (1997a: 547); in this instance, a woman.[16]

From the very beginning, Jefferson's reading makes clear that boxing is an activity that confers masculinity and also power to individual men. Moreover, 'choosing passivity' – failing to fight back when bullied by older boys at school – is crucial to Jefferson's interpretation of Tyson's 'unconscious' motivation to engage in activities that involve violence such as boxing and later gang behaviour and theft (1996b: 161). According to Jefferson, the 'undoubted "pull"' that attracts so many 'young, disadvantaged ghetto males' to boxing is owed to the idea that boxing is not simply 'a specific form of courageous violence' (1997b: 162). Citing Wacquant, Jefferson describes boxing as 'a true "blood sport" . . . [and] . . . fistic trade that puts a high premium on physical toughness and the ability to withstand – as well as dish out – pain and bodily arm [sic]'. Accordingly, it follows that '[t]he *specific honour* of the pugilist, like that of the ancient gladiator, consists in refusing to concede and kneel down'.[17]

Proceeding to discuss the significance of the various 'transformations' that took place during Tyson's life, it is also clear that these can be read as 'evidence' of Tyson's desire to move out of 'passivity', which he does by identifying with subject positions that confer masculinity – such as the 'bad' or 'tough' boy subject position – rather than those that confer femininity – such as the 'good' or 'fairy' boy subject position (1996b: 159).

The first transformation in Tyson's subjectivity took place during his early days, which were plagued with 'feelings of confusion' and were due to 'multiple sources':

> ...chronic poverty; an absent father; a mother who could not cope, who drank and who fought with her boyfriend; ...a genetic endowment that gave him [Tyson] a body and a head too big and bulky for either his years or his soft, lisping voice.
>
> (Jefferson 1996b: 155)

These factors produced the 'kind of combination' of feelings in the young Tyson that led him to be 'a constant target of bullying' (Jefferson 1996b: 155). As the above extract illustrates, Tyson's vulnerability stemmed from having a big head and a 'soft, lisping voice'. The implication is that, although Tyson physically appeared 'hyper masculine', he sounded feminine.

Following this early period of 'passivity', we are told that Tyson was involved in a series of activities during adolescence such as being a 'gang member' and a 'thief'. Tyson's motivation for engaging in such activities is understood by Jefferson as further 'evidence' that his 'feelings of confusions' were becoming insurmountable. Jefferson explains how this period of 'anxiety' was 'central' to and for 'understanding ... the young Tyson' as it signified the first and crucial transformation in Tyson's life when he no longer identified with the subject position of the 'fairy boy' (1996b: 155, 159).

At this point, it is worth saying something about Jefferson's own narrative, for it is one that is centred on an anxious and fragile young man who has been shown the rewards that come from being 'active' in the world (he joins a gang, consorts with thieves and so on), rather than what happens when one remains 'passive' (appearing to sound like a woman is equated with the apparently untenable position of the feminine). The pivotal moment that marks the turning point in this narrative as significant and that prompts Jefferson to conclude that the 'young Tyson' had moved on from his early 'passive days', is described as 'the infamous pigeon incident'. This incident involved Tyson punching a 'sadistic bully' who had ripped 'the head off one of Tyson's beloved pigeons' (Jefferson 1996b: 155).[18] Commenting how, on this occasion, an 'enraged Tyson turned and fought back' is for Jefferson 'in terms of anxiety', 'evidence' that 'Tyson's feelings of vulnerability and powerlessness' were becoming 'overwhelming, insupportable' but only temporarily 'assuaged in the fight back' (1996b: 159). Indeed, this moment in which Tyson finally 'fought back' is crucial for Jefferson's representation of the formulaic structure of the narrative, which so far has confirmed the 'social rewards' that inhere in the 'bad boy' subject position with which Tyson had apparently begun to identify at this point in his life (1996b: 160).

Jefferson's representation of this first sequence of events in Tyson's life is one in which he claims to 'discover' the cause of Tyson's later delinquent behaviour as located in a past history of feeling insulted during childhood; that is, in feeling named (and positioned) as like a woman (he was bullied at school, he had a head that was too big for his body, a soft, lisping voice and so on). 'Passivity', however, only has meaning in the sense that it carries with it the connotation of 'homosexuality' and, relatedly, as an object of penile penetration, one is rendered a 'passive' receptacle, *like a woman*. Having delineated the episodes of Tyson's life within this first narrative sequence (being bullied at school and later being a 'gang member' and a 'thief'), we must remember it is in retrospect that these events are construed as 'evidence' of Tyson's desire for a discursive positioning that is conferring of masculinity.

It is at this point in Tyson's life that he has, according to Jefferson, been shown 'the importance of social rewards ("empowerment") attaching to the bad boy image'. Accordingly, Jefferson argues that when Tyson's motivation to invest in the subject position of the 'bad boy' is (re)read through the 'tough guy' discourse, Tyson shifts from being an 'object' to a 'subject' of discourse (1996b: 160). When this same subject position – the 'bad boy' or 'tough guy' – is configured through the 'good/evil' discourse (as it has erroneously been construed by radical or victim feminism), Tyson's propensity for violence ends up (mis)interpreted as the acts of an abstracted subject who is no more and no less than the devalued term in a binary pair: 'woman-as-victim/-as-agent, man-as-oppressor/-as-guilty' (Jefferson 1997b: 282).

All becomes clear when it is explained that Tyson's subjectivity undergoes a second transformation that takes place during a time in Tyson's life when his psyche was split between two conflicting personae – between remaining a 'bully boy' and becoming 'Iron Mike', the 'compleat destroyer' (1996b: 160). Having already taken his 'first transforming step away from his passive withdrawn identity' (from 'little fairy boy' to 'bully' and then 'thief'), the 'second crucial step was his take-up of boxing at the age of 13' (Jefferson 1996b: 161). Drawing on French sociologist, Loïc Wacquant's 'brilliant portrayal of the boxer's world "from the native point of view"', and by concentrating on some of boxing's discursive meanings, Jefferson's more empathetic reading is one that 'understands' how boxing 'became meaningful to Tyson' (1996b: 161). Here, Jefferson makes use of Wacquant's distinction between 'the cowardly violence of the wife-beater' and 'the specific honour of the pugilist', which 'like that of the ancient gladiator, consists in refusing to concede and kneel down' (1993: 8, cited in Jefferson 1996b: 162). For Jefferson, 'the advantages boxing held out to' Tyson were both 'social' and 'psychic rewards ... a way of resolving the complex contradictions around "good/bad" and black/white by enabling him to be both good and bad simultaneously' (Jefferson 1996b: 162). Accordingly, Jefferson argues that '[w]ithout some notion of the "psychic release"', it is 'hard to understand' the 'burning intensity' of 'the commitment of some working-class males [such as Tyson] to becoming a boxer [like Muhammad Ali and Malcolm X]' (Jefferson 1996b: 163). This is only possible once we understand both sides of the picture: 'Tyson the bully boy on his way to becoming "Iron Mike", the "compleat destroyer" and what was also happening to the "little fairy boy"'. This requires us, argues Jefferson, to look further at 'Tyson's occasional passivity in the ring' that could only be 'temporarily' assuaged by the 'fight-back'. Apparently, Tyson's 'overwhelming passivity' that caused him to lose two important fights was 'conjoined' with 'fear' and a 'deep-rooted anxiety' that he was 'alone, unloved, and quite possibly unlovable' (Jefferson 1996b: 163–64). Although boxing offered Tyson an outlet through which to resolve 'the psychic anxiety underpinning ... [his] feared passivity', by 'destroying another man', we are also told that the signs were all there to show that his passivity might be 'fatal' (Jefferson 1996b: 165).

It would also appear that Tyson's (repressed) fears of 'passivity' could not be confined to the boxing ring. Not only was Tyson 'ill-equipped to deal with the fame and fortune that accompanies the heavyweight championships', he was beset by '[a]llegations of sexual assault by angry women, a stormy, short-lived marriage, brawling, the deaths of those closest to him ... the list goes on and on'. Having 'already lost his crown' (and presumably a good portion of his masculinity at this point), he was also struggling 'amidst constant media stories of a man careering out of control'. Then, we are told, 'came his downfall event: the sensational rape trial ... conviction and six-year gaol sentence'. Once again, the psychosocial approach assists Jefferson to catalogue 'the psychic roots of social "rage"' (Jefferson 1996b: 166) and better understand how Tyson's acts can be understood as inextricably linked to a desperate struggle to become masculine (Collier 1997). The task that Jefferson sets for himself is that of understanding whether there is 'a deeper, emotional truth' of 'the date that became a rape' behind the 'truth' of the legal discourse that pronounced Tyson 'guilty' (Jefferson 1997b: 287).

Not surprisingly, Jefferson begins by reiterating the inadequacies of radical feminist theorising, which is responsible for the current confusion that surrounds whether 'date-rape' is 'real-rape'. From this it follows that the 'problem with all these discourses on rape, traditional, feminist or legal' is that they 'assume too unitary and rational a subject (woman-as-victim/-as-agent, man-as-oppressor/-as-guilty) to capture the emotional confusions, inconsistencies and contradictions that lie behind human behaviour, especially where sexuality is somehow implicated' (Jefferson 1997b: 282). Jefferson promises to do 'justice to these more difficult, truths of the event' and, in doing so, offer an account of the 'rape' that totally downplays and ignores feminist accounts of male power and elevates instead the idea that it is a manifestation of psyches that are 'split', beset by 'tensions, conflicts and contradictions', 'held ambivalently', that is 'key' to understanding what really happened (Jefferson 1997b: 289).

According to Jefferson's representation of Tyson's story, it was one in which Tyson identified with both the 'super-stud' and 'being excessive' subject positions (Jefferson 1997b: 290). Tyson's motivation for investing in these two subject positions was as a result of 'the constant need to defend against feelings of powerlessness or anxiety'. Jefferson then poses the question of 'how else can we explain the desperately driven nature of the superstud's desire to fuck'. The answer is not, as Jefferson assures us, to be found in 'the law's "either/or" binarism'; rather, it lies in 'the "both/and" of psychoanalytic thinking' (Jefferson 1997b: 292). Jefferson suggests there are two things worth pondering about the evidence that was led at the trial: first, 'the meaning of laughter'; and, secondly, 'the notion that "no means yes"'. Proceeding from the view that 'meaning' is 'rarely straightforward', or at least not as straightforward as the law would have us believe, Jefferson proposes that the jury's verdict endorsed 'the either/or decision about the (legal) truth' as exemplified by the narrative mobilised by the prosecution. Apparently, during one of their exchanges, Tyson told Washington that he liked 'girls who say no' and laughed when he said it. According to Jefferson, when 'taken at face value' one would be forgiven for thinking that Tyson was simply a man who enjoyed 'rough sex, and mistakenly believes that she does too, or he is a sadistic bully'. But when understood 'from a psychoanalytic perspective', laughter can also 'signify a certain underlying nervousness or anxiety' and comments such as 'no means yes' can be understood as 'powerful, almost formulaic, masculinist' fantasies within a 'certain discourse of sexuality' (Jefferson 1997b: 291–92). Accordingly, Jefferson argues that 'fear of rejection' is transformed 'into the positive come-on; thus, it is important to hang on to both elements; to interpret this moment in terms of an unconscious attempt by Tyson to ward off anxiety as well as an example of his sadism'. As Jefferson reminds us, this more empathetic interpretation is one that has effectively replaced 'the law's "either/or" binarism' with 'the "both/and" of psychoanalytic thinking' (Jefferson 1997b: 292).

Let us not forget that Tyson is also alleged to have said 'you love me now, don't you' and 'don't fight me, mummy' in the moments prior to raping his victim. According to Jefferson's sympathetic reading, 'when (re)read through the discourse of (uncertain) love and (craved) intimacy' rather than through the lens of the radical feminist discourse of 'sexual conquest', Tyson's first comment can be understood as reflecting his 'confused thoughts around love and sex' and thwarted desire for intimacy. Moreover, the 'reference to mummy', we are told, 'is a slip of the tongue revealing an unconscious elision of the mother and other . . . a plea to have his infantile needs gratified, even if he has to take them by force'. All of this, Jefferson reminds us, 'reveals Tyson's similarity to, rather than his difference from, many men' (Jefferson 1997b: 292).

Not surprisingly, Jefferson has less to say about Washington's story and her 'ambivalence' but, according to his 'rough mapping of the salient discourses', this is only because he does not possess 'either a reservoir of similar experiences from which [he] might attempt an empathetic account of her discursive choices or sufficient indirect knowledge of being young, black and female in small-town Mid-America'; thus, he can only 'speculate about some of her identifications' because 'she was less of a public figure than Tyson' and therefore 'we know less about' her (Jefferson 1997b: 292). However, first we are told that Washington's story begins when she left behind her 'small-town' roots ('where she was a charming, friendly, popular, church-going beauty queen, with lots of friends and boyfriends') to make it in the 'big city'. Here her character is construed as naively unaware that her ambition to be a successful beauty queen meant that she inhabited a discursively incompatible subject-position, one that was construed through two discourses: the 'small-town provincial' discourse and the 'good time in the city' discourse:

> . . . the local beauty queen represents both the socially acceptable and doubtless proud expression of small-town sexuality ('our' girls are lovelier than yours), and the 'dangerous' stuff of subterranean male fantasies of sexual desire.
>
> (Jefferson 1997b: 293)

Next we are told that '[i]t is likely that the discourse of romance was also relevant', no doubt impacting on her investment in this subject-position but affecting how she would have been perceived by others, particularly men she met on the beauty queen circuit. Hence, the discourse of romance 'provided a unifying threat of sorts':

> The small-town girl moves to the bright lights and the city, achieving some fame, reward and recognition through a 'career' as a beauty queen, before romance and marriage herald her to return to her 'little house on the prairie' and the discourse of 'small-town provincial'.
>
> (Jefferson 1997b: 293)

According to Jefferson all three discourses (the 'small-town provincial', the 'good time in the city' and the romance discourses) are crucially important for highlighting the contradictions inherent in Washington's investment in her subject-position as each would have impacted on her decision to leave her 'small town' roots and make it in the 'big city'. Ultimately, however, we are to understand that it was the discourse of romance that provided a 'way of squaring the circle of conflicting accounts' that surrounded the reporting of the trial (Jefferson 1997b: 293).

On the one hand, Washington's character is narrated by Jefferson as that of 'a highly competitive beauty queen', who, despite being sexually assaulted, 'carried on competing after the rape because she was not a "quitter"' (Jefferson 1997b: 294). On the other hand, Jefferson explains, she had immersed herself in the 'heavily sexualized culture' of the beauty conquest in which 'to display' one's 'semi-naked' body is at some level willingly to treat oneself as a commodity (Jefferson 1997b: 294). At this point, we can see the creation of a key character in Jefferson's own narrative; one who is naive, ambitious, savvy and who ultimately brought the situation upon herself: she willingly agreed to a 'date' with Tyson; she regarded him as a 'sign of victory', as a way to achieve 'fame, however fleeting'; she also admitted she was 'flattered' by Tyson's invitation (1997b: 293–94). What is being hinted at here is made abundantly clear when he says: '[w]hichever way we think of Washington's acceptance of the date invitation, then, it would appear to hinge on her suppressing part of what she "knew" thereby overriding her doubts' (Jefferson 1997b: 294). While Jefferson concedes 'that Washington did not have sex on her mind when contemplating her date with Tyson', the 'assumption of agency on her part' – that she would be able to decide whether or not she wanted to have sex when the time came – meant she was an unwitting 'product of contemporary feminism', a testimony 'to her foolishness when viewed through the prism of masculinist common sense' (Jefferson 1997b: 296).

Consider the final abridged version of Jefferson's own narrative (Jefferson 1997b: 296), where he concedes Tyson's similarity to many men:

> It might have been a really beautiful evening. Tyson might have wined, dined, talked, danced and then charmed her into bed, after showering her with the kind of adoring attention that few of us, needy creatures that we are, can resist or willingly forego. His main motive may well have been sexual gratification ... Her main motivation might well have been different: perhaps to be 'special', if only for a night...

And further (1997b: 296–97).:

> ... [m]any successful dates are replete with such a mixture of motives, hypocrisy and self-deception, to say nothing of the confusion of feelings engendered ... [l]ike any and every man, he makes a pass ... She recoils...

One might be forgiven for wondering if Jefferson's empathetic reading is one in which he unconsciously identifies with Tyson.

Other criticisms have emerged of this particular strand of work on masculinity as it has developed in the area of crime and criminology. For these critics, the psychosocial approach can be found to 'stand in an uneasy relation to some essential conceptualizations of masculinity' (Collier 2004: 297, 2010a: 43; Hood-Williams 2001).[19] In terms expressed by Collier, while both the structured action account and psychosocial readings 'are clearly concerned with ... questions of power and politics', masculinity, whether 'accomplished' (in Messerschmidt's account) or 'performed' (in Jefferson's more poststructuralist account) ... 'continues to be deployed as a "reference point" against which a range of behaviour and identities might be evaluated'. Of relevance for Collier is the insight by McMahon (1993, 1999) that a marked feature of this approach is that the psyches of violent men are fragile and plagued by widespread feelings of insecurity and anxiety, troubled childhoods and a deep seated ambivalence to women (which can also translate to feminists and feminism more generally – or indeed any object perceived by a man to be unmanly or feminine) in their lives. For McMahon, this argument makes it possible to read the acts of violent men in a tragic light. It becomes not only possible to speak of the 'burdens of masculinity', but to speak of men as, at least through this psychoanalytic frame, 'at a disadvantage compared to women'. It also makes it possible to position men as the more vulnerable sex, because they have more problems with emotional attachment than do women and, as a result, are more likely to react with aggression and violence to perceived slights to their masculinity. Moreover, such accounts either 'implicitly or explicitly, construct a female "other" who is not emotionally damaged'. Rather, 'her emotional potential is intact, her emotional needs are acknowledged' (McMahon 1993: 688, 1999). As Collier explains, what is then effaced is the question of whether men should change their behaviour, of men's social power relative to women, and of men's individual and collective interest in maintaining present gender relations (2004: 298), a point I shall revisit in the concluding remarks in this chapter.

For present purposes, we can apply McMahon's insight to Jefferson's (re) reading of the biography of Mike Tyson, whose construction of the female 'other' is arguably one in which she ends up (re)positioned within Jefferson's own narrative as a culpable subject.[20] This point has been made much more strongly by Howe, who argues that: 'Jefferson's call for a focus on the troubled psyches of violent men has a number of disturbing effects', not the least of which is that in opening up the 'life-histories' of violent men it completely loses sight of – indeed ignores – the violence and suffering they inflict on the body of the victim (2008: 136–42). For Howe, a profound lack of empathy with women and an individualistic focus of attention on the 'insecure, vulnerable, anxious' man characterises the psychosocial approach (2008: 140).[21] This has led Collier to wonder whether all we are really 'dealing with here is little more than a reflection of the researcher's own projections (no more, or less, plausible than any other reading' (2010a: 42).[22] I couldn't agree more.

Despite the above criticisms of the psychodiscursive approach, what is also clear is that, in seeking to 'appreciate' the emotional ambivalence and contradictory nature of men's experiences over and above structured action theory, it has some political purchase (Collier 2004: 295). Critical of the tendency for Jefferson's readings of Tyson to rely on 'secondary' sources, 'notably media accounts and biographies written by a handful of aca-demically inclined journalists and psychotherapists', Gadd has argued, for instance, that by keeping 'in sight the psychic complexity' that comprises one man's 'experience' (eg Mike Tyson's), Jefferson ends up avoiding implying that all men, or all violent men, are quintessentially the same (eg violent) (2002: 66). The key point here for Gadd at least is the importance of showing how particular men take up 'discursive positions that represent themselves as different from violent, dangerous men'. In his discussion of the 'case histories' of four violent men he interviewed, Gadd concedes that '[]their female partners may have experienced these men's behaviours as part of a continuum of abuse', but suggests it is 'unlikely' that these men would have been able to do anything about it, such as, for instance, take responsibility for the violent acts they inflicted on their female victims. Apparently, this is because they would have been unable to 'recognize' their behaviour as violent since, we are given to assume, these violent men were so busy in their desperate struggle to identify as masculine (2003: 350).[23] On the one hand, the psychodiscursive approach and its positing of a 'defended subject' would appear to have developed a more 'sophisticated' or 'advanced' explanation for 'why brutal violence can emerge from apparently trivial disagreements and why so many men find their partner's emotionality so intolerable but are unable to face up to the emotionally charged nature of their own aggression' (Gadd 2003: 351). On the other hand, we are also asked to accept, on the basis that Gadd's observations 'fit neatly within the psychodiscursive approach', that we are one step away from developing a progressive politics of changing violent men (2003: 351, 2000: 430). As Gadd has argued, 'if we are also serious about pursuing the long road towards change among men we will have to engage with men's experiences at both social and psychic levels, pulling apart the issue of subjectivity as it relates to individuals' biographies and/or "criminal careers"' (2002: 75).

A key insight from within masculinities scholarship is that there is abundant evidence that men and masculinities are capable of change (Connell 2005; Dobash et al 2000; Kimmel 1987; Gadd 2004). However, many critics have also observed that the agenda for equality is much less clear (Ruxton 2004; Flood 2004). Over the past 10 years, there has been a growing focus on the vital role men can and do play in feminism (Segal 1990; Pease 1997, 2000; Tarrant 2009). There have been numerous efforts around the world to involve men and boys in the prevention of violence against women (Ferguson et al 2003; Jalmert 2003; Flood 2002–2003, 2005–2006). A growing consensus in violence prevention circles is that, to end this violence, it must involve men (Flood 2002–2003, 2011; Pease 2008a).[24] This idea that men should be involved in violence prevention work has become institutionalised in the philosophies of many international organisations (Flood et al 2010). In the Australian context, Pease has noted the recent shift within government organisations such as VicHealth from focusing on men as perpetrators of violence to involving them as partners in primary prevention (2008a: 39).

The concept of attitudes has also been an important component of campaigns to address men's violence against women (Flood and Pease 2008, 2009; Taylor and Mouzos 2006; Pease 2008b; Victorian Health Promotion Foundation 2009). Some efforts to shift attitudes that condone violence against women and children have been more focused on the role of education and the specific experiences of victims.[25] Since the growth of the women's movement and feminist activism, there has also been an explosion in campaigns that focus on education and attitudinal change among men and boys (World Health Organisation 2007).[26] As Flood and Pease have argued, such '[i]nterventions must address not only those attitudes which are overtly condoning of violence against women, but the wider social norms related to gender and sexuality which normalize and justify this violence' (2008: 558). However, as Dowd has also observed, within much of the masculinities scholarship, there is 'a position of despair' over whether men themselves are able to embrace equality given that so many men have much to 'gain from the perpetuation of their dominant position' (2008: 208).

Clearly, feminist analysis has much to learn from masculinities scholarship by, for example, 'de-essentializing men' in their work. At the same time, Dowd argues, masculinities theorists can benefit from 're-energizing the commitment to explore male power and strategize undermining that power and collaborating with as well as support women' (2008: 248). However, my assessment of much of this work harks back to an insight made by Smart more than 20 years ago. Smart warned of the dangers inherent in the 'quest for a feminist jurisprudence ... which seeks to replace one hierarchy of truth with another' (1989: 88–89). Just as Smart reminded us then that 'it is the law's power to define and to disqualify which should become the focus of feminist strategy rather than law reform as such' (1989: 164), I would argue that there is a similar power struggle going on around who gets to define the relationship between men, masculinities and male violence: masculinities theorists or feminist theorists. But as Howe quite rightly points out: 'talking about that massively resistant analytical object, "men's violence against women", is a very risky business indeed' (2008: 218–19).

Concluding remarks

There is little doubt that the biographical turn within the social sciences – which encompasses 'case- or life-history', 'socio-biological' and 'psychosocial' approaches to understanding individual men's lives – represents a renewed commitment to take the individual and subjectivity more seriously (Rustin in Chamberlayne et al 2000, 2004). The idea of the 'hegemonic masculine biography' has been enormously influential in criminology and Connell's work is among the most in-depth and insightful (Goodey 2000: 489).[27] More recently, the place of the 'biography' has seen something of a revival in criminology as illustrated by the work of Maruna (1997: 59–93), Halsey (2006: 147–81), Brown (2003: 421–37; 2007: 485–500) and Maruna and Matravers (2007: 427–42), to name but a few. In the editorial of the special issue of the international journal, *Theoretical Criminology*, it is noted that its aim is 'to revive academic interest in the criminological case study – the individual person – and especially psychosocial approaches to life narrative analysis'. According to the editors, the special issue is dedicated to the proponents of this approach; Clifford Shaw's *The Jack-Roller* (1930/1966) that featured the sociological autobiography of Stanley and who also featured in an autobiographical sequel by Jon Snodgrass, *The Jack-Roller at Seventy* (1982) (Maruna and Matravers, 2007: 427). In an article by Gadd and Jefferson, they argue, 'it is only through the prism of . . . [Stanley's] . . . unconscious defences against anxiety that both the particularities and typicality of his life can be properly grasped and the case's wider theoretical significance fully realized' (2007a: 443). It is interesting to note that, having 'taken seriously the nature of [Stanley's] inner world', Gadd and Jefferson trace his 'recurrent feelings of inferiority' to a 'difficult life' and also 'the loss of his real mother and her replacement by a "cruel" and "unjust" stepmother' who, along with his father (although to a lesser extent), 'became the recipient of all his bad feelings' (2007a: 448, 455, 460). Although their reading is one in which they examine 'all of Stanley's disclosures about his stepmother', they conclude that, in doing so, 'it is possible to detect a degree of ambivalence' that lay 'buried beneath his more dramatic expressions of outright contempt' (Gadd and Jefferson 2007a: 460). It is this more 'complex' rendering of Stanley's subjectivity that explains why he got into jack-rolling (eg '"stealing" . . . "strong arming" or deploying violence to accomplish the robbery; enticing a homosexual to a room with the promise of sex and then depriving him, violently or otherwise, of his property') in the first place (Gadd and Jefferson 2007a: 461). Again, all this seems to boil down to the same old story of (and individualistic focus on) a fragile, anxious violent man unconsciously defending himself against anxiety.

Over the last three decades, there has been a resurgence of interest in narrative and narrative methods in order that scholars can better understand how identity and the self are narratively configured and how narrative analysis can be used to analyse selves and identities (eg Bamberg 2012). As this chapter has argued and, in agreement with Bamberg, who insightfully observes that 'we plot our lives retrospectively when we pour it or its episodes into narrative format' (2004: 331), the authors of these narratives about other subjectivities and lives are also telling stories. In this chapter, I have considered some of the limitations with the psychosocial approach to individual biographies, that claims to offer a more progressive approach to masculine subjectivity as it relates to the individual's life history and, through psychoanalytic techniques, by making the 'role of the unconscious central, but without losing grip on the social'. As other critics have said, although psychoanalytic perspectives 'might offer a rich story for describing the effects of "discourses of masculinity" in particular contexts, these remain, ultimately, just that: stories' (Collier, 2010a: 42, 2004: 295–96). For Collier, it is difficult 'to see how the kinds of readings produced about the taking up of masculine subjectivity can be tested or proven in any meaningful way' (2010a: 42). While this particular strand of thinking about the relationship between men, masculinities and crime claims to be 'serious' about coming to terms with the 'gap' between representation (of masculinity) and reality (of men's violence), it would appear it still seeks to fill the 'gap' with one side of a binary pair, masculinity/masculinities. As this chapter has demonstrated, the present call being made for a focus on the troubled psyches of violent men in all their diversity, anxiety and confusion comes as a response to and disavowal of the feminine (and feminist theory), not only at the level of the represented object (masculinity), but also at the level of the represented theory itself (the narrative interview method). Thus, all that is achieved by taking a psychosocial approach to the problem of violent men is more stories that permit the long held cultural habit of reading male violence as an effect of anxiety and/or a latent and somewhat defensive response to feeling feminised. Moreover, according to this story, originary responsibility for these feelings is said to lie with a woman. What all this suggests to me is that the 'narrative turn' in psychosocial approaches to the study of men and masculinities is symptomatic of other issues: namely, a question of who gets to tell the story of masculine subjectivity (in all his anxiety, vulnerability, confusion and contradictory desires), masculinities theorists or feminist theorists? However, on this point I want to be clear. I am not saying this is the end of the story, nor am I saying that we should no longer continue our conversations with others about the relationship between masculinities and men's violence. First, and foremost, it means we should keep on asking 'the man question'.[28] As Dowd suggests, 'asking the man question means asking the other (gender) question in any situation' (2008: 235; see also 2010). And as Collier has said, this means engaging with questions of masculinity as part of a broader discursive attempt to stop the depiction of women as 'the problem' and deflect an objectifying gaze from women (2010a: 679).[29] For me, it means subjecting the stories about men, masculinities and male violence to continued scrutiny. It is my hope that this book takes us one step closer to challenging and subverting the exculpatory cultural narrative of a woman 'asking for it'. If all we have are our own and other people's stories, then the final aim of this book is to show why we must adopt a more critical strategy of rereading and rewriting them.

Notes

1 Buchbinder is referring to two books, one published by Susan Faludi in 1991 and another by Marilyn French, also in 1992.

2 Edwards has called this particular set of concerns 'the crisis from within' that 'centres precisely on a perceived shift in men's *experiences* of their position *as* men, their maleness, and what it means' (2006: 7–8, original emphasis).

3 According to Levant (1997), one of the reasons why so many men participated in rallies was as a result of an increasing awareness of pain. Thus, he argued that there were two key ways to help men take the next step and connect their pain to a critical examination and reconstruction of masculinity: first, by taking men's experiences seriously and adopting an empathetic approach to their pain and, secondly, to help men come to terms with the crisis and restore 'their lost sense of pride associated with being a man'.

4 For a discussion of the political implications of Bly's mythical approach see Bob Pease, 'The mythopoetic men's movement' (2000: 101–103) and Tim Edwards, 'From backlash to lashed backs and back again: Robert Bly and the politics of men's movements' (2006: 26–36).

5 Discussing the 'consciousness raising group' that developed in the early years of women's liberation, Connell writes that while these had several important strengths, not the least of which was how these operated '[a]s a technique for the reconstruction of femininity', a significant 'drawback' of these groups was the 'exclusion of men' which 'meant that heterosexual relationships were likely to be worked at from one end' (1987: 230–31).

6 This set of concerns generally fits with what Edwards called 'the crisis from without' that included 'some partially empirically documented concerns relating to the position of men within such institutions as the family, education and work'. Accordingly, Edwards argued that '[a] specific concern here is the perception that men have lost, or are losing, power or privilege relative to their prior status in these institutions' (2006: 7–8). Edwards also notes that the reaction of many men to feminism was deeply divided and, while some sought to address their concerns by becoming involved in the mythopoetic and/or men's movement, others turned to academia (2006: 25).

7 For an overview of his critique of role theory see Demetriou (2001: 337–40).

8 Discussing this aspect of masculinities research, Dowd has observed that the core elements of masculinity norms are negative ones; to be a man means not being a girl or woman and not being gay. From this it follows that a 'real' man must vigilantly defend 'against humiliation, underlying everything is fear' (Leverenz 1986, cited in Dowd, 2008: 209).

9 Biddulph has also complained that as 'an enlightened stance' in 'favour of women's worth, women's qualities and women's rights, feminism has 'sidelined' men (1995: 22). In his account, Biddulph notes that feminism 'asks men to change, but isn't for men'. Hence, the 'unspeakable reality' is that 'feminism does nothing for men'.

10 See also Seidler, who claims that many Western heterosexual men have responded to the challenges of feminist theory with confusion about what it means to be a man (1997: 1).

11 For an overview of psychosocial approaches to understanding criminality see Jones 2008.

12 Discussing how the relationship between men, masculinities and crime has become the 'very stuff' of the discipline, Collier refers to criminological work such as that by Pat Carlen and Tony Jefferson's *British Journal of Criminology (Special Issue)* 'Masculinities and crime' published in 1996, Maguire et al's *The Oxford Handbook of Criminology* published in 1997 and Sandra Walklate's *Gender and Crime: An Introduction* published in 1995 (2004: 285). For a detailed list of criminological work that has since utilised the

concept of masculinity and applied it to various and specific topics see Collier (2004: 288). For a discussion of the 'man question' in feminism and the new men's studies more generally see Pease (2000: 11–25).

13 As Collier has observed, not only do both authors remark on the influence of Connell repeatedly through their work, when writing the foreword to Messerschmidt's *Masculinities and Crime*, Connell praised it as 'a sign of the "conceptual revolution" within the social sciences', that 'thanks largely to [second wave] feminism, a "re-vitalized" criminology can now begin to critically engage with that which had been before it all along – the maleness of crime' (1998: 177).

14 Jefferson's psychosocial approach is also intended as a corrective to the concept of hegemonic masculinity and the tendency in criminology at least for the term to be reified so that it becomes effectively a fixed and negative characteristic (Jefferson 2002b). In defence of the usefulness of the concept, and remaining critical of the approach taken by Hall, Connell endorses Jefferson's psychological argument even though it lacks the rigour of more 'concrete case-study analyses' that can be found in Chodorow's work (2002: 93).

15 Discussing the notion of discourse implied by 'poststructuralism generally', Jefferson argues that it effectively 'obliterates' the subject. By reducing subjects to the effects of discourses, either to a sum of discursive positioning or to a product of the interplay of discourses, it effectively erases them; in so doing, poststructuralism echoes structuralism's corresponding reduction of subjects to the effects of structures (1994: 16). Hence, he stresses the importance of 'multiply divided subjects' (Jefferson 1994: 17).

16 In his discussion of other work that has taken a similar approach, Jefferson refers to Jackson's pamphlet on the James Bulger case in which he rereads the case of two 10-year-old boys who abducted, tortured and murdered two-year-old James Bulger in England in 1992. In his discussion of how Jackson takes 'up the neglected issue of masculinity', we are told that Jackson's reading of the killing showed how it 'could be understood as attempts to build up a more powerful sense of masculine identity . . . [and] . . . an attempt to master their own anxieties and fears about their own babyishness by violently projecting them on to James' (Jefferson 1997a: 547).

17 ibid 1997b: 162.

18 Jefferson understands the pigeon incident as 'undoubtedly an important moment of empowerment for the young Tyson, not just in the immediate sense, but in showing the rewards of another "active" way of being-in-the-world' (1996b: 159).

19 Discussing the advantages of the psychosocial approach over the sociological moorings of criminology, Collier has questioned the preference of a particular strand of Kleinian psychoanalysis and object relations theory in Jefferson's work, which for him, 'is itself premised on an unduly mechanistic model of personality formation' (2004; 296). Whereas Hood-Williams has shown that a more accurate reading of the Oedipus complex 'would hold that a central feature of Tyson's psyche, essential to his "tough *guy*" personality, would be the existence of a superego that is typically *feminine*' rather than masculine (2001: 52, original emphasis). In their more recent discussion of the relationship between rural men and violence, Carrington and Scott have observed how '[i]t is overly simplistic to explain violence as an activity involving abnormal or pathological individuals' as such accounts cannot appreciate 'variations in men's violence across time and space and between individuals' (2008: 655–56).

20 For an excellent discussion of the notion of hegemonic masculinity as it relates to guilty feminine bodies (culpable subjects) from the perspective of legal storytelling see Catherine Burns, *Sexual Violence and the Law in Japan* (2005).

21 Howe is also concerned with the ways in which the psychosocial approach misreads feminism and the nature of feminist work informed by postmodernism, including work on law and crime (2008: 136–42). Petersen's work *Unmasking the Masculine* in 1998 was similarly concerned with the ways in which studies of masculinity had yet to take seriously the work of feminist poststructuralist theorists.

22 This same point was made by Collier in his earlier work detailing the inadequacies of Messerschmidt's structured action account and the psychosocial approach to theorising masculinities and male violence where he offers that: 'notwithstanding the growing cultural salience of a desire to speak about the "maleness" crime, perhaps what we will continue to be left with is, regardless of approach adopted, just the same old story of "boys" doing [criminological] business"' (2004: 300).

22 See also Jefferson's argument about the importance of theorising masculinity in a way that men will "recognize" (1994: 29).

24 As Flood points out, there are three key elements to the feminist rationale that prevention work must engage men; the first is because it is largely men who perpetrate this violence; the second is that constructions of masculinity play a crucial role in shaping violence against women, particularly at an attitudinal level; and the third is that men have a positive role to play in helping to end violence against women (2011: 359). Pease notes that there a diverse range of entry points and forms of involvement that men can involve themselves in intervention: as men's behaviour change facilitators, anti-violence campaign organisers and activists, role models in community education, workshop and educational programme facilitators, facilitators of boys' programmes, policy-makers and programme administrators, intervention bystanders, egalitarian and non-violent men in families (2008a: 2–5).

25 The book *Blood on Whose Hands? The killing of women and children in domestic homicides* published in Australia in 1994 and written by the Women's Coalition Against Family Violence is an excellent example.

26 The most notable of these are the White Ribbon Day campaign available at http://www.whiteribbonday.org.au/ and the successful activist driven Not 1 more available at http://not1more.com/ campaign. The White Ribbon Day campaign is the only national violence prevention campaign, and it is unique in that it aims to raise awareness among Australian men and boys about the roles they can play to prevent violence against women. Not 1 more have now held two public rallies on White Ribbon Day, one in 2009 and one in 2010, to remember victims of family violence homicide; see http://indymedia.org.au/not-1-more-public-rally-to-remember-victims-of-family-violence-homicide. Similar versions of these programmes that hold regular activities for men now exist in Canada (White Ribbon Campaign); see http://ourfuturehasnoviolenceagainstwomen.blogspot.com/ and http://vod.journeyman.tv/s/Changing+Men (all accessed 1 March 2012).

27 Goodey provides a comprehensive overview of the autobiographical method and its deployment in criminology (2000: 476–80).

28 Dowd suggests that, first, feminist theorists must ask the man question. Secondly, they must go on to incorporate masculinities scholarship to help create gender-specific strategies to achieve equality. Thirdly, and finally, they need to identify and demonstrate how patriarchy constructs and infuses institutions (2008: 235–38). She then gives two examples – fatherhood and its place in work/family analysis, and boys in relationship to educational equity issues – to illustrate how the insights of masculinities scholarship might inform feminist scholars to approach and analyse these areas differently.

29 In his recent book, *Men, Law and Gender*, the first of its kind systematically to discuss what it means to speak of the 'man' of law or, more accurately, the 'men' of legal discourse,

Collier urges a return to work that is aligned methodologically with the 'postmodern turn', linking the personal with the political and highlighting the plural 'histories' of men, rather than the primacy of one grand historical narrative. Specifically, he is critical of what he believes is the 'tendency in relation to hegemonic masculinity . . . to assume the existence of culturally dominant values that individual men are, for a host of (unexplored) psychological imperatives, assumed to desire, achieve or accomplish'. For Collier, much of this work sits in an uneasy relation to essentialist conceptualisations of and presuppositions about masculinity, which has significant implications for the study of law and gender more generally. Considering aspects of what has not been said in debates about men, law and gender, Collier finally suggests that particular attention needs to be paid to the ways in which 'assumptions about the normative nature of heterosexuality have encoded and structured many aspects of everyday life' as well as the 'limits' of 'the concept of masculinity itself in approaching the idea of the gendered legal subject' (2010a: 43–52). Masculinity is not, as Collier (2010a: 51) is at pains to point out:

> . . . a fixed, homogenous or unchanging concept. Far from taking for granted what is meant by the term, locating its meaning in a grand narrative or 'big debate' of sociology (or, indeed, of any other discipline), it is more helpful to look at how it has been deployed in different contexts, in different ways and at different moments, as a particular kind of (inter)discursive construction.

Conclusion: the importance of rereading and rewriting

> Rereading, an operation contrary to the commercial and ideological habits of our society, which would have us 'throw away' the story once it has been consumed ... so that we can then move on to another story, buy another book ..., rereading is here suggested at the outset, for it alone saves the text from repetition (those who fail to reread are obliged to read the same story everywhere).[1]
>
> (Barthes 1974: 15–16)

In many ways, this book has sought to reflect on the question of whether the decision to abolish the partial defence of provocation will put an end to the mitigating culture of male violence. In doing so, it has offered both a detailed examination of that question, provided some answers and signposted possible future directions of enquiry. Furthermore, this book presents an account of the significance of literary devices and narrative conventions for a whole range of social, cultural and historical discourses; something which law has resisted. As I have previously stated, an understanding of law as storytelling has been central to feminists' efforts of exposing and unsettling law's truth claims. Some of the main aims of this book have been to acknowledge the feminist project of 'law as storytelling' while also expanding and reframing law as constituted through narrative. Rather than retelling the stories of the victims (the 'outsiders'), the primary thesis of this book situates itself along the lines of cultural studies and the scholars who argue for the need to approach the event of murder 'as a cultural phenomenon and that recognizes its inseparability from the plethora of mass-mediated representations of violence circulating throughout . . . society' (Black 2000: 780).[2]

Another aim of this book has been to take up Barthes's challenge of rereading, as illustrated by the quotation above. The analysis of legal narratives, in cases of intimate partner homicide in Chapters 2 and 3, revealed the intertextual histories in which legal categories, such as the criminal defence of provocation, are thoroughly embedded. The standard tale that is told in provocation cases, that 's/he asked for it', is anything but unique to the doctrine of the partial defence of provocation. This 'narrative of excuse' for male violence not only preoccupies, informs and shapes legal understandings of so-called provoked killings but it also operates more broadly as a feature of popular cinematic and literary culture (as illustrated in Chapter 2). The narrative (of insult) also works in areas where the 'complainant' is a centralised figure of the doctrinal drama of the rape trial. Since the early 1990s, feminist cultural scholars have demonstrated that legal attitudes are heavily influenced by conventional 'rape scripts' about 'unchaste' women who are guilty of arousing the sexual desires of their attackers, ultimately disqualifying their claims to sexual assault (Marcus 1992; Heath and Naffine 1994; Kaspiew 1995; Puren 1995; Lees 1997; Easteal 1998; Young 1998; Grix 1999; Galbraith 2000; Ehrlich 2001; Gotell 2002; Cossins 2003; Taylor 2004; Burns 2005; Comack and Peter 2005; Gavey 2005; Larcombe 2005; Bourke 2007; Temken and Krahe 2008). These scholars have shown not only how these exculpatory scripts are realised in popular culture but are also mobilised in the court room. As Gavey observes, both law and popular culture can be found to draw on 'dominant discourses of heterosexuality that positions women as relatively passive subjects who are encouraged to comply with sex with men, irrespective of their own sexual desire' (1992: 325). As such, the strategy of rewriting has been central to feminist engagements with the criminal law of rape. Such a strategy gives voice to an otherwise silenced subject, enabling an alternative account of women's experience. The future difficulty lies in resisting a reinscription of established orthodoxy. As recently noted by Larcombe, both 'rape law and romance fiction continue to reproduce conventionally gendered subjectivities' despite 'extensive feminist engagements with these texts over past decades' (2005: 1).

As I have demonstrated, there are numerous critical studies which extensively document the way in which exculpatory scripts about women who 'ask for it' interact with and challenge the legal process in the prosecution of sexual assault cases. In response to such studies, this book also presents a challenge. This challenge is directed specifically at the way in which these exculpatory scripts are reproduced across discursive sites. My thesis throughout this book regarding narrative – law's uncomfortable bedfellow – can be applied more broadly to the law of homicide and the operation of the criminal defence of provocation. Of specific interest in my thesis are cases where it is utilised by men who kill their current or former partners as a 'narrative of excuse' for men's violence against women. When the narratological underpinnings of law are laid bare, law's utilisation of the 'narrative of insult' becomes an obvious, and in many ways simple-minded, strategy. Once law is reframed through the lens of narrative, with its dependence on literary conventions, patterns of bias, chauvinism and bigotry come into focus, as this book has illustrated.

In Chapter 2, I demonstrated how attention to the effects and constraints of narrative theory, when applied to law, requires a critical awareness of its effects beyond the boundaries of legal discourse. Furthermore, I offered an examination of a range of historical and cultural materials that have portrayed the female body (and the mouth and tongue) as a sign of disorder and threat to certain ideals central to masculinity. In Chapter 3, I revealed the strategic courtroom advantage regarding the legal narrative of insult with its central trope of a woman 'asking for it'. Furthermore, I highlighted the way in which such tropes are mobilised by the defendant to claim the partial defence of provocation in order to receive reduction in culpability of the crime of murder. Chapter 4 considered the implications of the abolition of the provocation defence on legal responses (narrations) in recent Victorian cases of intimate partner homicide since the 2005 amendments. Chapter 5 then examined the turn to 'narrative' as the preferred method for understanding, and responding to, the problem of men's violence. This chapter also explored how a slew of individuals, from scholars and theorists of masculinity to the defence counsel, narrate stories regarding how women's words provoke men to kill women while also genuflecting to an essentialist notion that the unruly female body incites male violence.

What remains is to offer some suggestions for the way forward. My proposal, however, is a theoretical one because it necessarily involves an ongoing process of rereading and rewriting the claims made and written by others. In acknowledgement that these 'others' are implicated in the very knowledge structures that make rewriting possible (and sometimes impossible) indicates the extent to which such a project can be fraught with difficulties, particularly when the issues raised concern representations of sexed subjectivity and men's violence against women. As Threadgold reminds us, a critique, located through feminism or any other ideology 'is always a dialogue with significant others who claim, or have claimed, to know' (1997b: 34). Threadgold's insight is both a call for and response to rewriting strategies such as those adopted by de Lauretis (1984, 1987), in whose work she notes that '[f]ew of the current masters of philosophy and critical theory' have managed to 'escape her critique' (1997b: 35). It is the persistent refusal, on the part of male intellectuals, to engage with or only occasionally gesture to 'the epistemological contribution of feminism to the redefinition of subjectivity and sociality' that highlights the tenacity of their rigid thinking and the overwhelming inertia inherent in such gendered dogma (de Lauretis 1987: 24). Despite this, (or more possibly, because of this) Threadgold advocates that this should not 'prevent feminist theorists from reading and rewriting their (i.e. male intellectuals') works' (1997b: 35). Nowhere has the disavowal of feminist poststructuralist theory and its redefinition of sexed subjectivity (as a question and problem of its representation) been more apparent than within the burgeoning literature on men, masculinities and male violence within the area of crime and criminology. It is for this reason that one's 'tactics' for critique can and must be located at the site in which they are materially inscribed. For it is here, at the site of intersecting discourses, that power relations mark the body as a self-evident sexed body (Foucault 1978: 92–93). At the very least, a feminist strategy of rewriting ought to involve an account of the aesthetics of the legal text and its reception. From here we can begin to imagine an audience that, although inscribed and acted upon, starts reading (seeing and writing) otherwise. I end by providing an example of what such a strategy can achieve.

In the aftermath of the 2005 criminal trial of James Ramage, two books were published, one by Phil Cleary, former Independent member of the Federal Parliament of Australia and also former footballer and coach in the Victorian football league, and the other by Karen Kissane (a journalist with *The Age* newspaper). Phil Cleary's book, *Getting Away With Murder: The True Story of Julie Ramage's Death* (2005), provides a passionate and compelling account of the background to the *Ramage* case. The book 'retells' the story told at the trial of her killer (her estranged husband, James) from the point of view of the victim, Julie. Since the publication of his earlier book, *Just Another Little Murder* (2002),[3] Cleary has been an active campaigner against the legal system's treatment of violence against women.

Like her feature article in *The Age* newspaper, 'Honour killing in the suburbs', Kissane's text has been described as providing an equally 'damning critique of the provocation defence', one that is 'tenuously situated between the realms of law and literature'.[4] In its opening pages, we are told that what is written is 'Julie's story', the story of a middle-class woman, killed in the leafy Balwyn suburb one Monday morning, a story that exposes 'the brittleness of the middleclass veneer and the subtle viciousness of another kind of silent death: the abusive marriage' (2006: 7). Since Julie Ramage's murder, her twin sister, Jane Ashton, along with her family and friends, have struggled to come to terms with the pain, grief and loss of their loved one and friend. Following her sister's death, she vowed to help other women and children escape family violence. She now works as an anti-violence-against-women campaigner and communications coordinator with the Women's Domestic Crisis Violence Service. Like Phil Cleary, she is a White Ribbon ambassador and heavily involved in violence pre-vention programmes and campaigns aimed at engaging men and the wider community in changing attitudes that endorse or minimise violence against women (see McKay 2011). When her sister's killer was released from prison in July 2011, Ms Ashton said she hoped that the man who strangled her sister 'will never harm another woman'. She reflected how 'it had been a real journey for her family' and 'a steep learning curve around the law and violence against women' (Bucci 2011). For Cleary, while there has been considerable progress, violence against women is 'still a problem', as are the courts, the public narratives, 'the way media reports it' and 'the way police deal with it' (Anonymous 2011). To the extent that these books, along with media discourse, reinterpret and rewrite the murder of Julie Ramage, these counter stories stand to bring about (if they have not already) a significant challenge to existing attitudes that normalize men's violence against women within the legal community who are, as are we all, the authors and consumers of stories (both literary and legal).

In the Introduction, I referred to how the publication of *Blood on Whose Hands?* in 1994 told the story of the complicity of the legal system in 'the systematic silencing or trivializing of the long history of physical, emotional and sexual abuse experiences by the subjects of the study' (Otto 1994: 1134). I also noted how the authors linked this systemic failure to legal and community attitudes towards domestic violence that ignore or minimise its seriousness. In 2010, a national survey entitled *Changing Cultures Changing Attitudes*, the first national report card on the status of community attitudes to violence against women since 1995, found there was a decline in people who believe that women who are raped often ask for it (from 1 in 7 in 1995 to 1 in 20 in 2009). While the findings of the report show that attitudes about violence against women are changing for the better (VicHealth, Media Release (7 April 2010)), what is also clear is that more work needs to be done. But that is a book for another day. What these retellings (by Phil Cleary, Jane Ashton, Karen Kissane and those that appear in this book) signify is the power and instructive advantages of using different genres (true crime, academic writing), literary devices (such as first-person narrative), media representations, campaigns against family violence, cinema and so on to (re)interpret and ultimately *rewrite* the crime. In doing so, these acts of rereading and rewriting might help to dislodge the powerful exculpatory narratives currently at play.

Notes

1 I first came across this quotation in an article by Felman, who reflects on her place 'as a reader' of a lecture by Freud, entitled 'Femininity', which he intended to deliver to 'an audience gathered from all the Faculties of the University' (the University of Vienna) but was cancelled because he had undergone an operation for throat cancer. Felman's article opens with the following quotation from Freud's lecture: 'throughout history men have knocked their heads against the riddle of femininity ... Nor will *you* have escaped worrying over this question – those of you who are men; to those of you who are women, this will not apply – you are yourselves the problem'. Felman notes that the use of the 'you' in Freud's lecture reveals how it was originally intended to address a male audience. By representing the same quotation to a different audience, 'not the Viennese University public but a contemporary American audience gathered for a feminist colloquium at the University of Wisconsin-Milwaukee', Felman highlights that this 'different structure of address' ultimately interferes with Freud's text 'by disrupting the transparency and misleadingly self-evident universality of its male enunciation' (1981: 19–44).

2 Black's reference is in respect of three works, all published in 1998, that adopt such an approach: Karen Halttunen's *Murder Most Foul: The Killer and the American Gothic Imagination*, Sara L. Knox's *Murder: A Tale of Modern American Life* and Mark Seltzer's *Serial Killers: Death and Life in America's Wound Culture*.

3 A book which systematically details the injustice surrounding the decision by a Victorian Supreme Court jury to find his sister's ex-boyfriend and killer, Peter Keogh, guilty of manslaughter on the ground of provocation for her brutal stabbing outside the kindergarten where she worked in 1987.

4 I am indebted to one of the students who was enrolled in a third and fourth year criminology subject I was teaching at an Australian university in 2006 and who produced an excellent essay on the *Ramage* case with the title: 'From leafy Balwyn to lethal legacy: discursive constructions of the killing of Julie Ramage' (*Criminal Fictions* 2006). I am very grateful to the student for acknowledging the source of some of her ideas as deriving from an article I wrote on Kissane's book earlier that same year. Thus, I would like to return the gesture of collegiality and thank the student.

Bibliography

Adams, D. (2007) *Why Do They Kill? Men Who Murder Their Intimate Partners*, Nashville, TN: Vanderbilt University Press.

Alexander, G. (2004) 'Call it What it Was: Domestic Homicide', *The Age*, Letters and Opinion, 30 October.

Allen, H. (1987) *Justice Unbalanced: Gender,, Psychiatry and Judicial Decisions*, Milton Keynes, Philadelphia: Open University Press.

Allen, H. (1988) 'One Law For All Reasonable Persons', *International Journal of the Sociology of Law*, 16: 419–32.

Amsterdam, A. G. and Bruner, J. S. (2000) *Minding the Law*, Cambridge, M.A.: Harvard University Press.

Anderson, P. (2009) 'Accused Wife Killer Tells of Hen-pecked Torment', *The Herald Sun*, 23 October. Online. Available at http://www.heraldsun.com.au/news/victoria/accused-wife-killer-tells-of-hen-pecked-torment/story-e6frf7kx-1225790196337 (accessed 15 January 2011).

Anderson, P. (2010a) 'Prosecutor Argues Luke John Middendorp Be Given 11 year Sentence', *The Herald Sun*, 14 May. Online. Available at http://www.heraldsun.com.au/news/victoria/prosecutor-argues-luke-john-middendorp-be-given-11-year-sentence/story-e6frf7kx-1225866381908 (accessed 15 May 2010).

Anderson, P. (2010b) 'Luke John Middendorp Jailed Over the Stabbing Death of Jade Bownds', *The Herald Sun*, 19 May. Online. Available at http://www.heraldsun.com.au/news/luke-john-middendorp-jailed-over-the-stabbing-death-of-ex-lover/story-e6frf7jo-1225868587225 (accessed 20 May 2010).

Anderson, P. (2010c) 'Hulking Luke Middendorp Stabbed Tiny Jade Bownds – and Gets Off With Defensive Homicide', *The Herald Sun*, 20 May. Online. Available at http://www.dailytelegraph.com.au/news/national/hulking-luke-middendorp-stabbed-tiny-jade-bownds-and-gets-off-with-defensive-homicide/story-e6freuzr-1225868906818 (accessed 21 May 2010).

Anonymous. (1996) 'Judge's Racial Fears for Love Triangle Killer', *The Age*, 19 December, p A7.

Anonymous. (2007) 'Defence Can Blame Victim for a Crime', *The Courier Mail*, 6 July, p 26.

Anonymous. (2009a) 'Murder Accused Walks Free After Charges Dismissed', *ABC News*, 6 May. Online. Available at http://www.abc.net.au/news/stories/2009/05/06/2562766. htm (accessed 30 October 2009).

Anonymous. (2009b) 'Man Strangled Partner for Waking up Beloved Dog, Court Told', *The Age* 21 May. Online. Available at http://www.theage.com.au/national/man-strangled-partner-for-waking-up-beloved-dog-court-told-20090521-bgri.html (accessed 15 January 2011).

Anonymous. (2011) 'Phil Cleary on a Crusade', *Hobson's Bay Weekly*, 30 November. Online. Available at http://www.hobsonsbayweekly.com.au/news/local/news/general/phil-cleary-on-a-crusade/2376266.aspx?src=rss (accessed 2 December 2011).

Aristodemou, M. (1999) 'The Seduction of Mimesis: Theatre as Woman and the Play of Difference and Excess in Aeschylus's *Oresteia*', *Cardozo Studies in Law and Literature*, 11: 1–33.

Aristodemou, M. (2000) *Law & Literature: Journeys from Her to Eternity*, Oxford: Oxford University Press.

Arlidge, A. and Eady, D. (1982) *The Law of Contempt*, London: Sweet & Maxwell.

Armstrong, S. M. (2004) 'Is Feminist Law Reform Flawed? Abstentionists & Sceptics', *Australian Feminist Law Journal*, 20: 43–63.

Australian Law Reform Commission and New South Wales Law Reform Commission. (2010) *Family Violence: A National Legal Response* (ALRC Final Report 114; NSWLRC Final Report 128), Barton: Commonwealth of Australia.

Bacon, W. and Lansdowne, R. (1982) 'Women Who Kill Husbands: The Battered Wife on Trial', in C. O'Donnell and J. Craney (eds) *Family Violence in Australia*. Melbourne: Penguin.

Bagshaw, D. and Chung, W. (2000) *Men, Women and Domestic Violence*, Canberra: Office of the Status of Women, Commonwealth of Australia.

Baker, B. M. (1998) 'Provocation as a Defence for Abused Women Who Kill', *Canadian Journal of Law and Jurisprudence*, 11: 193–211.

Bakhtin, M. M. (1981) *The Dialogic Imagination*, Austin: University of Texas Press.

Bamberg, M. (2004) '"We are young, responsible, and male": Form and function of "slut-bashing" in the identity constructions in 15-year-old males, and Talk, small stories, and adolescent identities', *Human Development*, 47: 331–53.

Bamberg, M. (2012) 'Narrative Analysis', in H. Cooper (ed) *APA Handbook of Research Methods in Psychology: Vol. 2. Quantitative, Qualitative, Neuropsychological, and Biological*, Amercian Psychological Association.

Bandalli, S. (1995) 'Provocation – A Cautionary Note', *Journal of Law and Society*, 22: 398–409.

Bardsley, S. (2006) *Venomous Tongues: Speech and Gender in Late Medieval England*, Philadelphia: University of Pennsylvania Press.

Barthes, R. (1974) *S/Z*, New York: Hill and Wang.

Bauer, E. (1998) 'The Mouth and the Method: Interview with Quentin Tarantino', *Sight and Sound*, VIII: 6–9.

Bauman, R. (1983) *Let Your Words Be Few: Symbolism of Speaking and Silence Among Seventeenth-Century Quakers*, New York: Cambridge University Press.

Beasley, C. (2008) 'Rethinking Hegemonic Masculinity in a Globalizing World', *Men and Masculinities*, 11: 86–103.

Biddulph, S. (1995) *Manhood: An Action Plan for Changing Men's Lives*, Lane Cove: Finch Publishing Pty Limited.

Black, J. (2000) 'Murder: The State of the Art', *American Literary History*, 12: 780–793.

Blazina, C. (1997) 'The Fear of the Feminine in the Western Psyche and the Masculine Task of Disidentification: Their Effect on the Development of Masculine Gender Role Conflict', *Journal of Men's Studies*, 6: 55–67.

Bly, R. (1991) *Iron John: A Book About Men*, Shaftesbury, Dorset: Element.

Booker, J. (2011) 'Family's Bid to Honour Sophie', *The New Zealand Herald*, 11 June.

Boose, L. E. (1991) 'Scolding Brides and Bridling Scolds: Taming the Woman's Unruly Member', *Shakespeare Quarterly*, 42: 179–213.

Borochowitz, D. Y. (2008) 'The Taming of the Shrew: Batterers' Constructions of Their Wives' Narratives', *Violence Against Women*, 14: 1166–80.

Bourke, J. (2007) *Rape: Sex, Violence, History*, Emeryville, CA: Shoemaker & Hoard.

Boyd, S. (2008) 'Is Equality Enough? Fathers' Rights and Women's Rights', in R. Hunter (ed) *Rethinking Equality Projects in Law: Feminist Challenges*, Oxford and Portland: Hart Publishing.

Boyd White, J. (1973) *The Legal Imagination: Studies in the Nature of Legal Thought and Expression*, Boston: Little, Brown.

Boyle, C. (1990) 'The Battered Wife Syndrome and Self-Defence: *Lavallée v. R.*', *Canadian Journal of Family Law*, 9: 171–79.

Bradfield, R. (1998) 'Criminal Cases in the High Court of Australia: *Green v. The Queen*', *Criminal Law Journal* 22: 296–303.

Bradfield, R. (2000) 'Domestic Homicide and the Defence of Provocation: A Tasmanian Perspective on the Jealous Husband and Battered Wife', *University of Tasmania Law Review*, 19: 5–37.

Bradfield, R. (2001) 'Provocation and Non-violent Homosexual Advances: Lessons from Australia', *The Journal of Criminal Law*, 65: 76–84.

Bradfield, R. (2002) *The Treatment of Women Who Kill Their Violent Male Partners Within the Australian Criminal Justice System*, PhD, University of Tasmania.

Bradfield, R. (2003) 'Contemporary Comment: The Demise of Provocation in Tasmania', *Criminal Law Journal*, 27: 322–324.

Brooks, P. (1984) *Reading for the Plot: Design and Intention in Narrative*, New York: Knopf Press.

Brooks, P. (1993) *Body Work: Objects of Desire in Modern Narrative*, Cambridge, Massachusetts: Harvard University Press.

Brooks, P. (1996) 'The Law as Narrative and Rhetoric', in P. Brooks and P. Gewirtz (eds) *Law's Stories: Narrative and Rhetoric in the Law*. New Haven and London: Yale University Press.

Brooks, P. and Gewirtz, P. (eds) (1996) *Law's Stories: Narrative and Rhetoric in the Law*, New Haven and London: Yale University Press.

Brown, A. P. (2003) 'From Individual to Social Defences in Psychosocial Criminology', *Theoretical Criminology*, 7: 421–37.

Brown, A. P. (2007) 'Interpretation and the Case Study: the Challenge of a Relational Approach', *Theoretical Criminology*, 11: 485–500.

Brown, B. (1963) 'The Demise of the Chance Medley and the Recognition of Provocation as a Defence to Murder in English Law', *American Journal of Legal History*, 7: 310–18.

Brown, A., Williams, K. R. and Dutton, D. G. (1999) 'Homicide between intimate partners: A 20-year review', in M. D. Smith and M. A. Zahn (eds) *Homicide: A sourcebook of social research*, Thousand Oaks, CA: Sage.

Bucci, N. (2011) '"I'm Not Scared of Him": Sister Backs Killer's Balwyn Ban', *The Age*, 8 July.

Buchbinder, D. (1994) *Masculinities and Identities*, Carlton: Melbourne University Press.

Bumiller, K. (1988) *The Civil Rights Society: The Social Construction of Victims*, Baltimore, Maryland: The John Hopkins University Press.

Burman, M. (2010) 'The Ability of Criminal Law to Produce Gender Equality: Judicial Discourses in the Swedish Criminal Justice System', *Violence Against Women*, 16: 173–88.

Burns, C. (2005) *Sexual Violence and the Law in Japan*, London: Routledge.

Burton, M. (2003) 'Case Note. Sentencing Domestic Homicide Upon Provocation: Still "Getting Away with Murder"', *Feminist Legal Studies*, 11: 279–89.

Burton, K., Crofts, T. and Tarrant, S. (2011) *Principles of Criminal Law in Queensland and Western Australia*, Pyrmont: Law Book Company.

Busch, R. (1994) '"Don't Throw Bouquets at Me . . . (Judges) Will Say We're In Love": An analysis of New Zealand Judges' Attitudes Towards Domestic Violence', in J. Stubbs (ed) *Women, Male Violence and the Law*, Sydney: The Institute of Criminology.

Butler, J. (1990) *Gender Trouble: Feminism and the Subversion of Identity*, New York and London: Routledge.

Butler, J. (1993) *Bodies That Matter: On the Discursive Limits of 'Sex'*, New York and London: Routledge.

Butler, J. (1997) *Excitable Speech: A Politics of the Performative*, New York and London: Routledge.

Campbell, J. C. (1992) '"If I Can't Have You, No One Can": Power and Control in Homicide of Female Partners', in J. Radford and D. E. H. Russell (eds) *Femicide: The Politics of Woman Killing*, New York: Twayne Publishers.

Canadian Association of Elizabeth Fry Societies (2000) *Response to the Department of Justice re: Reforming Criminal Code Defences: Provocation, Self-Defence and Defence of Property*, Ottawa: Canadian Association of Elizabeth Fry Societies.

Capper, S. and Crooks, M. (2010) 'New Homicide Laws Have Proved Indefensible', *The Sunday Age*, 23 May, p 21.

Carlen, P. and Jefferson, T. (1996) *British Journal of Criminology: Special Issue – Masculinities and Crime*, 33.

Carline, A. (2005) 'Women Who Kill Their Abusive Partners: from Sameness to Gender Construction', *Liverpool Law Review*, 26: 13–44.

Carrick, D. (2010) 'The Defence of Provocation', *The Law Report*. Online. Available at http://www.abc.net.au/rn/lawreport/stories/2010/3051056.htm (accessed 15 January 2011).

Carrington, K. and Scott, J. (2008) 'Masculinity, Rurality and Violence', *British Journal of Criminology*, 48.

Castel, J. R. (1990) 'Discerning Justice for Battered Women Who Kill', *Toronto, Faculty of Law Review*, 48: 229–58.

Chamberlayne, P., Bornat, J., Wengraf, T. (eds) (2000) *The Turn to Biographical Methods in Social Science: Comparative Issues and Examples*, New York: Routledge.

Chamberlayne, P., Bornat, J. and Apitzsch, U. (2004) *Biographical Methods and Professional Practice: An International Perspective*, Bristol: Polity Press.

Cheah, P. and Grosz, E. (1996) 'The Body of Law: Notes Towards a Theory of Corporeal Justice', in P. Cheah, D. Fraser and J. Grbich (eds) *Thinking Through the Body of the Law*, St Leonards NSW: Allen & Unwin.

Chesterman, M. R. (1984) *Public Criticism of Judges*, Sydney: Australian Law Reform Commission.

Chesterman, M. R. (1987) 'Disorder in the Court: The Judge's Response', *University of New South Wales Law Journal*, 10: 32–46.

Clare, A. (2000) *On Men: Masculinity in Crisis*, London: Arrow Books.

Cleary, P. (2002) *Just Another Little Murder*, Crows Nest, NSW: Allen & Unwin.

Cleary, P. (2004) 'Julie's Judicial Betrayal', *The Herald Sun*, 29 October, p 4.

Cleary, P. (2005) *Getting Away with Murder: The True Story of Julie Ramage's Death*, Crows Nest, NSW: Allen & Unwin.

Cleary, P. (2006) 'Grave Insult to Murdered Wives', *The Herald Sun*, 23 February, p 21.

Cleary, P. (2009) 'Politics' Online. Available at http://www.philcleary.com.au/politics_2009_white_ribbon.html (accessed 15 January 2011).

Cleary, P. (2010) 'Women Out in the Cold', *The Age*, 24 April. Online. Available at http://www.theage.com.au/national/letters/lets-remember-the-huge-sacrifices-20100423-tj1y.html (accessed 28 April 2010).

Clough, A. (2010) 'Comment: Loss of Self-Control as a Defence: The Key to Replacing Provocation', *The Journal of Criminal Law*, 74: 118–26.

Clover, C. J. (1998) 'Law and the Order of Popular Culture', in A. Sarat and T. R. Kearns (eds) *Law in the Domains of Culture*, Ann Arbor: The University of Michigan Press.

Coker, D. K. (1992) ' Heat of Passion and Wife Killing: Men Who Batter / Men Who Kill', *Review of Law and Women's Studies*, 2: 71–130.

Collier, R. (1995) *Masculinities, Law and the Family*, London: Routledge.

Collier, R. (1996) '"Coming Together?": Post-Heterosexuality, Masculine Crisis and the New Men's Movement', *Feminist Legal Studies*, IV: 3–48.

Collier, R. (1997) 'After Dunblane: Crime, Corporeality, and the (Hetero-)Sexing of the Bodies of Men', *Journal of Law and Society*, 24: 177–98.

Collier, R. (1998) *Masculinities, Crime and Criminology: Men, Heterosexuality and the Criminal(ised) Other*, London: Sage.

Collier, R. (2004) 'Masculinities and Crime: Rethinking the "Man Question"?', in C. Sumner (ed) *The Blackwell International Companion to Criminology*, Oxford: Blackwell.

Collier, R. (2010a) *Men, Law and Gender: Essays on the 'Man' of Law*, London: Routledge.

Collier, R. (2010b) 'In Search of the "Good Father": Law, Family Practices and the Normative Reconstruction of Parenthood', *Studies in Law, Politics and Society*, 22.

Collier, R. and Sheldon, S. (2006) 'Fathers' Rights, Fatherhood and Law Reform – International Perspectives', in R. Collier and S. Sheldon (eds) *Fathers' Rights Activism and Legal Reform*, Oxford: Hart Publishing.

Collier, R. and Sheldon, S. (2008) *Fragmenting Fatherhood: A Socio-Legal Study*, Oxford: Hart Publishing.

Comack, E. and Peter, T. (2005) 'How the Criminal Justice System Responds to Sexual Assault Survivors: The Slippage Between Responsibilization and Blaming the Victim', *Canadian Journal of Women and the Law*, 17: 283–309.

Comstock, G. (1992) 'Dismantling the Homosexual Panic Defence', *Law and Sexuality*, 2: 81–102.

Connell, R. W. (1985) 'Theorizing Gender', *Sociology*, 19: 260–72.

Connell, R. W. (1987) *Gender and Power: Society, the Person and Sexual Politics*, Stanford: Stanford University Press.

Connell, R. W. (1994) 'Psychoanalysis on Masculinity', in H. Brod and M. Kaufman (eds) *Theorizing Masculinity*, Thousand Oaks: Sage.

Connell, R. W. (1995) *Masculinities*, Berkeley: University of California Press.

Connell, R. W. (1998) 'Introduction: Studying Australian Masculinities', *Journal of Interdisciplinary Gender Studies*, 3: 1–8.

Connell, R. W. (2000) *The Men and the Boys*, St Leonards: Allen & Unwin.

Connell, R. W. (2002) 'On Hegemonic Masculinity and Violence: Response to Jefferson and Hall', *Theoretical Criminology*, 6: 89–99.

Connell, R. W. (2005) 'Change Among the Gatekeepers: Men, Masculinities, and Gender Equality in the Global Arena', *Signs: Journal of Women in Culture and Society*, 30: 1801–25.

Connell, R. W. and Messerschmidt, J. W. (2005) 'Hegemonic Masculinity: Rethinking the Concept', *Gender & Society*, 19: 829–59.

Coss, G. (1991) '"God is a Righteous Judge, Strong and Patient: and God is Provoked Every Day": A Brief History of the Doctrine of Provocation in England', *Sydney Law Review*, 13: 570–604.

Coss, G. (2005) 'Editorial: Provocation's Victorian Nadir: The Obscenity of Ramage', *Criminal Law Journal*, 29: 133–38.

Coss, G. (2006) 'The Defence of Provocation: An Acrimonious Divorce from Reality', *Current Issues in Criminal Justice*, 29: 133–38.

Cossins, A. (2003) 'Saints, Sluts and Sexual Assault: Rethinking the Relationship between Sex, Race and Gender', *Social & Legal Studies*, 12: 77–103.

Côté, A. December 1 2006. Letter to Right Honourable Stephen Harper.

Côté, A., Sheehy, E. and Majury, D. (2000) *Stop Excusing Violence Against Women: NAWL's Brief on Defence of Provocation*, Ontario: National Association of Women and the Law (NAWL).

Cover, R. (1986) 'Violence and the Word', *Yale Law Journal*, 92: 1601–29.

Crooks, M. (2004) 'It's Time Women Had a Better Deal From the Law', *The Age*, Letters and Opinion, 1 November, p 17.

Crofts, T. (2006) 'Wilful Murderers in Western Australia: Soon to get away with Murder?', *Alternative Law Journal*, 31: 203–05.

Crofts, T. (2008) 'Two Degrees of Murder: Homicide Law Reform in England and Western Australia', *Oxford University Commonwealth Law Journal*, 8: 187–210.

Csefalvay, K. Z. (2006) 'Taunts, Chapati Pans and the Case of the Reasonable Glue-Sniffer: An Examination of the Normative Test in Provocation after *Smith* and *Holley*', *Cambridge Student Law Review*, 2: 45–52.

Culler, J. (1981) *The Pursuit of Signs: Semiotics, Literature, Deconstruction*, Ithaca, New York: Cornell University Press.

Culler, J. (1988) *Framing the Sign: Criticism and Its Institutions*, Oxford: Basil Blackwell.

Daly, M. and Wilson, M. (1988) *Homicide*, New York: Aldine.

Davies, M. (2003) 'Legal Theory and Law Reform: Some Mainstream and Critical Approaches', *Alternative Law Journal*, 28: 168–71.

Dawson, M. and Gartner, R. (1992) *Woman Killing: Intimate Femicide in Ontario, 1974–1990*, Toronto, Canada: Women We Honour Action Committee.

Dawson, M. and Gartner, R. (1998) 'Differences in the Characteristics of Intimate Femicides: the Role of Relationship State and Relationship Status', *Homicide Studies*, 2: 378–99.

Delgado, R. (1989) 'Storytelling for Oppositionists and Others: A Plea for Narrative', *Michigan Law Review*, 87: 2411–41.

Demetriou, D. Z. (2001) 'Connell's Concept of Hegemonic Masculinity: A Critique', *Theory and Society*, 30: 337–61.

Department of Justice (Victoria) (2010) *Review of the Offence of Defensive Homicide: Discussion Paper, Criminal Law – Justice Statement*, Melbourne: Department of Justice Victoria.

Department of Justice and Attorney-General (Queensland) (2007) *Discussion Paper Audit on Defences to Homicide: Accident and Provocation*, Brisbane: Queensland.

Dick, C. (2009) *A Tale of Two Cultures: Intimate Femicides, Cultural Defences, and the law of Provocation*, Annual Meeting of the Canadian Political Science Association, Ottawa, Canada.

Dijkstra, B. (1996) *Evil Sisters: The Threat of Female Sexuality and the Cult of Manhood*, New York: Alfred A. Knopf.

Dinovitzer, R. and Dawson, M. (2007) 'Family-Based Justice in the Sentencing of Domestic Homicide', *British Journal of Criminology*, 47: 655–70.

Dobash, R. P., Dobash, R. E., Cavanaugh, K. and Lewis, R. (2000) *Changing Violent Men*, Thousand Oaks, CA: Sage.

Dobash, R. E., Dobash, R. P., Cavanagh, K. and Lewis, R. (2004) 'Not an Ordinary Killer – Just an Ordinary Guy', *Violence Against Women*, 10: 577–605.

Dobash, R. E., Dobash, R. P., Cavanaugh, K. and Medina-Ariza, J. (2007) 'Lethal and Nonlethal Violence Against an Intimate Female Partner', *Violence Against Women*, 13: 329–53.

Dobash, R. P., Dobash, R. E. and Gutteridge, S. (1986) *The Imprisonment of Women*, Oxford: Basil Blackwell.

Domestic Violence Resource Centre Victoria (2010) 'Defensive Homicide: Is it Working for Victims of Violence?', *DVRCV Newsletter*, Edition 4 – Summer: 16.

Douglas, H. A. (2006) 'Assimilation and Authenticity: The "Ordinary Aboriginal Legal Person" and the Provocation Defence', *Adelaide Law Review*, 27: 199–226.

Douglas, H. A. (2008) 'The Demise of the Provocation Defence and the Failure of Equality Concepts', in R. Hunter (ed) *Rethinking Equality Projects in Law: Feminist Challenges*. Oxford and Portland: Hart Publishing.

Douzinas, C. and Nead, L. (1999) *Law and the Image: The Authority of Art and the Aesthetics of Law*, Chicago and London: The University of Chicago Press.

Dowd, N. E. (2008) 'Masculinities and Feminist Legal Theory', *Wisconsin Journal of Law, Gender & Society*, 23: 201–48.

Dowd, N. E. (2010) 'Asking the Man Question: Masculinities Analysis and Feminist Theory', *Harvard Journal of Law & Gender*, 33: 415–30.

Dressler, J. (1995) 'When "Heterosexual" Men Kill "Homosexual" Men: Reflections on Provocation Law, Sexual Advances, and the "Reasonable Man"', *Journal of Criminal Law and Criminology*, 85: 726–63.

Drew Griffith, R. (1995) 'A Homeric Metaphor Cluster Describing Teeth, Tongue, and Words', *American Journal of Philology*, 116: 1–5.

Dyer, C. (2002) 'Attorney-General Seeks Tougher Sentences For Domestic Killings', *The Guardian*, 4 December.

Eades, D. (2008) 'Telling and Retelling Your Story in Court: Questions, Assumptions and Intercultural Implications', *Current Issues in Criminal Justice*, 20: 209–30.

Earle, A. M. (1907) *Curious Punishments of Bygone Days*, New York: Duffield & Company.

Easteal, P. W. (1993a) *Killing the Beloved: Homicide Between Adult Sexual Intimates*, Canberra: Australian Institute of Criminology.

Easteal, P. W. (1993b) 'Sentencing Those Who Kill Their Sexual Intimates: an Australian Study', *International Journal of the Sociology of Law*, 21: 189–218.

Easteal, P. W. (1994) 'Homicide Between Adult Sexual Intimates in Australia: Implications for Prevention', *Studies on Crime and Justice Prevention*: 24–40.

Easteal, P. W. (1998) *Balancing the Scales: Rape, Law Reform and Australian Culture*: Sydney: Federation Press.

Easteal, P. W. (2001) *Less Than Equal*, Sydney: Butterworths.

Eburn, M. (2001) 'A New Model of Provocation in New South Wales', *Criminal Law Journal*, 25: 206–14.

Edmistone, L. (2007a) 'Verdicts Provoke Debate', *The Courier Mail*, 3 July.

Edmistone, L. (2007b) 'State Lags on Provocation', *The Courier Mail*, 5 July.

Edwards, S. (2003) 'Injustice That Puts Low Price On a Woman's Life', *The Times*, 2 September.

Edwards, S. S. M. (1984) *Women on Trial*, Manchester: Manchester University Press.

Edwards, S. S. M. (1987) '"Provoking Her Own Demise": From Common Assault to Homicide', in J. Hanmer and M. Maynard (eds) *Women, Violence and Control*, Hampshire: The Macmillan Press.

Edwards, S. S. M. (1996) *Sex and Gender in the Legal Process*, London: Blackstone Press Limited.

Edwards, S. S. M. (2006) 'Descent into Murder: Provocation's Stricture – The Prognosis for Women Who Kill Men Who Abuse Them', *The Journal of Criminal Law*, 71: 342–61.

Edwards, T. (2006) *Cultures of Masculinity*, Abingdon, Oxon: Routledge.

Ehrlich, S. (2001) *Representing Rape: Language and Sexual Consent*, London: Routledge.

Elliott, C. (2000) 'The Partial Defence of Provocation: The House of Lords Decision in Smith', *Journal of Criminal Law*, 64: 594–600.

Elms, E. (2008) 'On the Use of Classical Allusions in Judgment Writing', *University of New South Wales Law Journal*, 31: 56–79.

Erlich, S. (2001) *Representing Rape: Language and Sexual Consent*, London: Routledge.

Estrich, S. (1988) *Real Rape: How the Legal System Victimizes Women Who Say No*, Cambridge, M.A.: Harvard University Press.

Evans, S. (9 August 2010) 'Chiltern Murder Victim's Father Supports Homicide Law Review', *The Border Mail*, 9 August. Online. Available at http://www.bordermail.com.au/news/local/news/general/chiltern-murder-victims-father-supports-homicide-law-review/1907590.aspx (accessed 15 January 2011).

Ewick, P. and Silbey, S. S. (1995) 'Subversive Stories and Hegemonic Tales: Toward a Sociology of Narrative', *Law & Society Review*, 29: 197–226.

Fairall, P. A. and Yeo, S. (2005) *Criminal Defences in Australia*, Sydney: LexisNexis Butterworths.

Faludi, S. (1991) *Backlash: the Undeclared War against American Women*, New York: Crown.

Faludi, S. (1999) *Stiffed: The Betrayal of the American Man*, London: Chatto & Windus.

Farouque, F. (2005) 'Husband Killer Set to get Out of Jail', The Age, 11 June. Online. Available at http://www.theage.com.au/news/National/Husband-Killer-set-to-get-out-of-jail/2005/06/10/1118347600887.html (accessed 17 May 2012).

Federal Department of Justice Canada. (1998) *Reforming Criminal Code Defences: Provocation, Self-Defence and Defence of Property: A Consultation Paper*, Ontario: Federal Department of Justice Canada.

Felman, S. (1981) 'Rereading Femininity', *Yale French Studies*, 62: 19–44.

Fenstermaker, S. and West, C. (eds) (2002) *Doing Gender, Doing Difference: Inequality, Power and Institutional Change*, London and New York: Routledge.

Ferguson, H., Hearn, J., Gullvåg Holter, O., Jalmert, L., Kimmel, M., Lang, J. and Morrell, R. (2003) *Ending Gender-Based Violence: A Call for Global Action to Involve Men*, Sida, Stockholm: Swedish Agency for International Development Cooperation.

Fineman, M. A. (1991) *The Illusion of Equality: The Rhetoric and Reality of Divorce Law Reform*, Chicago: The University of Chicago Press.

Finkel, N. (1995) 'Achilles Fuming, Odysseus Stewing, and Hamlet Brooding: On the Story of the Murder/Manslaughter Distinction', *Nebraska Law Review*, 74: 742–803.

Flood, M. (2002/2003) 'Engaging Men: Strategies and Dilemmas in Violence Prevention Education Among Men', *Women Against Violence: A Feminist Journal*, 13: 25–32.

Flood, M. (2004) 'Men's Collective Struggles for Gender Justice: The Case of Antiviolence Activism', in M. Kimmel, J. Hearn and R. Connell (eds) *Handbook of Studies on Men and Masculinities*, Thousand Oaks, CA: Sage.

Flood, M. (2005/2006) 'Changing Men: Best Practice in Sexual Violence Education', *Women Against Violence: A Feminist Journal*, 18: 26–36.

Flood, M. (2011) 'Involving Men in Efforts to End Violence Against Women', *Men and Masculinities*, 14: 358–77.

Flood, M., Peacock, D., Stern, O., Barker, G. and Greig, A. (eds) (2010) *World Health Organization Men and Gender Policy Brief: Policy approaches to involving men and boys in achieving gender equality and health equity*, Johannesburg: Sonke Gender Justice Network.

Flood, M. and Pease, B. (2006) 'Undoing Men's Privilege and Advancing Gender Equality in Public Sector Institutions', *Policy and Society*, 24.

Flood, M. and Pease, B. (2008) 'Rethinking the Significance of "Attitudes" in Challenging Men's Violence Against Women', *Australian Journal of Social Issues*, 43: 547–61.

Flood, M. and Pease, B. (2009) 'Factors Influencing Attitudes to Violence Against Women', *Trauma, Violence, Abuse*, 10: 125–42.

Flynn, A. (2007) 'Carl Williams: Secret Deals and Bargained Justice – the Underworld of Victoria's Plea Bargaining System', *Current Issues in Criminal Justice*, 19: 120–26.

Flynn, A. (2009) 'Sentence Indications for Indictable Offences: Increasing Court Efficiency at the Expense of Justice – a Response to the Victorian Legislation', *Australian and New Zealand Journal of Criminology*, 42: 244–68.

Forell, C. (2006) 'Gender Equality, Social Values and Provocation Law in the United States, Canada and Australia', *Journal of Gender, Social Policy and the Law*, 14: 27–71.

Foucault, M. (1978) *The History of Sexuality: Volume 1, An Introduction*, translated by R. Hurley, New York: Penguin Books.

Foucault, M. (1980) 'Two Lectures', in C. Gordon (ed) *Power/Knowledge: Selected Interviews and Other Writings 1972–77*, New York: Pantheon Books.

Fyfe, M. (2010) 'Young Male Killers Using Defence Law', *The Age*, 8 August. Online. Available at http://www.theage.com.au/victoria/young-male-killers-using-defence-law-20100807-11pi2.html (accessed 15 January 2011).

Gadd, D. (2000) 'Masculinities, Violence and Defended Psychosocial Subjects', *Theoretical Criminology*, 4: 429–49.

Gadd, D. (2002) 'Masculinities and Violence Against Female Partners', *Social & Legal Studies*, 11: 61–80.

Gadd, D. (2003) 'Reading Between the Lines: Subjectivity and Men's Violence', *Men and Masculinities*, 5: 333–54.

Gadd, D. (2004) 'Criminal Careers: Desistance and Subjectivity: Interpreting Men's Narratives of Change', *Theoretical Criminology*, 8: 123–56.

Gadd, D. and Jefferson, T. (2007a) 'On the Defensive: a Psychoanalytically Informed Psychosocial Reading of the Jack Roller', *Theoretical Criminology*, 11: 443–67.

Gadd, D. and Jefferson, T. (2007b) *Psychosocial Criminology*, London: Sage.

Galbraith, J. (2000) 'Processes of Whiteness and Stories of Rape', *Australian Feminist Law Journal*, 14: 71–90.

Gavey, N. (1992) 'Technologies and Effect of Heterosexual Coercion', *Feminism and Psychology*, 2: 325–51.

Gavey, N. (2005) *Just Sex? The Cultural Scaffolding of Rape*, London and New York: Routledge.

Gewirtz, P. (1996a) 'Narrative and Rhetoric in the Law', in P. Brooks and P. Gewirtz (eds) *Law's Stories: Narrative and Rhetoric in the Law*, New Haven and London: Yale University Press.

Gewirtz, P. (1996b) 'Victims and Voyeurs at the Criminal Trial', *Northwestern University Law Review*, 90: 863–97.

Giddens, A. (1976) *New Rules of Sociological Method: A Positive Critique of Interpretative Sociologies*, London : Hutchinson.

Giddens, A. (1991) *Modernity and Self-Identity: Self and Society in the Late Modern Age*, Cambridge: Polity Press.

Gillis, J., Jebely, P., Ostovich, E., Sagarti, S. and Mandell, D. (2006) 'Systemic Obstacles to Women's Participation in the Judicial System', *Violence Against Women*, 12: 1150–68.

Goffman, E. (1979) *Gender Advertisements*, Cambridge, M.A.: Harvard University Press.

Golder, B. (2004a) '"It Forced Me to Open More Than I Could Bear": HAD, Paedophilia, and the Discursive Limits of the Male Heterosexual Body', in A. T. Kenyon and P. Rush (eds) *An Aesthetics of Law and Culture: Texts, Images, Screens*, Amsterdam: Elsevier.

Golder, B. (2004b) 'The Homosexual Advance Defence and the Law/Body Nexus: Towards a Poetics of Law Reform', *E-Law Murdoch University Electronic Journal of Law*, 11: paras 1–67.

Goodey, J. (2000) 'Biographical Lessons for Criminology', *Theoretical Criminology*, 4: 478–98.

Goodrich, P. (1986) *Reading the Law: A Critical Introduction to Legal Method and Techniques*, Oxford and New York: Basic Blackwell.

Goodrich, P. (1987) *Legal Discourse: Studies in Linguistics, Rhetoric and Legal Analysis*, Houndmills, Basingstoke, Hampshire and London: The Macmillan Press Ltd.

Goodrich, P. (1990) *Languages of Law: From Logics of Memory to Nomadic Masks*, London: Wiedenfeld and Nicolson.

Goodrich, P. (1995) *Oedipus Lex: Psychoanalysis, History, Law*, Los Angeles, London: University of California Press.

Goodrich, P. (1996) *Law in the Courts of Love: Literature and Other Minor Jurisprudences*, London and New York: Routledge.

Goodrich, P. (1997) 'Epistolary Justice: The Love Letter as Law', *Yale Journal of Law & the Humanities*, 9: 245–95.

Gorman, W. (1999) 'Provocation: The Jealous Husband Defence', *Criminal Law Quarterly*, 42: 478–500.

Gotell, L. (2002) 'The Ideal Victim, the Hysterical Complainant, and the Disclosure of Confidential Records: The Implications of the *Charter* for Sexual Assault Law', *Osgoode Hall Law Journal*, 40: 252–96.

Gough, D. (2004) 'Ramage Manslaughter Verdict Under Attack', *The Age*, 30 October, p 3.

Gower, P. (2009) 'Sophie's Father Says Judge Censored Him', *New Zealand Herald*, 13 November.

Gowing, L. (1996) *Domestic Dangers: Women, Words, and Sex in Early Modern London*, Oxford: Clarendon Press.

Grant, I. (1991) 'The Syndromization of Women's Experiences', *University of British Colombia Law Review*, 25: 51–68.

Graycar, R. (1996) 'Telling Tales: Legal Stories About Violence Against Women', *Cardozo Studies in Law and Literature*, 8: 297–315.

Graycar, R. and Morgan, J. (1990) 'Injuries to Women: Gendered Harms', *Refractory Girl*, 36: 7–12.

Graycar, R. and Morgan, J. (1996) 'Legal Categories, Women's Lives and the Law Curriculum OR: Making Gender Examinable', *Sydney Law Review*, 18: 431–50.

Graycar, R. and Morgan, J. (2002) *The Hidden Gender of Law*, Leichhardt, NSW: The Federation Press.

Graycar, R. and Morgan, J. (2005) 'Women's Lives, Legal Categories, and the Law Curriculum OR Making Gender Examinable?', *Sydney Law Review*, 18: 431–450.

Graycar, R. and Morgan, J. (2006) 'One Step Forward or Two Steps Back?', *Australian Feminist Law Journal*, 20: 23–40.

Graycar, R. and Morgan, J. (2008) 'Equality Rights: What's Wrong?', in R. Hunter (ed) *Rethinking Equality Projects in Law: Feminist Challenges*, Oxford and Portland: Hart Publishing.

Greene, J. (1989) 'A Provocation Defence for Battered Women who Kill', *Adelaide Law Review*, 12: 145–63.

Grix, J. (1999) 'Law's Truth and Other Lies: Women, Sexual Assault and the Criminal Justice System', *Australian Feminist Law Journal*, 12: 83–95.

Hachamovitch, Y. (1997) 'The Dummy: An Essay on Malice Prepensed', in P. Rush, S. McVeigh and A. Young (eds) *Criminal Legal Doctrine*, Aldershot: Ashgate.

Hagan, K. and Russell, M. (2009) 'Manslaughter Verdict as Jury Accepts Strangler's Abuse Defence', *The Age*, 1 November. Online. Available at http://www.theage.com.au/national/manslaughter-verdict-as-jury-accepts-stranglers-abuse-defence-20091031-hqto.html (accessed 5 November 2009).

Hall, A. (2010) 'Chief Justice Warns of Ethnic Honour Crimes', *ABC News*, 1 April. Online. Available at http://www.abc.net.au/news/stories/2010/04/16/2874376.htm (accessed 18 April 2010).

Halsey, M. J. (2006) 'Negotiating Conditional Release: Juvenile Narratives of Repeat Incarceration', *Punishment and Society*, 8: 147–81.

Hamer, D. (2008) 'Admissibility and the Use of Relationship Evidence in *HML v The Queen*: One Step Forward, Two Steps Back', *Criminal Law Journal*, 32: 351–67.

Hayward, A. (2008) 'Homicide Laws Overhauled', *WA Today*, 31 July. Online. Available at <http://www.watoday.com.au/wa-news/homicide-laws-overhauled-20080731-3nod.html (accessed 15 December 2008).

Hearn, J. (1996) 'Is Masculinity Dead? A Critique of the Concept of Masculinity/Masculinities', in M. Mac an Ghaill (ed) *Understanding Masculinities: Social Relations and Cultural Arenas*, Buckingham: Open University Press.

Hearn, J. (1998) 'Men Will Be Men: The Ambiguity of Men's Support for Men Who Have Been Violent to Known Women', in J. Hearn, J. Popay and Edwards, J. (eds) *Men, Gender Divisions and Welfare*, London: Routledge.

Hearn, J. (2004) 'From Hegemonic Masculinity to the Hegemony of Men', *Feminist Theory*, 5: 49–72.

Heath, M. and Naffine, N. (1994) 'Men's Needs and Women's Desires: Feminist Dilemmas About Rape Law Reform', *Australian Feminist Law Journal*, 30: 30–52.

Heidensohn, F. (1985) *Women and Crime*, London: Macmillan.

Henriques, J., Hollway, W., Urwin, C., Venn, C. and Walkerdine, V. (1984) *Changing the Subject: Psychology, Social Regulation and Subjectivity*, London and New York: Methuen & Co Ltd.

Higgins, C. (1997) 'Legal Language as Discursive Formation', in C. O'Farrell (ed) *Foucault: The Legacy*, Kelvin Grove: Queensland University of Technology Press.

Hinsliff, G. (2003) 'Crime of Passion is No Defence', *The Guardian*, 19 January. Online. Available at http://www.guardian.co.uk/politics/2003/jan/19/ukcrime.prisonsand-probation (accessed 15 January 2011).

Holland, W. (2007) 'Murder and Related Issues: an Analysis of the Law in Canada', in J. Horder (ed) *Homicide Law in Comparative Perspective*, Oxford and Portland.

Hollway, W. (1984) 'Gender Difference and the Production of Subjectivity', in J. Henriques, W. Hollway, C. Urwin, C. Venn and V. Walkerdine (eds) *Changing the Subject: Psychology, Social Regulation and Subjectivity*, London: Methuen.

Hollway, W. (1989) *Subjectivity and Method in Psychology: Gender, Meaning and Science*, London: Sage.

Hollway, W. and Jefferson, T. (1997) 'Eliciting Narrative Through the In-depth Interview', *Qualitative Inquiry*, 3: 53–70.

Hollway, W. and Jefferson, T. (1998) '"A Kiss is Just a Kiss": Date Rape, Gender and Subjectivity', *Sexualities*, 1: 405–23.

Hollway, W. and Jefferson, T. (1999) 'Gender, Generation, Anxiety and the Reproduction of Culture: a Family Case Study', in R. Josselson and A. Lieblich (eds) *Making Meaning of Narratives in the Narrative Study of Lives*, London: Sage.

Hollway, W. and Jefferson, T. (2000a) 'Biography, Anxiety and the Experience of Locality', in P. Chamberlayne, J. Bornat and T. Wengraf (eds) *The Turn to Biographical Methods in Social Science: Comparative Issues Examples*, London: Routledge.

Hollway, W. and Jefferson, T. (2000b) *Doing Qualitative Research Differently: Free Association, Narrative and the Interview Method*, London: Sage.

Hood-Williams, J. (2001) 'Gender, Masculinities and Crime: From Structures to Psyches', *Theoretical Criminology*, 5: 37–60.

Hopkins, A. and Easteal, P. (2010) 'Walking in Her Shoes: Battered Women Who Kill in Victoria, Western Australia and Queensland', *Alternative Law Journal*, 35: 132–37.

Horder, J. (1989) 'Sex, Violence, and Sentencing in Domestic Provocation Cases', *Criminal Law Review*: 546–54.

Horder, J. (1992a) *Provocation and Responsibility*, Oxford: Clarendon Press.

Horder, J. (1992b) 'The Duel and the English Law of Homicide', *Oxford Journal of Legal Studies*, 12: 419–30.

Hore, E., Gibson, J. and Bordow, S. (1996) *Domestic Homicide*, Sydney: Family Court of Australia.

Howe, A. (1994) 'Provoking Comment: The Question of Gender Bias in the Provocation Defence', in N. Grieve and A. Burns (eds) *Australian Women: Contemporary Feminist Thought*, Melbourne: Oxford University Press.

Howe, A. (1997) 'More Folk Provoke Their Own Demise: (Homophobic Violence and Sexed Excuses – Rejoining the Provocation Law Debate, Courtesy of the Homosexual Advance Defence)', *Sydney Law Review*, 19: 336–65.

Howe, A. (1998) 'The Provocation Defence: Finally Provoking its Own Demise? *Green v R* case note', *Melbourne University Law Review*, 22: 466–90.

Howe, A. (1999) 'Reforming Provocation (More or Less)', *Australian Feminist Law Journal*, 12: 127–37.

Howe, A. (2000) 'Homosexual Advances in Law: Murderous Excuse, Pluralized Ignorance and the Privilege of Unknowing', in C. Stychin and D. Herman (eds) *Sexuality in the Legal Arena*, London: Athlone.

Howe, A. (2002) 'Provoking Polemic – Provoked Killings and the Ethical Paradoxes of the Postmodern Feminist Condition', *Feminist Legal Studies*, 10: 39–64.

Howe, A. (2004a) 'Managing "Men's Violence" in the Criminological Arena', in C. Sumner (ed) *The Blackwell International Companion to Criminology*, Oxford: Blackwell.

Howe, A. (2004b) 'Provocation In Crisis – Law's Passion at the Crossroads? New Directions for Feminist Strategists', *The Australian Feminist Law Journal*, 21: 53–77.

Howe, A. (2008) *Sex, Violence and Crime: Foucault and the "Man" Question*, London: Routledge-Cavendish.

Howe, A. (2010) 'Another Name for Murder', *Sydney Morning Herald*, 24 May. Online. Available at http://www.smh.com.au/opinion/society-and-culture/another-name-for-murder-20100523-w3w0.html (accessed 26 May 2010).

Hubble, G. (1997) 'Feminism and the Battered Woman: The Limits of Self-Defence in the Context of Domestic Violence', *Current Issues in Criminal Justice*, 9: 113–24.

Hulls, R. (2010a) 'Probe Into New Law on Homicide', *The Age*, 30 May. Online. Available at http://www.theage.com.au/national/probe-into-new-law-on-homicide-20100529-wmli.html (accessed 31 May 2010).

Hulls, R. (2010b) 'Fighting Family Violence May Require Further Reform', *The Age*, 30 May.

Hunt, E. (2008) 'Henpecked Hubby "Snapped" Over Upset Dog', *The Herald Sun*, 16 September. Online. Available at http://forum.dadsontheair.com/viewtopic.php?t= 30678andstart=0andpostdays=0andpostorder=ascandhighlight=andsid=1d5421f98 b67e93486c6fe87e005799d (accessed 15 January 2010).

Hunter, R. C. (1996) 'Gender in Evidence: Masculine Norms vs. Feminist Reforms', *Harvard Women's Law Journal*, 19: 127–68.

Hunter, R. C. (2006a) 'Narratives of Domestic Violence', *Sydney Law Review*, 28: 733–76.

Hunter, R. C. (2006b) 'Law's (Masculine) Violence: Reshaping Jurisprudence', *Law and Critique*, 17: 27–46.

Hunter, R. C. (ed) (2008) *Rethinking Equality Projects in Law: Feminist Challenges*, Oxford and Portland: Hart Publishing.

Iaria, M. (2009) 'Anthony Sherna "Killed Partner For Waking Up Dog"', 21 May. Online. Available at http://www.news.com.au/breaking-news/anthony-sherna-killed-partner-for-waking-up-dog/story-e6frfku0-1225714103936 (accessed 15 January 2009).

Jackie Brown (1997, directed by Quentin Tarantino), United States: Miramax Films.

Jackson, B. S. (1990) 'Narrative Theories and Legal Discourse', in C. Nash (ed) *Narrative in Culture: The Uses of Storytelling in the Sciences, Philosophy, and Literature*, London: Routledge.

Jalmert, L. (2003) *The Role of Men and Boys in Achieving Gender Equality: Some Swedish and Scandinavian Experiences*, Paper presented at the Expert Group Meeting, United Nations Development Programme, Brasilia, Brazil, 21–24 October.

Jefferson, T. (1994) 'Theorising Masculine Subjectivity', in T. Newburn and E. A. Stanko (eds) *Just Boys Doing Business? Men, Masculinities and Crime*, London: Routledge.

Jefferson, T. (1996a) 'Introduction to Masculinities, Social Relations and Crime', *The British Journal of Criminology: Delinquency and Deviant Social Behaviour*, 36: 337–47.

Jefferson, T. (1996b) 'From "Little Fairy Boy" to "The Compleat Destroyer": Subjectivity and Transformation in the Biography of Mike Tyson', in M. Mac an Ghaill (ed) *Understanding Masculinities: Social Relations and Cultural Arenas*, Buckingham: Open University Press.

Jefferson, T. (1997a) 'Masculinities and Crime', in M. Maguire, R. Morgan and R. Reiner (eds) *The Oxford Handbook of Criminology*, Oxford: Clarendon Press.

Jefferson, T. (1997b) 'The Tyson Rape Trial: The Law, Feminism and the Emotional "Truth"', *Social and Legal Studies*, 6: 281–301.

Jefferson, T. (1998) '"Muscle, "Hard Men" and "Iron" Mike Tyson: Reflections on Desire, Anxiety and the Embodiment of Masculinity', *Body and Society*, 4: 77–98.

Jefferson, T. (2002a) 'For a Psychosocial Criminology', in K. Carrington and R. Hogg (eds) *Critical Criminologies: An Introduction*, Cullumpton, Devon: Willan Publishing.

Jefferson, T. (2002b) 'Subordinating Hegemonic Masculinity', *Theoretical Criminology*, 6: 63–88.

Jefferson, T. (2004) 'From Cultural Studies to Psychosocial Criminology: an Intellectual Journey', in J. Ferrel, K. Hayward, W. Morrison and M. Presdee (eds) *Cultural Criminology Unleashed*, London: Glasshouse Press.

Johnson, C. (2009a) 'Teenager in Court Over Gruesome Killing of Stepdad', *The Age*, 31 January. Online. Available at http://www.theage.com.au/national/teenager-in-court-over-gruesome-killing-of-stepdad-20090112-7f8m.html (accessed 2 February 2009).

Johnson, C. (2009b) 'Murder Charges Dropped Against "Sex Slave" Teen', *The Age*, 27 October. Online. Available at http://www.theage.com.au/national/murder-charged-dropped-against-sex-slave-teen-20090327-9czp.html (accessed 30 October 2009).

Johnson, H. and Dawson, M. (2011) *Violence Against Women in Canada*, Oxford: Oxford University Press.

Johnson, J. and Hotton, T. (2003) 'Losing Control: Homicide Risk in Estranged and Intact Intimate Relationships', *Homicide Studies*, 7: 58–84.

Johnson, P. (1996) '"More than Ordinary Men Gone Wrong": Can the Law Know the Gay Subject?', *Melbourne University Law Journal*, 20: 1152–92.

Jones, D. W. (2008) *Understanding Criminal Behaviour: Psychosocial Approaches to Criminality*, Cullompton: Willan Publishing.

Jones, K. (2006) *Gender and Petty Crime in Late Medieval England: the Local Courts in Kent 1460–1560*, Woodbridge: Boydell Press.

Julius, A. (1999) 'Introduction', in M. Freeman and A. Lewis (eds) *Law and Literature*, New York: Oxford University Press.

Kahan, D. M. and Nussbaum, M. C. (1996) 'Two Conceptions of Emotion in Criminal Law', *Columbia Law Review*, 96: 269–374.

Kamensky, J. (1996) 'Talk Like a Man: Speech, Power, and Masculinity in Early New England', *Gender & History*, 8: 22–47.

Kamensky, J. (1997) *Governing the Tongue: The Politics of Speech in Early New England*, Oxford and New York: Oxford University Press.

Kaspiew, R. (1995) 'Rape Lore: Legal Narrative and Sexual Violence', *Melbourne University Law Review*, 20: 350–82.

Katz, J. (1988) *Seductions of Crime*, New York: Basic Books.

Kaufman, M. (1994) 'Men, Feminism and Men's Contradictory Experiences of Power', in H. Brod and M. Kaufman (eds) *Theorizing Masculinities*, Thousand Oaks: Sage.

Kaye, M. and Tolmie, J. (1998) 'Discoursing Dads: The Rhetorical Devices of Fathers' Rights Groups', *Melbourne University Law Review*, 22: 162–94.

Kennedy, R. (2002) 'Legal Sensations: Sexuality, Textuality and Evidence in a Victorian Murder Trial', in M. Thornton (ed) *Romancing the Tomes: Popular Culture, Law and Feminism*, London: Cavendish Publishing Limited.

Kersten, J. (1996) 'Culture, Masculinities and Violence against Women', *British Journal of Criminology*, 36: 318–95.

Kimmel, M. S. (ed) (1987) *Changing Men: New Directions in Research on Men and Masculinity*, London: Sage.

Kimmel, M. S. and Kaufman, M. (1995) 'Weekend Warriors: The New Men's Movement', in M. S. Kimmel (ed) *The Politics of Manhood*, Philadelphia: Temple University Press.

Kirkwood, D. (2000) *Women Who Kill: A Study of Female Perpetrated Homicide in Victoria Between 1985 and 1995*, PhD, Monash University.

Kirkwood, D. (2010) 'Access to Justice: Heather Osland's Fight for Justice', *Alternative Law Journal*, 35: 168–69.

Kissane, K. (2004a) 'Jammed Scales And a Blunt Sword', *The Herald Sun*, 30 October, p 32.

Kissane, K. (2004b) 'Honour Killing in the Suburbs', *The Age*, Insight, 6 November, p 4 –5.

Kissane, K. (2006) *Silent Death: the Killing of Julie Ramage*, Australia: Hodder.

Kissane, K. (2008) 'New Approach to Provocation in Sentencing Urged', *The Age*, 7 February. Online. Available at http://www.theage.com.au/news/national/new-approach-to-provocation-in-sentencing-urged/2008/02/06/1202233951254.html (accessed 15 January 2010).

Klineberg, J. (2002) 'Anger and Intent for Murder: The Supreme Court Decision in *R. v. Parent*', *Osgoode Hall Law Journal*, 41: 37–73.

Knox, S. L. (1998) *Murder: A Tale of Modern American Life*, Durham: Duke University Press.

Lacey, N., Wells, C. and Quick, O. (2010) *Reconstructing Criminal Law: Text and Materials*, Cambridge: Cambridge University Press.

Larcombe, W. (2005) *Compelling Engagements: Feminism, Rape Law and Romance Fiction*, Sydney: The Federation Press.

Lauretis, T. de (1984) *Alice Doesn't: Feminism, Semiotics, Cinema*, Bloomington: Indiana University Press.

Lauretis, T. de (1987) *Technologies of Gender: Essays of Theory, Film, and Fiction*, Bloomington and Indianapolis: Indiana University Press.

Law Commission UK (2004) *Partial Defences to Murder: Final report*, United Kingdom: Law Commission.

Law Reform Commission New Zealand (2000) *Battered Defendants: Victims of Domestic Violence Who Offend, A Discussion Paper*, Wellington: Law Reform Commission New Zealand.

Law Commission of New Zealand (2001) *Some Criminal Defences with Particular Reference to Battered Defendants Report No 73*, Wellington: Law Commission of New Zealand.

Law Commission UK (2006) *Bringing the Law of Homicide Into the 21st Century*, Press Release, 29 November, London: Law Commission UK.

Law Reform Commission of Victoria (1991) *Homicide: Report No 40, Homicide Prosecutions Study,* Appendix 6 to Report No 40, Homicide, Melbourne: Law Reform Commission of Victoria.

Law Reform Commission of Western Australia (2007) *Final Report: Review of the Law of Homicide* (Project 97), Perth: Law Reform Commission of Western Australia.

Leader-Elliott, I. (1997) 'Passion and Insurrection in the Law of Sexual Provocation', in N. Naffine and R. Owens (eds) *Sexing the Subject of Law*, Sydney: Sweet & Maxwell.

Lee, C. (2003) *Murder and the Reasonable Man: Passion and Fear in the Criminal Courtroom*, New York: New York University Press.

Lee, C. (2008) 'The Gay Panic Defense', *UC Davis Law Review*, 42: 471–566.

Lees, S. (1992) 'Naggers, Whores, Libbers: Provoking Men to Kill', in J. Radford and D. E. H. Russell (eds) *Femicide: The Politics of Woman Killing*, New York: Twayne Publishers.

Lees, S. (1997) *Ruling Passions: Sexual Violence, Reputation and the Law*, Buckingham: Open University Press.

Levant, R. F. (1997) 'The Masculinity Crisis', *Journal of Men's Studies*, 5: 221–28.

Lunny, A. M. (2003) 'Provocation and "Homosexual Advance": Masculinized Subjects As Threat, Masculinized Subjects Under Threat', *Social & Legal Studies*, 12: 311–33.

MacDonald, V. (2010) 'Rally for Tougher Murder Laws', *The Border Mail*, 7 August. Online. Available at http://www.bordermail.com.au/news/local/news/general/rally-for-tougher-murder-laws/1906996.aspx (accessed 15 January 2011).

Mackay, R. D. (2010) 'The *Coroners and Justice Act* 2009 – partial defences to murder (2) The new diminished responsibility plea', *Criminal Law Review*, 4: 290–302.

Mackenzie, G. and Colvin, E. (2009) *Homicide in Abusive Relationships: A Report on Defences*, Robina: Faculty of Law Bond University.

Maguigan, H. (1991) 'Battered Women and Self-Defense: Myths and Misconceptions in Current Reform Efforts', *University of Pennsylvania Law Review*, 140: 379–486.

Maguigan, H. (1998) 'More than Victims: Battered Women, the Syndrome Society, and the Law [Review]', *Criminal Justice Ethics*, 17: 50–57.

Maharaj, Z. (1995) 'A Social Theory of Gender: Connell's *Gender and Power*', *Feminist Review*, 49: 50–65.

Maher, J., Segrave, M., Pickering, S. and McCulloch, J. (2005) 'Honouring White Masculinity: Culture, Terror, Provocation and the Law', *Australian Feminist Law Journal*, 23: 147–76.

Mahoney, M. R. (1991) 'Legal Images of Battered Women: Redefining the Issue of Separation', *Michigan Law Review*, 90: 1–94.

Marcus, S. (1992) 'Fighting Bodies, Fighting Words: A Theory and Politics of Rape Prevention', in J. Butler and J. W. Scott (eds) *Feminist Theorize the Political*, London and New York: Routledge.

Martin, W. (1986) *Recent Theories of Narrative*, Ithaca: Cornell University Press.

Martinson, D. (1999) '*Lavallée v. R.*: The Supreme Court of Canada Addresses Gender Bias in the Courts', *University of British Colombia Law Review*, 24: 381–96.

Martinson, D., MacCrimmon, M., Grant, I. and Boyle, C. (1991) 'A Forum on *Lavallée v. R*: Women and Self-Defence', *University of British Colombia Law Review*, 23–68.

Maruna, S. (1997) 'Going Straight: Desistance from Crime and Life Narratives of Reform', in A. Lieblich and R. Josselson (eds) *The Narrative Study of Lives*, London: Sage.

Maruna, S. and Matravers, A. (2007) 'Criminology and the Person', *Theoretical Criminology*, 11: 427–42.

Matsuda, M. (1987) 'Looking to the Bottom: Critical Legal Studies and Reparations', *Harvard Civil Rights-Civil Liberties Law Review*, 22: 323–399.

Matsuda, M. J., Lawrence III, C. R., Delgado, R. and Williams Crenshaw, K. (eds) (1993) *Words That Wound: Critical Race Theory, Assaultive Speech, and the First Amendment*, Boulder: Westview Press.

McBarnet, D. J. (1981) *Conviction: Law, the State and the Construction of Justice*, London: Macmillan.

McColgan, A. (1993) 'In Defence of Battered Women Who Kill', *Oxford Journal of Legal Studies*, 13: 508–29.

McColgan, A. (2000) 'General Defences', in D. Nicolson and L. Bibbings (eds) *Feminist Perspectives on Criminal Law*, London: Cavendish Publishing Limited.

McDonald, B. and Smith, S. (1999) *Zero Tolerance Against Violence: The Klassen Case* Online. Available at http://zerotolerance.ca/ (accessed 9 December 2008).

McDonald, E. (1993) 'Provocation, Sexuality and the Actions of "Thoroughly Decent Men"', *Women's Studies Journal*, 9: 126–47.

McIntosh, M. K. (1998) *Controlling Misbehaviour in England, 1370–1600*, Cambridge: Cambridge University Press.

McKay, H. (2011) 'Ribbon of Hope for Balwyn Woman', *Progress Leader*, 25 November.

McMahon, A. (1993) 'Male Readings of Feminist Theory: The Psychologization of Sexual Politics in the Masculinity Literature', *Theory and Society*, 22: 675–95.

McMahon, A. (1999) *Taking Care of Men: Sexual Politics in the Public Mind*, Melbourne, Australia: Cambridge University Press.

McQuillan, M. (2000) *The Narrative Reader*, London: Routledge.

McSherry, B. (2005) 'It's a Man's World: Claims of Provocation and Automatism in "Intimate" Homicides', *Melbourne University Law Journal*, 28: 905–29.

Merry, S. E. (1992) 'Culture, Power, and the Discourse of the Law', *New York Law School Law Review*, 37: 209–25.

Messerschmidt, J. W. (1993) *Masculinities and Crime: Critique, and Reconceptualization of Theory*, Maryland: Rowan & Littlefield.

Messerschmidt, J. W. (1994) 'Schooling, Masculinities and Youth Crime by White Boys', in T. Newburn and E. Stanko (eds) *Just Boys Doing Business: Men, Masculinities and Crime*, London: Routledge.

Messerschmidt, J. W. (1997) *Crime as Structured Action*, London: Sage.

Messerschmidt, J. W. (1999) 'Making Bodies Matter: Adolescent Masculinities, the Body, and Varieties of Violence', *Theoretical Criminology*, 3: 197–220.

Messerschmidt, J. W. (2000) 'Becoming "Real Men": Adolescent Masculinity Changes and Sexual Violence', *Men and Masculinities*, 2: 286–307.

Messerschmidt, J. W. (2008) 'And Now, the Rest of the Story... A Commentary on Christine Beasley's "Rethinking Hegemonic Masculinity in a Globalising World"', *Men and Masculinities*, 11: 104–108.

Meure, D. (2001) 'Homo Panic in the High Court: The High Court in *Green v R*', *Griffith Law Review*, 10: 240–55.

Miller, C. J. (2000) *Contempt of Court*, Oxford: Oxford University Press.

Mills, S. (1995) *Feminist Stylistics*, London: Routledge.

Mills, L. G. (2003) *Insult to Injury: Rethinking Our Responses to Intimate Abuse*, Princeton: Princeton University Press.

Mills, L. G. (2008) *Violet Partners: A Breakthrough Plan for Ending the Cycle of Abuse*, New York: Basic Books.

Milovanovic, S. (2010a) 'Osland Should Be Released, Hulls Was Told', *The Age*, 24 June.

Milovanovic, S. (2010b) 'Husband Killer Wins Legal Battle Over Pardon', *The Age*, 23 June.

Ministry of Justice UK (2008) *UK Murder Law Reforms: Provocation Not An Excuse*, Media Release, 29 July, London: Ministry of Justice.

Mison, R. B. (1992) 'Homophobia in Manslaughter: The Homosexual Advance as Insufficient Provocation', *California Law Review*, 80: 133–78.

Model Criminal Code Officers Committee of the Standing Committee of Attorneys-General (1998) *Chapter 5, Fatal Offences Against the Person*, Canberra: Model Criminal Code Officers Committee of the Standing Committee of Attorneys-General.

Morgan, J. (1997) 'Provocation Law and Facts: Dead Women Tell No Tales, Tales Are Told About Them', *Melbourne University Law Review*, 21: 237–76.

Morgan, J. (2002) *Whom Kills Whom and Why: Looking Beyond Legal Categories*, Melbourne: Victorian Law Reform Commission.

Morrissey, B. (2003) *When Women Kill: Questions of Agency and Subjectivity*, London and New York: Routledge.

Mouzos, J. (2000) *Homicidal Encounters: A Study of Homicide in Australia 1989–1999*, Canberra: Australian Institute of Criminology.

Mouzos, J. (2001) *Indigenous and Non-Indigenous Homicides in Australia: A Comparative Analysis*, Canberra: Australian Institute of Criminology.

Munro, I. (2009a) 'Jury Deadlock Over Wife Strangle Case', *The Age*, 2 June. Online. Available at http://www.theage.com.au/national/jury-deadlock-over-wife-strangle-case-20090602-btu6.html (accessed 3 June 2009).

Munro, I. (2009b) 'Manslaughter Verdict a Scandal, Says Activist', *The Age*, 5 November. Online. Available at http://www.theage.com.au/national/manslaughter-verdict-a-scandal-says-activist-20091104-hxzg.html (accessed 6 November 2009).

Murphy, P. (2010) 'And He Said it Was Self-defence', *The Herald Sun*, 12 May, p 13.

Naffine, N. (1990) *Law and the Sexes: Explorations in Feminist Jurisprudence*, Sydney: Allen & Unwin.

Naffine, N. (1994) 'Possession: Erotic Love in the Law of Rape', *The Modern Law Review*, 57: 10–37.

Naffine, N. (1995) 'Criminal Conversation', *Law and Critique*, VI: 193–207.

Naffine, N. (2003) 'The "Man Question" of Crime, Criminology and Criminal Law', *Criminal Justice Matters*, 53: 10–11.

Nelson, C. A. (2002) '(En)Raged or (En)Gaged: The Implications of Racial Context to the Canadian Provocation Defence', *University of Richmond Law Review*, 35: 1007–1083.

New South Wales Law Reform Commission (1997) *Partial Defences to Murder: Provocation and Infanticide, Report No 83*, Sydney: New South Wales Law Reform Commission.

Newburn, T. and Stanko, E. (1994) *Just Boys Doing Business? Men, Masculinities and Crime*, London: Routledge.

New Zealand Government (2009a) *Provocation Bill Gets Unanimous Support*, Media Statement, 19 August.

New Zealand Government (2009b) *Partial Defence of Provocation Abolished*, Media Statement, 27 November.

New Zealand Labour Party (2009a) *National Blocks Move to Remove Provocation*, Media Statement, 23 July.

New Zealand Labour Party (2009b) *Labour Welcomes Repeal of Provocation*, Media Statement, 27 November.

Ng, F. S. (2003) 'Marriage and Discipline: The Place of Women in Early Quaker Controversies', *Seventeenth-Century*, 18: 113–40.

Ng, F. S. (2007) *Literature and the Politics of Family in Seventeenth-Century England*, Cambridge: Cambridge University Press.

Nicolson, D. (1995) 'Telling Tales: Gender Discrimination, Gender Construction and Battered Women Who Kill', *Feminist Legal Studies*, III: 185–206.

Nicolson, D. (2000) 'What the Law Giveth, It Also Taketh Away: Female-Specific Defences to Criminal Liability', in D. Nicolson and L. Bibbings (eds) *Feminist Perspectives on Criminal Law*, London: Cavendish Publishing.

Nicolson, D. and Sanghvi, R. (1993) 'Battered Women and Provocation: the Implications of *R v Ahluwalia*', *Criminal Law Review*, October: 728–38.

Norrie, A. (2010) 'The Coroners and Justice Act 2009 – partial defences to murder (1) Loss of control', *Criminal Law Review*, 4: 275–89.

Norton, M. B. (1987) 'Gender and Defamation in Seventeenth-Century Maryland', *William and Mary Quarterly*, 44: 3–39.

Nourse, V. (1997) 'Passion's Progress: Modern Law Reform and the Provocation Defense', *The Yale Law Journal*, 106: 1325–408.

Nova Scotia Advisory Council on the Status of Women (1998) *Response to Department of Justice Consultation Paper on Provocation, Self-Defence and Defence of Property*, Nova Scotia: Nova Scotia Advisory Council on the Status of Women.

O'Donovan, K. (1991) 'Defences for Battered Women Who Kill', *Journal of Law and Society*, 18: 219–40.

Office of the Attorney-General Victoria (4 October 2005) *Hulls announces major reform to homicide laws*, Media release.

Office of the Attorney-General Victoria (2005) *Hulls Announces Major Reform to Homicide Laws*, Media Release, 4 October.

Office of the Attorney-General Western Australia (2008) *Tough New Homicide Laws for Western Australia*, Media Release, 18 March.

Office of the Deputy Premier and Attorney-General Queensland (2011) 'Legal Loopholes Closed After Tough New Laws Passed', Media Release, 24 March, Brisbane: Department of Justice and Attorney-General.

Office of Women (2000) *Report of the Taskforce on Women and the Criminal Code*. Online. Available at http://www.communities.qld.gov.au/women/resources/resource-types/women-and-the-criminal-code (accessed 19 April 2012).

Osthoff, S. and Maguigan, H. (2005) 'Explaining Without Pathologizing: Testimony on Battering and its Effects', in D. R. Loseke, R. J. Gelles and M. M. Cavanaugh (eds) *Current Controversies on Family Violence*, London: Sage.

Otto, D. (1994) 'Blood on Whose Hands? The Killing of Women and Children in Domestic Homicides' Women's Coalition Against Family Violence, Melbourne, 1994, pages i–xiii, 1–146, notes 147–55. Price $10.00 (soft cover). ISNB 0 646 17924 1. *Melbourne University Law Review*, 19: 1134–36.

Packham, B. and Ross, N. (2004) 'Sister Slams Verdict', *Herald Sun*, 30 October, p 16.

Papke, D. R. (1991) *Narrative and the Legal Discourse: A Reader in Storytelling and the Law*, Liverpool: Deborah Charles.

Parfett, J. (2001) 'Beyond Battered Woman Syndrome Evidence: An Alternative Approach to the Use of Abuse Evidence in Spousal Homicide Cases', *Windsor Review of Legal and Social Issues*, 12: 55–96.

Parker, P. (1989) 'On the Tongue: Cross Gendering and the Art of Words', *Style*, 23: 445–65.

Pasquale, S. de (2002) 'Provocation and the Homosexual Advance Defence: The Deployment of Culture as a Defence Strategy', *Melbourne University Law Review*, 26: 110–44.

Paster, G. K. (1987) 'Leaky Vessels: The Incontinent Women of City Comedy', *Renaissance Drama*, 18: 45–65.

Paton, A. (1958) *Cry: The Beloved Country, A Story of Comfort in Desolation*, Harmondsworth: Penguin.

Pease, B. (1997) *Men and Sexual Politics: Towards a Profeminist Practice*, Adelaide, Australia: Dulwich Centre Publications.

Pease, B. (2000) *Recreating Men: Postmodern Masculinity Politics*, London: Sage.

Pease, B. (2002) '(Re)Constructing Men's Interests', *Men and Masculinities*, 5: 165–77.

Pease, B. (2003) 'Men and Masculinities: Profeminist Approaches to Changing Men', in B. Pease, L. Briskman and J. Allan (eds) *Critical Social Work: An Introduction to Theories and Practices*, Crows Nest, NSW: Allen & Unwin.

Pease, B. (2008a) 'Engaging Men in Men's Violence Prevention: Exploring the Tensions, Dilemmas and Possibilities', *Australian Domestic & Family Violence Clearinghouse*, August: 1–20.

Pease, B. (2008b) 'Rethinking the Significance of Attitudes in Preventing Men's Violence Against Women', *Australian Journal of Social Issues*, 43: 547–61.

Petersen, A. (1998) *Unmasking the Masculine: 'Men' and 'Identity' in a Sceptical Age*, London: Sage.

Petrie, A. (2010a) '17 years' Jail for Man Who Beat Wife "to Pulp"', *The Age*, 29 June.

Petrie, A. (2010b) 'Jealous Man Gets 17 years for Clubbing Wife to Death', *The Age*, 30, June.

Philadelphoff-Puren, N. (2005) 'Contextualising Consent: The Problem of Rape and Romance', *Australian Feminist Studies*, 20: 31–42.

Philadelphoff-Puren, N. and Rush, P. (2003) 'Fatal (F)Laws: Law, Literature and Writing', *Law and Critique*, 14: 191–211.

Phillips, M. M. (1981) 'Erasmus on the Tongue', *Erasmus of Rotterdam Society Yearbook One*, 113–25.

Phillips, A. (2003) 'When Culture Means Gender: Issues of Cultural Defence in the English Courts', *The Modern Law Review*, 66: 510–31.

Polk, K. (1994) *When Men Kill: Scenarios of Masculine Violence*, Cambridge: Cambridge University Press.

Polk, K. and Ranson, D. (1991a) 'The Role of Gender in Intimate Homicide', *Australian and New Zealand Journal of Criminology*, 24: 15–24.

Polk, K. and Ranson, D, (1991b) 'Patterns of Homicide in Victoria', in D. Chappell, P. Grabosky and H. Strang (eds) *Australian Violence: Contemporary Perspectives*, Canberra: Australian Institute of Criminology.

Puren, N. (1995) 'Hymeneal Acts: Interrogating the Hegemony of Rape and Romance', *Australian Feminist Law Journal*, 5: 15–27.

Puren, N. and Young, A. (eds) (1999) 'Signifying Justice: Law, Culture and the Questions of Feminism', *Australian Feminist Law Journal*, 13: 3–13.

Queensland Law Reform Commission (2008) *A Review of the Defence of Accident and the Defence of Provocation Report No 64*, Brisbane: Queensland Law Reform Commission.

Radford, J. (1984) '"Womanslaughter": A Licence to Kill? The Killing of Jane Asher', in P. Scraton and P. Gordon (eds) *Causes for Concern*, Harmondsworth: Penguin Books.

Radford, J. and Russell, D. E. H. (eds) (1992) *Femicide: The Politics of Woman Killing*, New York: Twayne Publishers.

Ramsey, C. (2010) 'Provoking Change: Comparative Insights on Feminist Homicide Law Reform', *Criminal Law & Criminology*, 100: 33–108.

Rawlinson, P. (2010) *From Fear to Fraternity: A Russian Tale of Crime, Economy and Modernity*, London: Pluto Press.

Reilly, A. (1997) 'Loss of Self-Control in Provocation', *Criminal Law Journal*, 21: 320–35.

Rix, K. (2001) '"Battered Woman Syndrome": and the Defence of Provocation: Two Women with Something More in Common', *The Journal of Forensic Psychiatry*, 12: 131–49.

Rollinson, M. (2000) 'Re-Reading Criminal Law: Gendering the Mental Element', in D. Nicolson and L. Bibbings (eds) *Feminist Perspectives on Criminal Law*, London: Cavendish Publishing Limited.

Roth, L. (2007) *Provocation and Self-Defence in Intimate Partner and Homophobic Homicides*: New South Wales Parliamentary Library Research Service.

Rozenberg, J. (2008) 'Homicide Reforms Would be "Nightmare" for Juries, Says Top Law Lord', *Telegraph*, 7 November.

Rudland, S. (2001) 'Trauma and Mercy: Reading the Law through the Narrative of Trauma', *Australian and Feminist Law Journal*, 15: 80–105.

Rush, P. (1992) *The Trials of Men: Sexuality and Socio-Legal Politics*, PhD, Faculty of Law, University of Edinburgh.

Rush, P. (1997) *Criminal Law*, Melbourne: Butterworths.

Ruxton, S. (ed.) (2004) 'Gender Equality and Men: Learning from Practice', Oxford: Oxfam GB, 1–235.

Sarat, A. and Kearns, T. R. (eds) (1998) *Law in the Domains of Culture*, Ann Arbor: The University of Michigan Press.

Sarat, A. and Simon, J. (2001) 'Beyond Legal Realism?: Cultural Analysis, Cultural Studies, and the Situation of Legal Scholarship', *Yale Journal of Law & the Humanities*, 13: 3–32.

Sarmas, L. (1994) 'Storytelling and the Law: A Case Study of *Louth v Diprose*', *Melbourne University Law Journal*, 19: 701–27.

Scheppele, K. L. (1989) 'Foreword: Telling Stories', *Michigan Law Review*, 87: 2073–98.

Schneider, E. M. (1980) 'Equal Rights to Trial for Women: Sex Bias in the Law of Self-Defence', *Harvard Civil Rights–Civil Liberties Law Review* 15: 623.

Schneider, E. M. (2000) *Battered Women and Feminist Law-Making*, New Haven: Yale University Press.

Schofield, M. A. (1987) '"Women's Speaking Justified": The Feminine Quaker Voice, 1662–1797', *Tulsa Studies in Women's Literature*, 6: 61–77.

Schuller, R. A., Wells, E., Rzepa, S. and Klippenstine, M. A. (2004) 'Rethinking Battered Woman Syndrome Evidence: The Impact of Alternative Forms of Expert Testimony on Mock Jurors' Decisions', *Canadian Journal of Behavioral Science*, 36: 127–36.

Schwartz, J. D. and DeKeseredy, W. S. (1993) 'The Return of the "Battered Husband Syndrome" Through the Typification of Women As Violent', *Crime Law and Social Change*, 20: 249–365.

Scutt, J. (2005) 'Judges Need to be Taught', *Law Institute Journal of Victoria*, 79: 28–29.

Segal, L. (1990) *Slow Motion: Changing Masculinities, Changing Men*, London: Virago.

Seidler, V. J. (1989) *Rediscovering Masculinity: Reason, Language and Sexuality*, London: Routledge.

Seidler, V. J. (ed) (1991) *The Achilles Heel Reader: Men, Sexual Politics and Socialism*, London: Routledge.

Seidler, V. J. (1997) *Man Enough: Embodying Masculinities*, London: Sage.

Seldon, J. (1610) *The Duello, Or, Single Combat: From Antiquity Derived Into this Kingdom of England, with seuerall kindes, and ceremonious formes thereof from good authority described*, London: G[eorge] E[ld] for I. Helme.

Serran, G. and Firestone, P. (2004) 'Intimate Partner Homicide: a Review of the Male Proprietariness and the Self-defence Theories', *Aggression and Violent Behaviour*, 9: 1–15.

Seuffert, N. (1999) 'Domestic Violence, Discourses of Romantic Love, and Complex Personhood in the Law', *Melbourne University Law Review*, 23: 211–40.

Shackelford, T. K. and Mouzos, J. (2005) 'Partner-Killing by Men in Cohabiting and Marital Relationships: A Comparative, Cross-National Analysis of Data from Australia and the United States', *Journal of Interpersonal Violence*, 20: 1310–24.

Shaffer, M. (1997) 'The Battered Woman Syndrome Revisited: Some Complicating Thoughts Five Years after *R v Lavallée*', *University of Toronto Law Journal*, 47: 1–33.

Shakespeare, W. (1594) *The Taming of the Shrew*; updated edition with introduction by A. Thompson (2003), Cambridge: Cambridge University Press.

Shaw, C. (1930) *The Jack Roller*, Chicago: University of Chicago Press.

Sheehy, E. A. (1991) 'Women and Equality Rights in Canada: Sobering Reflections; Impossible Choices', in S. Bazilli (ed) *Putting Women on the Agenda*, Johannesburg: Raven Press.

Sheehy, E. A. (1994) 'Developments in Canadian Law after *R. v. Lavallée*', in J. Stubbs (ed) *Women, Male Violence and the Law*, Sydney: Institute of Criminology.

Sheehy, E. A. (2001) 'Battered Women and Mandatory Minimum Sentencing', *Osgoode Hall Law Journal*, 39: 529–54.

Sheehy, E. A., Stubbs, J. and Tolmie, J. (1992) 'Defending Battered Women on Trial: The Battered Woman Syndrome and its Limitations', *Criminal Law Journal*, 16: 369–94.

Sheneman, P. (1993) 'The Tongue as a Sword: Psalms 56 and 63 and the Pardoner', *The Chaucer Review*, 27: 396–400.

Sherwin, R. K. (2000) *When Law Goes Pop: The Vanishing Line between Law and Popular Culture*, Chicago: University of Chicago Press.

Simmons, J. L. (1977) 'The Tongue in Its Office', *The Revenger's Tragedy*, 92: 56–68.

Simone, C. J. (1997) '"Kill(er) Man Was a Battered Wife" – The Application of Battered Woman Syndrome to Homosexual Defendants: *The Queen v McEwen*', *Sydney Law Review*, 19: 230–39.

Sing, J. J. (1999) 'Culture as Sameness: Toward a Synthetic View of Provocation and Culture in the Criminal Law', *The Yale Law Journal*, 108: 1845–84.

Slack, J. (2008) 'Go Soft on Killer Wives: Women Who Kill in Cold Blood Could Escape Murder Charge', *Daily Mail*, 29 July.

Slack, J. and Doherty, S. (2009) 'Jealousy No Defence For Killer Husbands, But Abused Wives Can Escape a Murder Charge', *Mail Online*, 1 January. Online. Available at http://www.dailymail.co.uk/news/chapter-1114714/Jealousy-defence-killer-husbands-abused-wives-escape-murder-charge.html (accessed 17 January 2010).

Smart, C. (1978) *Women, Sexuality, and Social Control*, London: Routledge.

Smart, C. (1989) *Feminism and the Power of Law*, London: Routledge.

Smart, C. (1990) 'Law's Power, the Sexed Body and Feminist Discourse', *Journal of Law and Society*, 17: 194–210.

Smart, C. (1992) *Regulating Womanhood: Historical Essays on Marriage, Motherhood and Sexuality*, London: Routledge.

Smart, C. (1992) 'The Woman of Legal Discourse', *Social & Legal Studies*, 1: 29–44.

Snedaker, K. H. (1986–1987) 'Storytelling in Opening Statements: Framing the Argumentation of the Trial', *American Journal of Trial Advocate*, 10: 15–45.

Snodgrass, J. (1982) *The Jack-Roller at Seventy: A Fifty-Year Follow-Up*, Boston: Lexington Books.

Snyder, T. L. (2003) *Brabbling Women: Disorderly Speech and the Law in Early Virginia*, Ithaca: Cornell University Press.

Spargo, J. W. (1944) *Juridical Folklore in England: Illustrated by the Cuckingstool*, Durham, N.C.: Duke University Press.

Special Issue (2008) 'Hegemonic Masculinities in International Politics', *Men and Masculinities*, 10: 383–518.

Spindel, D. J. (1995) 'The Law of Words: Verbal Abuse in North Carolina to 1730', *The American Journal of Legal History*, XXXIX: 25–42.

St George, R. B. (1984) '"Heated" Speech and Literacy in Seventeenth-Century New England', in D. D. Hall and D. G. Allen (eds) *Seventeenth-Century New England*, Boston: Colonial Society of Massachusetts.

Stallybrass, P. (1987) 'Reading the Body: The Revenger's Tragedy and the Jacobean Theatre of Consumption', *Renaissance Drama*, 18: 121–48.

Stanko, E. A. (1994) 'Challenging the Problem of Men's Individual Violence', in T. Newburn and E. A. Stanko (eds) *Just Boys Doing Business? Men, Masculinities and Crime*, London: Routledge.

Statham, B. (1999) 'The Homosexual Advance Defence: "Yeah, I Killed Him, But He Did Worse To Me": Green v R', *University of Queensland Law Journal*, 20: 301–311.

Stevens, K. (2009) 'Breakthrough Case – Dismissed Murder Charge Defence Successful Under New Laws', *Shepparton News*, 8 May, p 3.

Stewart, K. (2004) 'Women Are Angry', *The Age*, 30 October, Letters and Opinion, p 10.

Stewart, F. and Freiberg, A. (2008a 1st edn) *Provocation in Sentencing (Research Report)*, Melbourne: Sentencing Advisory Council.

Stewart, F. and Freiberg, A. (2008b) 'Provocation in Sentencing: A Culpability-Based Framework', *Current Issues in Criminal Justice*, 19: 283–308.

Stewart, F. and Freiberg, A. (2009 2nd edn) *Provocation in Sentencing (Research Report)*, Melbourne: Sentencing Advisory Council.

Stigwood, E. (2007) 'Sebo Acquittal Sparks Calls For Law Reform', *The Gold Coast Bulletin*, 4 July, p 12.

Straton, J. C. (1994) 'Research Note: The Myth of the "Battered Husband Syndrome"', *Masculinities*, 2: 79–82.

Stubbs, J. (1992) 'Battered Woman Syndrome: An Advance for Women or Further Evidence of the Legal System's Inability to Comprehend Women's Experiences', *Current Issues in Criminal Justice*, 3: 267–70.

Stubbs, J. and Tolmie, J. (1994) 'Battered Woman Syndrome in Australia: A Challenge to Gender Bias in the Law?', in J. Stubbs (ed) *Women, Male Violence and the Law*, Sydney: The Institute of Criminology.

Stubbs, J. and Tolmie, J. (1995) 'Race, Gender, and the Battered Woman Syndrome: An Australian Case Study', *Canadian Journal of Women and the Law*, 8: 122.

Stubbs, J. and Tolmie, J. (1999) 'Falling Short of the Challenge? A Comparative Assessment of the Australian Use of Expert Evidence on the Battered Woman Syndrome', *Melbourne University Law Review*, 23: 709–48.

Stubbs, J. and Tolmie, J. (2005) 'Defending Battered Women on Charges of Homicide: The Structural and Systemic Versus the Personal and Particular', in W. Chan, D. E. Chunn and R. Menzies (eds) *Women, Mental Disorder and the Law*, London: Glasshouse Press.

Stubbs, J. and Tolmie, J. (2008) 'Battered Women Charged With Homicide: Advancing the Interests of Indigenous Women', *The Australian and New Zealand Journal of Criminology*, 41: 138–61.

Swanwick, T. (2010) 'Susan Falls Found Not Guilty of Murdering Husband Rodney Falls', *Perth Now*, 4 June. Online. Available at http://www.perthnow.com.au/news/susan-falls-found-not-guilty-of-murdering-husband-rodney-falls/story-e6frg12c-1225875463636 (accessed 29 October 2010).

Sweetman, T. (2010) 'Rage No Defence in Act of Homicide', *The Courier Mail*, 17 September.

Symposium (1989) 'Legal Storytelling', Michigan Law Review, 87: 2073.

Tang, K. (2003) 'Battered Woman Syndrome Testimony in Canada: Its Developments and Lingering Issues', *International Journal of Offender Therapy and Comparative Criminology*, 47: 618–29.

Tarantino, Q. (1997) *Jackie Brown: Quentin Tarantino*, London: Faber & Faber.

Tarrant, S. (1990) 'Something is Pushing Them to the Side of Their Own Lives: A Feminist Critique of Law and Laws', *Western Australian Law Review*, 20: 573–606.

Tarrant, S. (1996) 'The "Specific Triggering Incident" in Provocation: Is the Law Gender Biased?', *Western Australian Law Review*, 26: 190–206.

Tarrant, S. (2009) *Men and Feminism*, Berkeley, CA: Seal Press.

Taylor, N. and Mouzos, J. (2006) *Community Attitudes to Violence Against Women Survey: A Full Technical Report (Paper One)*, Canberra: Australian Institute of Criminology.

Taylor, S. C. (2004) *Court Licensed Abuse: Patriarchal Lore and the Legal Response to Intrafamilial Sexual Abuse of Children*, New York: Peter Lang Publishing.

Temken, J. and Krahe, B. (2008) *Sexual Assault and the Justice Gap: A Question of Attitude*, Oxford: Hart Publishing.

Thornton, M. (1989) 'Hegemonic Masculinity and the Academy', *International Journal of the Sociology of Law*, 17: 115–30.

Thornton, M. (1991) 'Feminism and the Contradictions of Law Reform', *International Journal of the Sociology of Law*, 19: 453–74.

Thornton, M. (1996) *Dissonance and Distrust: Women in the Legal Profession*, Oxford: Oxford University Press.

Threadgold, T. (1994) 'Re-Writing Law as Postmodern Fiction: The Poetics of Child Abuse', in J. Neville Turner and P. Williams (eds) *The Happy Couple: Law and Literature*, Sydney: Federation Press.

Threadgold, T. (1997a) 'Performativity, Regulative Fictions, Huge Stabilities: Framing Battered Woman's Syndrome', *Law Text Culture*, 3: 210–31.

Threadgold, T. (1997b) *Feminist Poetics: Poiesis, Performance, Histories*, London and New York: Routledge.

Threadgold, T. (2002) 'Lawyers Reading Law/Lore as Popular Culture: Conflicting Paradigms of Representation', in M. Thornton (ed) *Romancing the Tomes: Popular Culture, Law and Feminism*, London: Cavendish Publishing Limited.

Tolmie, J. (1991) 'Provocation or Self-Defence for Battered Women Who Kill?', in S. M. H. Yeo (ed) *Partial Excuses to Murder*, Sydney: The Federation Press.

Tolmie, J. (1997) 'Pacific-Asian Immigrant and Refugee Women Who Kill Their Batterers: Telling Stories that Illustrate the Significance of Specificity', *Sydney Law Review*, 19: 472–513.

Tolmie, J. (2002) 'Battered Defendants and the Criminal Defences to Murder – Lessons from Overseas', *Waikato Law Review*, 10: 91–114.

Tolmie, J. (2009) 'Defence of Provocation Has Its Place', *The New Zealand Herald*, 7 September.

Tolson, A. (1977) *The Limits of Masculinity*, Indiana University: Tavistock.

Tomsen, S. (1994) 'Hatred, Murder & Male Honour: Gay Homicides and the "Homosexual Panic Defence"', *Criminology Australia*, 6: 2–7.

Tomsen, S. (1998) '"He Had to be a Poofter or Something": Violence, Male Honour and Heterosexual Panic', *Journal of Interdisciplinary Gender Studies*, 3: 44–57.

Tomsen, S. (2002) 'Victims, Perpetrators and Fatal Scenarios: A Research Note on Anti-Homosexual Male Homicides', *International Review of Victimology*, 9(3): 253–71.

Trenwith, C. (2010) 'Queensland's Domestic Killing Defence an Australian First', *The Brisbane Times*, 10 February.

Tyler, I. (2008) '"Chav Mum, Chav Scum": Class Disgust in Contemporary Britain', *Feminist Media Studies*, 8: 17–34.

Tyson, D., Capper, S. and Kirkwood, D. (2010) *Review of the Offence of Defensive Homicide*, Submission to the Department of Justice, Victoria.

Underdown, D. E. (1985) 'The Taming of the Scold: the Enforcement of Patriarchal Authority in Early Modern England', in A. Fletcher and J. Stevenson (eds) *Order and Disorder in Early Modern England*, Cambridge: Cambridge University Press.

Victorian Health Promotion Foundation (2009) *National Survey on Community Attitudes to Violence Against Women 2009: Changing Cultures, Changing Attitudes – Preventing Violence Against Women*, Carlton: Victorian Health Promotion Foundation.

VicHealth (2010) 'Young People Hold the Key to Ending Violence Against Women', Media Release, VicHealth.

Victorian Law Reform Commission (2003) *Defences to Homicide: Options Paper*, Melbourne: Victorian Law Reform Commission.

Victorian Law Reform Commission (2004) *Defences to Homicide: Final Report*, Melbourne: Victorian Law Reform Commission.

Virueda, M. and Payne, J. (2010) *Homicide in Australia: 2007–08 National Homicide Monitoring Program Annual Report*, Canberra: Australian Institute of Criminology.

Volpp, L. (1994) '(Mis)Identifying Culture: Asian Women and the "Cultural Defense"', *Harvard Women's Law Journal*, 17: 57–101.

Wacquant, L. J. D. (1993) *From the Native's Point of View: How Boxers Think and Feel About Their Trade*, working paper, New York: Russell Sage Foundation.

Wade, A. (2010) 'Mother's Bid to Tackle Abuse', *The New Zealand Herald*, 7 October.

Walker, C. (1985) 'Scandalising in the Eighties', *The Law Quarterly Review*, 101: 359–84.

Walker, L. E. (1989) *The Battered Woman Syndrome*, New York: Springer Publishing Co.

Walker, L. E. (1990) *Terrifying Love: Why Battered Women Kill and How Society Responds*, New York: Harper Perennial.

Walklate, S. (1995) *Gender and Crime: An Introduction*, Hemel Hempstead: Prentice Hall/Harvester Wheatsheaf.

Wallace, A. (1986) *Homicide: The Social Reality*, Sydney: Bureau of Crime Statistics and Research.

Websdale, N. (1999) *Understanding Domestic Homicide*, Boston: Northeastern University Press.

Wells, C. (1994) 'Battered Woman Syndrome and Defences to Homicide: Where Now?', *Legal Studies*: 266–76.

Wells, C. (2000) 'Provocation – the Case for Abolition', in A. Ashworth and B. Mitchell (eds) *Re-Thinking English Homicide Law*, Oxford: Oxford University Press.

Wells, C. and Quick, O. (2006) 'Getting Tough with Defences – Law Commission Proposals to Reform Homicide-defences', *Criminal Law Review*, June: 514–26.

West, C. and Fenstermaker, S. (1993) 'Power, Inequality, and the Accomplishment of Gender: An Ethnomethodological View', in P. England (ed) *Theory on Gender/ Feminism on Theory*, New York: Aldine de Gruyter.

West, C. and Zimmerman, D. H. (1987) 'Doing Gender', *Gender & Society*, 1: 125–51.

White, J. B. (1973) *The Legal Imagination: Studies in the Nature of Legal Thought and Expression*, Boston: Little Brown.

White, J. B. (1985) *The Legal Imagination*, Chicago: The University of Chicago Press.

Whitehead, S. M. (2002) *Men and Masculinities*, Cambridge: Polity Press.

Wiener, M. J. (2004) *Men of Blood: Violence, Manliness, and Criminal Justice in Victorian England*, Cambridge: Cambridge University Press.

Williams, M. (1999) '*Tess of the D'Urbervilles* and the Law of Provocation', in M. Freeman and A. D. E. Lewis (eds) *Law and Literature: Current Legal Issues*, Oxford: Oxford University Press.

Williams, P. J. (1991) *The Alchemy of Race and Rights*, Cambridge, Mass.: Harvard University Press.

Wilson, L. (2010) 'Murder Victim's Mother Slams Self-defence Homicide Law', *The Australian*, 20 May. Online. Available at http://www.theaustralian.com.au/national-affairs/state-politics/murder-victims-mother-slams-self-defence-homicide-law/story-e6frgczx-1225868885556 (accessed 22 May 2010).

Wilson, M. and Daly, M. (1993) 'Spousal homicide risk and estrangement', *Violence and Victims*, 8: 3–16.

Wilson, M. and Daly, M. (1998) 'Lethal and Nonlethal Violence Against Wives and the Evolutionary Psychology of Male Sexual Proprietariness', in R. E. Dobash and R. P. Dobash (eds) *Rethinking Violence Against Women*, Thousand Oaks, CA: Sage.

Wilson, M., Daly, M. and Daniele A. (1995) 'Familicide: The Killing of Spouse and Children, *Aggressive Behavior*, 21: 275–91.

Withey, C. (2011) 'Loss of Control, Loss of Opportunity?', *Criminal Law Review*, 4: 263–79.

Women's Coalition against Family Violence (1994) *Blood on Whose Hands? The Killing of Women and Children in Domestic Homicides*, Brunswick: Women's Coalition Against Family Violence.

Wood, L. (2010) 'Taking the Long Road', *The Age*, 29 May. Online. Available at http://www.theage.com.au/victoria/taking-the-long-road-20100528-wll6.html (accessed 6 September 2010).

Wooding, D. (2008) 'Nagging's Not Murder Defence', *The Sun*, 29 July.

World Health Organization. (2007) *Engaging Men and Boys in Changing Gender-Based Inequity in Health: Evidence from Programme Interventions*, Geneva: World Health Organization.

Yeo, S. (1987a) 'Ethnicity and the Objective Test in Provocation', *Melbourne University Law Review*, 16: 67–82.

Yeo, S. (1987b) 'Provoking the "Ordinary" Ethnic Person: A Juror's Predicament', *Criminal Law Journal*, 11: 96–104.

Yeo, S. (1996) 'Sex, Ethnicity, Power of Self-Control and Provocation Revisited', *Sydney Law Review*, 18: 304–22.

Yeo, S. (2010) 'English Reform of Partial Defences to Murder: Lessons for New South Wales', *Current Issues in Criminal Justice*, 22: 1–18.

Young, A. (1990) *Feminity in Dissent*, London: Routledge.

Young, A. (1993) 'Conjugal Homicide and Legal Violence: A Comparative Analysis', *Osgoode Hall Law Journal*, 31: 761–809.

Young, A. (1994) 'Caveat sponsa: violence and the body in law', in J. Brettle and S. Rice (eds) *Public Bodies/Private States*, Manchester: Manchester University Press.

Young, A. (1996) *Imagining Crime: Textual Outlaws and Criminal Conversations*, London: Sage.

Young, A. (ed) (1997) *Femininity as Marginalia: Conjugal Homicide and the Conjugation of Sexual Difference*, Aldershot: Ashgate.

Young, A. (1998) 'The Waste Land of the Law, the Wordless Song of the Rape Victim', *Melbourne University Law Review*, 22: 442–65.

Young, A. (2001) '"Into the Blue": The Image Written on Law', *Yale Journal of Law & the Humanities*, 31: 305–27.

Zemon Davis, N. (1975) *Society and Culture in Early Modern France*, Stanford: Stanford University Press.

Index